*Approaching Difference Differently* is both timely and timeless. At a moment when polarised exchanges so often dominate, Amanda Ridings offers a fresh way of meeting one another – one that feels deeply relevant now, yet rooted in wisdom that endures.

The writing itself is spacious and invitational. Rather than presenting abstract theory, Amanda invites reflection and offers simple practices that, when repeated, become woven into the fabric of daily life. In this way, the book becomes both a guide and a companion, one that nurtures attentiveness, resilience and openness in our work with others.

*Approaching Difference Differently* is practical and restorative. It affirms that when we meet difference with curiosity, respect and embodied awareness, we open the door to creativity, connection and transformation. A resource to return to again and again, it is a book for anyone committed to leading, listening and living with presence and courage.

> Dr Eunice Aquilina, author of *Embodying Authenticity* and *Stepping Into Your Power*

'This conversation is feeling a bit stuck and I don't know how to move it on'.

If this statement resonates, then *Approaching Difference Differently* is the book for you. Whether it's a difficult conversation or a tricky situation, at work or at home, Amanda talks you through how you might handle the situation by 'collecting yourself' and interacting with it in a different way. I deliberately use the phrase 'Amanda talks you through' as this is a book in which you're in conversation with her. This makes it a delight to read, with plenty of pauses for reflection and practice.

From my personal experience, these approaches really work and it's amazing how they can positively change the dynamics of situation. A theme of the book is: 'it takes practice'. And so, you'll return to this book, time and time again.

> Scott Heald, Director, Public Health Scotland

If more of us understood the difference between debate and dialogue, the world would be a better place. It's easy to get stuck in our own opinions, and Amanda Ridings shows us how to get unstuck and face challenging conversations with both strength and openness. Unique to her approach is the use of powerful embodied practices to explore how shifting your posture and focus shifts your state from stubborn to curious. These practices not only make you a better leader, but also make you a better human being.

I can think of no wiser guide than Amanda. She distils decades of experience into this rich, clear and inviting book.

> Anouk Brack, Lead Trainer, Leadership Embodiment Europe

*Approaching Difference Differently* is both practical and hopeful. It invites us to see difference not as a threat but as a source of energy, creativity, and transformation. Amanda's earlier work, *Pause for Breath*, weaves together dialogue theory, mindfulness and reflection to offer leaders concrete tools for handling difficult conversations and, whilst it contains a chapter on difference, this theme now comes to the fore. The result is a deeper, richer, more coherent account of how we can engage with difference skilfully and constructively.

The insights in this book reach far beyond leadership conversations: they are applicable wherever purposeful conversations take place. I wholeheartedly recommend *Approaching Difference Differently* to anyone who wants to lead, learn and live with greater skill in our divided world.

Timothy B. Kelly, Professor of Social Work (Emeritus)

# Approaching Difference Differently

## Practices for transforming leadership conversations

## Amanda Ridings

Originate Books

The moral right of the author has been asserted.

Published in 2025 by Originate Books

Originate Books is an imprint of Originate: www.originate.org.uk

Edited by Helen Bleck
Diagrams by Sai Cook
Designed and typeset by Raspberry Creative Type

Printed by IngramSpark

ISBN 978-1-0686609-2-4

Also available as an e-book: ISBN 978-1-0686609-4-8

British Library Cataloguing in Publication Data.

A catalogue record for this book is available from the British Library.

This book is dedicated to:


Wendy Palmer (1947–2022) in gratitude for her
inspiring work, which informs everything I do.
I've lost a teacher, Dharma sister and friend.

*Dialogue is a conversation with a center, not sides.
It is a way of taking the energy of our differences
and channeling it toward something that has never
been created before.*

William Isaacs
*Dialogue and the art of thinking together*

# Contents

# Preface

This is my second book in the field of dialogue. The first, *Pause for Breath*,[1] looked at some of the principles and practices of dialogue through the lens of mind, body and spirit. This time, my intention is to invite you into an exploration of the way we can use the practices of dialogue to approach difference differently. We'll engage with this ground as a leadership development activity. Together, we'll explore the 'how' of conversations alongside the 'what', reflecting a theme of my work in recent years. As we do so, I encourage you to use what you find in these pages to gain insight into why your conversations play out the way they do, and then to make changes to your practice.

There's an important distinction between gaining new knowledge and changing practice. One is an activity of mind. The other is an embodied activity, a physiological process of building neural pathways. It's more like refining a golf swing or learning to play a musical instrument than understanding a subject: it takes time and practice.

When we meet difference in our conversations, the embodied element of our experience matters. Our physiology is wired to put us on alert whenever we encounter something unfamiliar or potentially hazardous – whether a threat to life, livelihood, ideas or identity. And so, when differences arise, our body tries to intervene to keep us safe, often prompting us to attack or defend. This affects the way we engage with others and limits our options. To approach difference differently and transform our leadership conversations, we attend to our body as well as our mind.

As I begin, I'm thoughtful about both *what* I want to write about and *how* I intend to write it.

What I want to write about is shaped by a world in which it seems increasingly relevant to be able to handle ourselves skilfully when differences arise. In condensed exchanges such as those prevalent on social media, where much is expressed through 'short form' means such as TikTok, Twitter/X and texting – and through even more concise vehicles like hashtags and emojis – meaning is often lost to a trending headline. As momentum gathers and polarises around a summary phrase and its rebuttal, it can be increasingly hard to honour differences. Nuance, ambiguity and context are often overlooked in the course of restating what's believed to be certain, absolute and true. When this happens, differences tend to be reinforced, to the detriment of all.

This is disturbing enough. Even more troubling is an apparent increase in intolerance of difference itself, evidenced by the emergence of trolling, cancel culture and no-platforming. When we find something challenging, distasteful or just plain wrong, I understand that it can be easier to attack or avoid it, rather than explore it. However, I'm not sure this serves us, individually or collectively. With less appetite for our differences, the potential for creativity, innovation and shared understanding diminishes. Further, the skills for handling diverse ideas seem to be falling into disuse and, without them, our world is shrinking.

Many commentators have described this societal trend, a sense that we're becoming less able to engage skilfully with dissenting voices. Often, their solution is to call for better debate, this being the predominant form of conversation in many Western cultures. As you'll discover, I'm not sure that more debate – even if it's better debate – can resolve this predicament. As a conversational form, debate amplifies difference by arguing for and against a position.

What if, instead, we were to become *interested* in our differences, and to explore how they arise? Rather than focusing on what divides us, what if we asked: what connects us? This represents a change in orientation that calls for greater awareness of, and skilfulness in, dialogue.

My personal interest in dialogue was catalysed by William Isaacs' book, *Dialogue and the Art of Thinking Together*.[2] In it, dialogue is described as a conversation in which we seek greater shared understanding. In dialogue, we harness the energy of difference to generate new possibilities. To foster this transformation, we attend to the 'hows' of a conversation: how we set it up; how we carry ourselves in it; and

how we nurture the conditions in which difference can be explored. Individually, we can support this transformation by developing our capacity to *embody* dialogue practices, by which I mean to 'live them' and make them integral to the way we speak and listen.

This sets the scene for this book: this is *what* I want to write about.

In terms of *how* I intend to write, I want the means to reflect the ends. This presents the challenge of enfolding the principles of dialogue practices into my words *and* into the relationship forged with you, the reader. Isaacs acknowledged this challenge when he wrote: 'Writing a book about dialogue is in some respects a contradiction in terms.'

In an email exchange, a leading practitioner went further: 'Writing cannot be dialogic.'

'Perhaps not,' I replied, 'but it *can* be conversational.'

We agreed to differ.

Then, with impeccable timing, an unsolicited endorsement came from a reader of *Pause for Breath*, who wrote:

> What I also enjoyed while reading was the sense we were in a conversation together. By using your personal experiences to explain and also the style you chose, it felt as if you were talking to me.

And so, deliberately, I intend to write in a way that invites you into conversation with me. I believe this to be important for our subject matter, although it may mean that this book is somewhat unconventional in form.

As well as writing as if I'm talking to you, I'll regularly be saying 'over to you' and inviting you to pause, reflect and connect to your personal experience. I want to draw you into conversation with yourself, and invite you to consider how you might try out some of the approaches outlined in these pages. For this is not simply a book of ideas, easily grasped. Rather, it aims to engage you in the hard graft of changing your practice in your conversations.

This book builds on the material set out in *Pause for Breath*, and explores the complexities of putting it into practice. With this emphasis, you may get the most from what's on offer if you already have some knowledge and/or experience of dialogue. If so, and whatever your route into this field, I hope you'll find that what you discover in these pages stands alone. If, instead, you're completely new to dialogue, *Pause for Breath* might offer a suitable starting point.

As you read, I encourage you to assess what I've written in two ways. First, examine my views in the context of your current frames of reference. Whether you agree with my words or not, take time to consider the provenance of your opinion: what prompts you to accept or reject what you're reading? How did you come to see the world in the way you do? Are you willing to further assess both my perspective and your own?

Second, test what I offer by exploring what happens in practice. This involves a shift from weighing the balance between your ideas and mine to considering what you do in your conversations and whether you get the outcomes you're seeking. This means holding yourself to account and being honest about your part in any exchange. While you may attribute some of what occurs to others, you'll always influence what transpires, even if you say or do nothing. This can sometimes be hard to accept – and yet, it's a necessary first step towards changing your practice.

The book-based conversation that lies ahead is set out in four parts. In Part I we begin with some scene-setting about leadership, conversations and our differences, and introduce dialogue as a form of conversation. We also consider what might be involved if we're to change our practice. We then use the dialogue practice of check-in to connect with ourselves and to establish our relationship to the extent that our context allows. This prepares the ground for engaging with the challenges of approaching difference differently.

Towards the end of Part I, we start to explore three tenets that, over the years, have become the foundation of my leadership development work in the field of dialogue. They represent themes that I found myself repeating as I described how we can embody the dialogue practices that support us to work creatively with the energies of difference. While the tenets are fairly simple to state, it's not easy to inhabit them.

In Part II, we'll prepare the ground for a deeper exploration of the three tenets by considering the relationship between neat ideas and the messy realities of being human. I see this relationship as similar to that between a map and the terrain beneath our feet: the map provides useful context and data for a walk, but the experience of walking may be easier or harder than we imagine. To explore the interface between ideas and realities, we'll blend frameworks, a case study, embodied practices and opportunities to reflect. In the process, our appreciation for how we might approach difference differently will grow.

In Part III, we'll look into the complexities of bringing the three tenets to life. We'll see that engaging with our differences can give rise to tensions and flash points, and we'll explore some of the resources that can support us to navigate these challenges.

Finally, in Part IV, we'll take time to reflect on our book-based conversation. We'll look at an approach for recognising which types of conversation might benefit from the additional time, energy and preparation involved in creating the conditions for dialogue. We'll clarify what it takes to change our practice, and consider how this process might continue beyond the book. Then we'll bring our conversation to a close.

Taking all this together, I hope this book will entice you into conversation with me, with yourself and with the world around you, and inspire you to embody dialogue practices.


In working with mind, body and spirit in conversation, I draw on a plethora of sources and have benefited from the guidance of many teachers: I'm utterly grateful to them. Beyond my formal teachers, I've been influenced by numerous others, such as all those who've taken part in my dialogue programmes over many years. Without teachers, mentors and other learning partners, my approach to dialogue would have remained rooted in ideas and theory – and the casualties of my own conversations would have been even greater in number and gravity. I remain a work in progress.

Throughout this book, I draw on the models and concepts of others and I intend to be respectful of their work. However, I also want to be honest about my own learning process: in bringing the approaches of others into my practice, I've often adapted them so I can use them authentically. I apologise unreservedly where, in doing this, I've misunderstood or misrepresented original intentions. I've referenced my sources and, as you develop your own practice, I encourage you to access them.

Finally, I believe the blend of approaches in this book to be unique even though there's nothing fundamentally new in the underlying material. I've done my utmost to credit sources where I know of them. However, I haven't researched the field systematically and it's possible that I've used a phrase, word or motif that others claim. My intent is only to share my experience and provide a resource: if I've inadvertently adopted your words without acknowledgement then it's simply because I'm unaware of your material. If you let me know, I'll put it right.

# Part I

## Preparation and beginning

# Chapter 1    Preparation and beginning: introduction

In preparation for the developmental journey ahead, what follows is a brief outline of my perspective on the connections between leadership, conversations and the way we navigate our differences. This offers a first glimpse of the relationship between dialogue and a desire to approach difference differently. With a sense of our context, we'll take a step towards understanding the challenges of changing our practice in conversations.

## Leadership, conversations and our differences

While it's not always possible, I try to talk about leadership rather than leaders. This is because, regardless of position or seniority, my focus is on the activities that bring out the best in ourselves and others, and on finding a good response to any situation. I believe that leadership begins with self: holding ourselves to account, continuing to learn and keeping ourselves healthy in mind, body and spirit. Our self-leadership shows up in the way we communicate and act, whether in a profession, organisation, community or family. I see leadership in support staff who find the courage to speak out when things aren't right. I see leadership in those who meet the most adverse events with grace. I see leadership in those who *do* hold positions of power, yet have the humility to admit that they don't have answers, who listen to others without judgement and are willing to change their minds.

The medium in which leadership is most often conducted and expressed is conversation. Whether we're in a meeting, giving or receiving a presentation, or engaging one-to-one (formally or informally), our focus is usually on *what* we're saying: we tend to concentrate on the subject matter and getting our thoughts in order. Many of us pay less attention to the 'how' of our conversations, the look and feel of our interactions, and the way these factors enable or limit what's possible. We don't always give due consideration to how we'll create the conditions for exchanges that generate *both* good outcomes *and* healthy rapport and confidence amongst those present. A central theme of the journey ahead is paying attention to the 'how' of our important conversations.

In addition, we don't tend to take account of the way our personal demeanour and energy affect a conversation. Sometimes this doesn't matter. And sometimes we go into a room intending to be collaborative and constructive, yet quickly become resistant, frustrated, uneasy or defensive. We explode (or implode) and the conversation becomes strained and edgy. We'll maximise our impact if we're able to steward our mind, body and spirit so that we carry ourselves well, even in difficult circumstances.

In essence, we can bring leadership to two less-considered aspects of our interactions:

- how we bring the best of ourselves to a conversation; and

- how we create conditions that support others to bring the best of themselves to that conversation.

These things go hand in hand. If we carry ourselves well but don't set things up so that others can participate fully, our voice (or the voices of others) may get lost or be discounted. Equally, if we establish a positive climate but can't maintain our own composure and presence when things don't go our way, it can affect the tenor of the whole conversation.

The way we set up a conversation and carry ourselves within it is particularly important when we encounter difference because the way we navigate it will affect how the conversation unfolds. Difference occurs naturally and takes many forms – the most obvious being different opinions. It may also be present in the form of different cultures and languages. More subtly, it can arise within a shared language, due to different dialects or idioms, or to attributing different meaning to a word or phrase.

In addition, the way we each perceive our experience leads to different interpretations of the same events. Such differences arise because each of us has personal preferences for how we take in and process information, and this subtly influences what we pay attention to. We also tend to filter for things that matter to us, influenced by our values, principles, preconceptions and/or interests. All this is simply part of being human, as is the tendency to have expectations about what a conversation will yield, and this too will vary from one person to another.

When we pause and reflect, we realise that difference will always be present – even when people think they agree. If we don't surface our differences and examine them, they may fester and emerge at a later time and/or in an inconvenient way. And so, what kind of conversation will create space for differences to be spoken, heard and held in a constructive climate so that they can be explored?

This brings us to dialogue and its role in approaching difference differently. Dialogue is an ordinary word, often used interchangeably with debate, discussion and other descriptors of conversation. However, in my world it has a particular meaning, defined by William Isaacs in *Dialogue and the Art of Thinking Together*[2] as:

> a conversation with a center, not sides. It is a way of taking the energy of our differences and channeling it toward something that has never been created before.

In referring to the energy of our differences, this definition places dialogue in the realm of embodied experience. Rather than the differences themselves, it's the heightened energy that we bring to them – the passion, the conviction – that can derail a conversation. This heightened energy is rooted in our innate human reaction to difference, which is an impulse to fight, flee or freeze. This impulse is generated by our physiology, and is a primal reaction to the risk that's inherent in anything unfamiliar. It limits what's possible in a conversation and calls for a physiological, or embodied, remedy. To work skilfully with the energies of difference, we look inwards and build our capacity to engage skilfully with both our own heightened energy and that of others. This involves settling our human system so that we can be curious, inclusive and responsive. This is the embodied element of the journey ahead.

If dialogue is the medium in which the energy of our differences is transformed, then it's the conversational form that supports us to approach difference differently. With a few tweaks of language, I offer a corollary to Isaacs' definition of dialogue:

Approaching difference differently, and channelling its energy into new possibilities, calls for dialogue, a conversation with centre, not sides.

In summary, dialogue transforms the energy of our differences and so, when difference arises, we navigate it by embodying dialogue practices.

## Changing practice

For most of us, this calls for a change in practice, which is the terrain of this book. In these pages, we'll:

- explore frameworks and practices from the field of dialogue to gain insight into the shape and quality of our conversations;

- use embodied practices distilled from the principles of martial arts to examine the energy we bring to our conversations; and

- combine these two elements to build our capacity for holding conversations in which the energy of difference can be harnessed to create something new.

As we proceed, I'll encourage you to explore the structures and patterns in your conversations through a blend of frameworks, embodied practices and examples from my own experience and that of my clients. We'll pay attention to the shape and quality of our conversations and, as 'content' becomes less prominent, we'll gain insight into factors that might otherwise go unnoticed. Along the way, I'll be asking questions that invite you to reflect on your own experiences and, perhaps, to reframe them. As you recognise your conversational habits, you'll distinguish between those that serve you and those that don't. As you change your perception of conversations and the part you play in them, you may be inspired to experiment with different approaches and to discover how they work for you.

Changing practice is a form of first-person action research, because there isn't a single 'right way' to bring dialogue practices to life. Briefly, the process involves:

- identifying personal stumbling blocks and what you might change;

- road-testing the approaches you might adopt; and

- refining, embedding and embodying the practices that make a difference.

Only you can decide what's relevant to you and how you'll work with what you find in these pages. The direction of travel is to explore which approaches have the greatest impact, whilst allowing you to be yourself.

And now, to be faithful to my intention to be in conversation with you and to invite you to be in conversation with yourself, it's time to pause and reflect. This is the first of many opportunities to connect what I'm saying to your own experience. Each of these pauses offers an interlude in which to make some notes, review, go for a walk and/or make your own sense of my words. So ... over to you.

## Over to you ...

You're already a practitioner in the field of conversation, with a lot of experience and history. Take some time to reflect on this – in which conversations have you been most able to be yourself, warts and all? What made this possible? What was the outcome?

And, in those conversations where you were guarded, adamant or weary, what prompted this? What was the impact on you and others?

What initial conclusions might you draw about what supports you to bring the best of yourself to your conversations?

As we begin to develop the themes outlined in this chapter, it feels important to clarify that I use the term 'dialogue practices' in two ways: generally; and to reference a suite of four specific dialogue practices. Used generally, the phrase really means 'the practices of dialogue', which include approaches such as check-in (Chapters 3 and 4), creating a container for a conversation (Chapters 22 to 26), and balancing advocacy and inquiry (Chapter 7). To embody these approaches, we embrace them, explore them and embed them into the way we engage in our conversations, so that they become part of who we are.

Used specifically, the phrase refers to four practices that underpin dialogue: listening, respecting, suspending judgement and authentic voicing. These practices are described in *Dialogue and the Art of Thinking Together* and, when we inhabit the spirit of them, it permeates how we talk and listen. They become a way of being, rather than something we do. In this book, the four dialogue practices appear in a variety of ways from Chapter 12 onwards. In addition, in Chapter 20, we'll explore what it means to embody them.

## Preparation and beginning

To bring this chapter to a close, I'd like to explain the phrase 'preparation and beginning', which I've used as the title for Part I. It comes from T'ai Chi Chuan, a martial art that I've practised since 1998. It's through T'ai Chi that I've learned the value of practice and experienced the way that an activity changes, often subtly, when it's repeated mindfully over time. It's the medium in which I've become familiar with the boredom and frustration inherent in repetition, and developed strategies for coaching myself through them. Most of us have experienced this kind of tenacity: when the going gets tough and we face tedium, dissatisfaction or even pain, we dig in and carry on. Oddly, this kind of grit seems to be required when we make changes to our practice in conversations. How can we prepare for this?

Most people recognise T'ai Chi as a series of flowing movements, and 'preparation and beginning' alludes to the moment before moving (preparation) and the first movement (beginning). The preparation element is a process of settling into a 'ready' stance, softening, collecting ourselves and becoming alert in body, mind and spirit. Only then do we begin.

More generally, the way we prepare depends on the activity we're about to undertake. We prepare differently for a hill walk in winter conditions than for a stroll along a beach. We prepare differently for a crucial formal presentation than for an informal briefing. And our preparation for engaging in, and/or creating the conditions for, dialogue will be significantly different to that required for an everyday conversation.

In the context of exploring the way that embodying dialogue practices can support us to approach difference differently, this chapter is the first stage of our preparation. The next stage is to set the scene for what lies ahead and to describe my approach to dialogue more fully. Then, in Chapters 3 and 4, I'll introduce the dialogue practice of check-in, mirroring the way I begin my dialogue programmes. In a conventional setting, checking in readies us to engage in conversation – let's discover how it works with a book-based conversation.

# Chapter 2 Preparation: setting the scene for my approach to dialogue

In the decade or so since I wrote *Pause for Breath,*[1] my approach to bringing the practices of dialogue to leadership conversations has shifted. I now accentuate the role of personal and collective energy and focus on changing practice. Whilst there's great simplicity in this, it also brings challenges, one being that the discipline of dialogue doesn't offer a set of tools or techniques for getting what we want from a conversation. Instead, dialogue is a way of being, a way of carrying ourselves and relating to others. It's an embodied practice, which takes time to develop. This can present a stumbling block for those who seek immediate results.

The essence of this book is to invite you to engage in the effort of cultivating new habits in your conversations. Like most people, you'll have developed habitual ways of communicating, and these will come with unique strengths and shortcomings. This personal style means that some aspects of what you find in these pages will have more relevance than others – as you identify approaches that you think might enhance your repertoire, versatility and impact, please try them out and reflect on what changes. Where the material resonates less with your own development needs, it may offer insight into the way that other people communicate and support you to engage with them more skilfully.

## Engaging with difference

As we discovered in Chapter 1, dialogue is a conversation in which we actively engage with difference in a way that supports the emergence of new possibilities. As we embark on an exploration of how we handle difference, it's important to consider our personal relationship to it. This can be a tricky area – we may think our attitude towards difference takes a certain form, but our emotional and behavioural reality may not reflect this. For example, we may believe (and say) that we welcome diverse views, fresh thinking, challenge and/or dissent. Yet, in reality, we may find we only welcome this kind of input from certain people. When others offer it, we may be critical, resistant and/or dismissive – without meaning to, we put them down, question their credentials or simply ignore them.

Examining the relationship between our words and what we embody in our actions is an important aspect of the work ahead. When we discover an inconsistency and examine the internal experience that underlies it, we may not like what we find. It takes courage to acknowledge that the way we behave doesn't accord with what we believe about ourselves – and to see that difference is present within us. When we're aware of the disparities and incongruities in our own make-up, we can navigate difference in our conversations more skilfully. If we don't attend to our inner differences, they may derail us. Let's pause to gain insight into the way you relate to difference.

## Over to you …

Give some thought to what happens when someone opposes you – something you've said is questioned or even disputed. What impulse arises within you? Do you tend to push back, give way, appease …? Does this vary, depending on who the 'someone' is?

Similarly, when you disagree with something that's been said, what impulse arises within you? Do you tend to wade in, let it go, ask for more information …? Does this vary, depending on who the 'someone' is?

What have you discovered about your relationship to difference?

We each view the world through a unique bundle of preconceptions, preoccupations and experiences and so, as I become your guide in the terrain of dialogue, it's important to describe what influences the way I see this field. An appreciation of this wider context will, I believe, support you to clarify your own perspective on the role of dialogue practices in your leadership conversations.

## My approach to dialogue

My journey with dialogue began as personal development. First, at the turn of the century, I read *Dialogue and the Art of Thinking Together.* Then, over several years, I took part in a number of development programmes offered by Dialogue Associates.[3] During this time, I reflected on my own interactions and conversations and tried out different approaches. Alongside this, I started to include some dialogue frameworks in my coaching and consultancy work. I also began to write about dialogue, a process of reflection and sense-making that eventually became *Pause for Breath,* and continued in my blog posts.[4]

The activities of personal reflection, writing and sharing my learning with others continued as my own conversational practice evolved. In fact, these activities are ongoing: they're interdependent and somewhat iterative, and they support me to move between theory and practice in a developmental way. In essence, my path towards dialogue is rooted in my interpretation of work done by others, enriched by experience and reflective practice. My dialogue work is therefore founded on a practice-based approach. This may or may not suit you – whichever is the case, I encourage you to find your own way, just as I've found mine.

One aspect of finding my own way is that my approach to dialogue has diverged from the original concept of working with a 'whole system' and gathering a group of forty or more people to *think together.* My 'big picture' mind was inspired by the potential of this. And yet, when I took part in conversations that aspired to be dialogic in nature, I found that I was unable to sit with the challenges, dissonances and energies of such conversations.

What usually happened was that, when I was invited to listen deeply and to leave space between one spoken contribution and another, I sat quietly for a while … and, gradually, energy began to build within me. At some point, the pressure to make my point would erupt, and I'd blurt out a torrent of unformed thinking, judgement and strident opinions. I was often lacking in respect, more caught up in my own thinking than in properly listening to what others had to say. Driven by impulse and preoccupation, I was unable to play my part in holding a space in which different perspectives could be explored. This kind of experience had a huge influence on the form my dialogue work began to take.

Later, I came to understand the nature of the gap between my strong belief in the potential of dialogue and my inability to embody the practices. At the time, I was simply frustrated that I couldn't access the promise of dialogue. In addition, I could see a clear connection between my reaction in dialogue settings and my embodied experience of partner work in the martial art of T'ai Chi Chuan – I just didn't know how to make use of it. Knowing that I was unlikely to be uniquely challenged in this way, I began to explore this ground. Over time, my quest to *embody* dialogue practices has come to define the way I contribute to the field.

## Over to you …

What's the parallel for you? In your conversations, what do you aspire to and yet find yourself unable to put into practice? Perhaps you intend to be collaborative and yet often make unilateral decisions in order to move quickly? Perhaps you intend to be open and inclusive but discount what others say without much consideration? Perhaps you intend to listen properly, but your mind has already moved on?

Which of these experiences would you most like to change?

Dialogue became more central to my work from around 2006. The process began with a small group of friends and colleagues who'd also participated in the programmes offered by Dialogue Associates. We decided to form 'something like' an action-learning set: our aim was to explore how we might collectively deepen our understanding of dialogue practices and more often put them to use. I took a lead on designing our sessions, partly because I'd been on more of the programmes and partly because, as an independent coach and consultant, I had the experience to do it.

The other group members were employed in senior leadership roles in public services. What was most relevant to them was finding ways to use the insights and practices of dialogue to improve their *everyday* conversations. The sticking point in most of these conversations was difference – disagreeing about the nature of an issue, about what mattered, about how to take action … and so on.

The essence of this prototype programme was that we concentrated on 'putting on our own oxygen masks' before trying to help others. The beauty of this approach was that we each had plenty of real material to work with – conversations or meetings that had stalled, imploded or worse. In focusing on our own part in these conversations, we gained insight into our interactions with others. This helped us to see what we could change, and we each became more skilful in navigating difference.

Over the years, the seeds planted by this group became the core of my dialogue programmes. As the programmes evolved, I met Wendy Palmer and discovered her Leadership Embodiment (LE) work.[5] LE practices offered a way to bring embodied approaches into my dialogue work and to explore the gap between what we know and our ability to put it into practice. We'll touch on this theme lightly in Chapter 4, and then develop it more fully in Chapter 9.

Meanwhile, we'll continue our preparation with the practice of check-in.

# Chapter 3 Preparation: checking in with each other

As mentioned in the Preface, I intend to invite you into conversation with me. In this chapter, we'll use the dialogue practice of check-in to connect with each other in preparation for this. Then, in the next chapter, we'll continue checking in as we consider what we'll do together and how we'll approach it.

In a book-based conversation, there are obvious constraints to checking in with each other and with a shared purpose and approach. However, we can touch on the principles of check-in and engage with the process to some extent, pausing and becoming more present to the way we're engaging with the work we're doing together.

With an invitation to suspend any disbelief for a moment, let's work through the process and see what happens.

## Checking in – phase one

First, we check in with ourselves. In groups, I usually support this process with a tailored 'Pause for Breath' mindfulness practice. The aim of the practice is to turn our attention to our posture and breath, and to scan our body, heart and mind to get a sense of our mood. Towards the end of the practice, I ask a question such as: what called you to be here? Or, how are you as you arrive? Or, what matters to you today? The practice supports us to settle into being present and to set down any preoccupations. We connect with ourselves and with our readiness to engage with others and the work ahead. There's an example of this kind of practice at Appendix A – we can use this, or a similar approach, to begin conference calls, in-person conversations or virtual gatherings on platforms such as Zoom or MS Teams.

21

After the 'Pause for Breath' practice, those present take it in turns to check in and to share something about who they are and how they are as the conversation begins. This allows each person to speak, to bring themselves into the gathering. It also begins the second phase of checking: getting a sense of who's in the room.

In terms of our book-based conversation, if you engaged with the 'Over to you …' elements of Chapters 1 and 2, you've started to check in with yourself. Let's expand on this.

## Over to you …

Take a moment to check in with yourself and reflect on what inspired you to acquire this book. Use a short mindfulness practice if you have ready access to one. Then ask: what am I looking for from this book, both today and in the longer term? How might I use what I discover to transform my leadership conversations? And today, what's my capacity to take things in and make sense of them?

These questions invite you to connect to your sense of self, your relationship to this book and your bandwidth for reading, in this moment. If you find the questions valuable, you might make a note of them and use them to check in with yourself each time you pick up the book.

This sort of inquiry represents the first phase of an approach to fostering trust that's outlined in *Pause for Breath*. It's based on the work of Jack Gibb,[6] and a premise that, when we enter a new process, group or conversation, we hold questions about how we fit in. We may also hold questions about the purpose of the shared activity and its relevance and/or value. Sometimes these concerns aren't conscious but, if they're not acknowledged and addressed, they tend to inhibit wholehearted engagement.

In the first phase of the Gibb approach, we're essentially asking: who am I in this situation? There are three further phases, which I presented in linear form in *Pause for Breath*. However, I now understand the process to be cyclical in nature – when circumstances change, such as when someone joins or leaves a group, or an unsettling event occurs, we may have to 'begin again'. This updated interpretation is reflected in the diagram below.

## Engaging with each other
### First phase

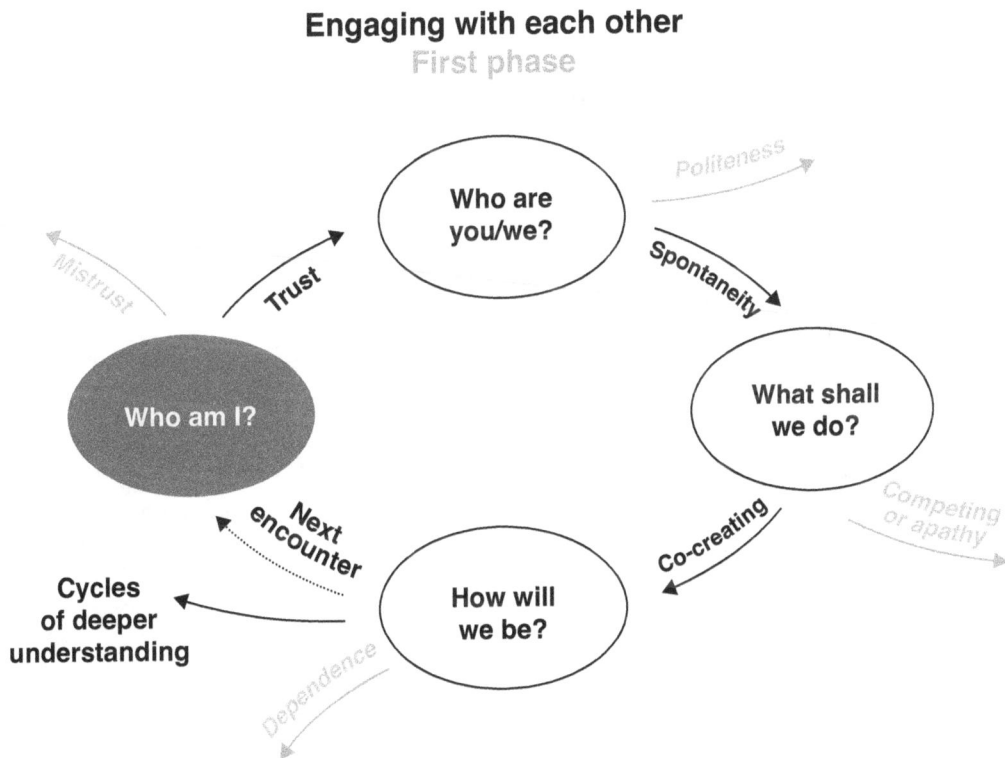

Based on the work of Jack Gibb

## Checking in – phase two

When we've connected with ourselves and have some sense of our place in a group, we turn our attention to others. This reflects the second phase of Gibb's approach: we wonder about who else is present and how *they* fit in. In essence, we're asking: who are you? Can I give credence to what you say? While we may want to know the names and roles of others, we also want to get a sense of their nature and character.

**Engaging with each other**

Second phase

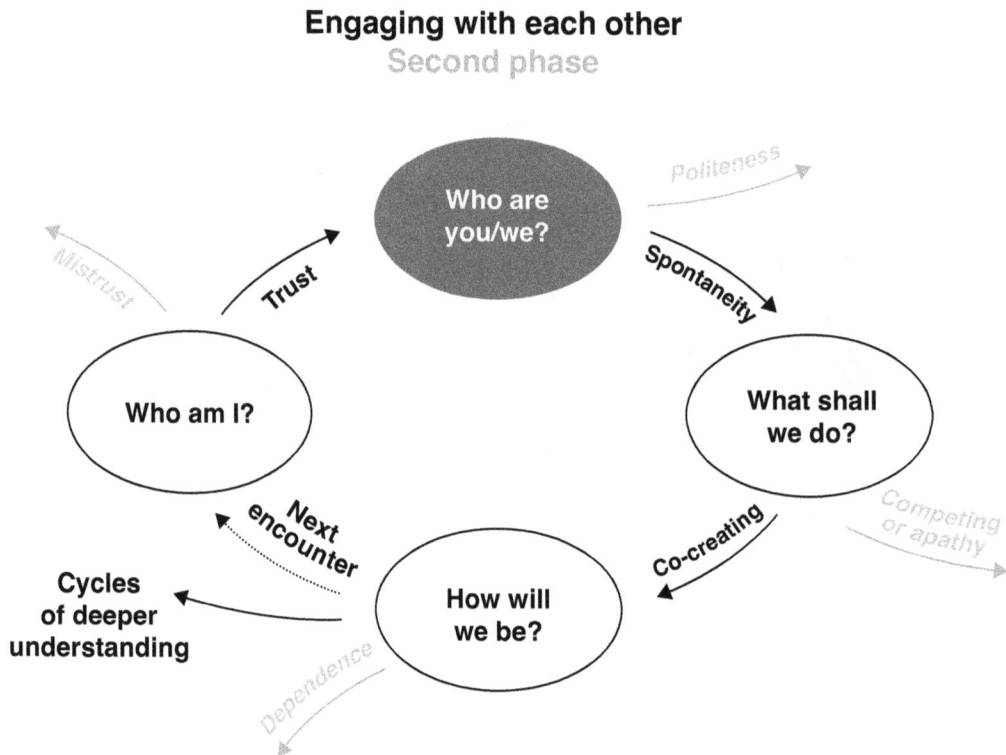

Based on the work of Jack Gibb

In a conversation, meeting or workshop group, this phase might involve sharing some headlines about how you are today and/or your appetite for what lies ahead. If those present are candid, some will be enthused and/or excited whilst others may be tired, preoccupied and/or resistant. The ability to be honest depends on the quality of the environment or 'holding space' for the conversation. In the early stages, responsibility for this often falls largely on a host, convenor or chairperson. However, if trust is carefully fostered, group members begin to take on this responsibility, and to participate in collectively holding the space. This is the development of a 'container', which we'll begin to explore in Chapter 4.

If we begin to have confidence that everyone present has something of value to contribute, it's human nature to engage more fully and spontaneously with each other. If we don't find this confidence, we may retreat into politeness and/or paying lip service to others. And so, for example, you might set this book aside if my words don't connect with you. Let's take a moment to reflect on the human aspect of checking in.

## Over to you …

Think of a time when you established, or joined, a new group or team. In this unfamiliar setting, what do you recall about your thoughts, feelings and engagement? What did you notice about the way other people navigated their new circumstances? What enabled people to find their place?

To what extent does your experience reflect the first two phases of the Gibb approach?

We'll continue our exploration of the Gibb approach in Chapter 4. In the meantime, we'll return to the process of checking in for our book-based conversation. To do this, I'll share a little more about myself and what has shaped my approach to life, work and conversations.

## Me, my work and my conversations

To give you a flavour of 'who I am': I live in the Cairngorms National Park and enjoy walking, mainly in Scotland. I'm a student of Buddhism and I practise T'ai Chi Chuan as a martial art. Both disciplines have been crucial in helping me to understand the reactions that underpin my combative nature. In terms of character, I like to learn from every experience and I strive to walk my talk.

I feel privileged to work as an executive coach and coach supervisor, and to offer leadership development programmes that explore how we can embody dialogue practices. I came to this work after a career in finance, which started in the dealing rooms of the City of London and culminated in being a director of finance in the National Health Service. During the finance years, my conversations were often terse, direct and argumentative – I took no prisoners.

I began to move towards working in leadership development in the late 1990s, when I won a scholarship to do a full-time MBA at Lancaster University. What I learned there strengthened my existing interest in organisational change, leadership and systems thinking. I was particularly inspired by *The Fifth Discipline*[7] and the practice guides that followed.[8] The material in these books seemed to come from an orientation towards learning, and this began to shape my thinking and my conversations.

After the MBA, I became an independent consultant, drawing on some of the approaches in *The Fifth Discipline*, neuro-linguistic programming (NLP), personality inventories such as the Myers-Briggs type indicator and other well-known frameworks. However, none of them really defined my work. The essential, delineating disciplines came in the form of dialogue practices rooted in the thinking of David Bohm,[9] and embodied practices developed by Wendy Palmer.[10] Together, these practices helped me to transform my conversations: dialogue approaches expanded my repertoire and Leadership Embodiment helped me to attend to the energetic impact of what I said and did. As a result, my conversations became more exploratory, open and curious.

## My outlook

Two things materially shape my outlook: my early study of pure mathematics and my recent study of Tibetan Buddhism. Pure mathematics is conceptual and systemic in nature and this has had a profound influence on how I think, and how I make sense of what I see and hear. Whilst it's difficult to explain, it seems that, in my conversations, I listen for patterns, deep structures and an underlying order in what's being said. This shapes what I notice – and what I miss.

Tibetan Buddhism has helped me to understand how my perceptions determine my reality. Two principles feel particularly relevant to our journey into dialogue. The first is that each moment conditions the next. For good or ill, the choices we make and enact set in motion everything that follows. This applies both individually and collectively. So, if I treat a colleague badly, it's likely that they'll be less willing to help me in the future. If a team covers up a mistake, they sow the seeds for a more general breakdown in trust. And, of course, if we treat someone with kindness and respect, it's likely that our relationship with them will flourish.

The second principle is that we're largely responsible for how an event affects us. In particular, we can make an adverse experience worse by taking it personally and complaining or raging. As an alternative, we can relate to the same experience by accepting the hand we've been dealt and seeking to play it well. For example, I have a strong tendency to anger. In the past, when I felt wronged and became angry, I'd fuel the anger with blame, self-justification, resentment, self-righteousness and judgement of others. This kept it smouldering – sometimes for weeks. Instead, I've learned to apply myself to de-escalating my experience of anger until (usually) I realise that I'm most often angry with myself.

In these two principles, I find strong motivation to take self-leadership seriously. When we recognise the inevitable consequences of our actions, it can motivate us to behave with integrity, generosity, courage and/or similar values. When we truly inhabit such positive qualities, we may inspire others to rise to them too. When we take ownership of our reactions to difficult people, situations and moments, and handle them well, we significantly reduce the likelihood that we'll lay our shortcomings at the feet of others. This has the potential to make our interactions more positive.

These themes will appear in different guises throughout this book. For now, let's pause and reflect.

## Over to you …

What qualities do you generally look for in a guide and/or fellow traveller? To what extent do I seem to reflect these qualities?

To what extent do you have faith in what I'm offering? What will support you to be open to my words and curious about them, even if you initially question or reject them?

What reservations do you have about me, this book and/or the work ahead? What will enable you to persevere, despite them?

As we engage with the second phase of the Gibb approach I am, of course, curious about you. What prompted you to acquire this book? What inspires you? What stretches you? How do you contribute to life on this planet? How might the approaches in these pages enhance this? As I write, I hold a whole range of readers in my mind and sincerely hope that you can hear my voice as clearly as if I was sitting next to you.

For now, we've reached the end of the 'preparation' element of our work: we have a sense of our context and have checked in with ourselves and each other. We've settled into a 'ready' stance, as described in Chapter 1. We can now begin.

Let's turn to our subject matter and check in with our purpose and then attend to how we'll engage with the development work that lies ahead.

# Chapter 4    Beginning: checking in with our purpose and approach

In the context of dialogue, we use the practice of check-in each time we meet. If we're using the Gibb approach as a guide, this means beginning each conversation by checking in with self and each other. We then turn our attention to our shared purpose and to the way we intend to 'hold' our conversation – we'll explore these two phases in this chapter.

## Checking in – phase three

To check in with our purpose, subject matter or task, we consider the third question in Gibb's approach to developing trust: what shall we do together? In a conversation, workshop setting or project team meeting, this phase is concerned with understanding why those present have come together. To do this, we invite each person to briefly outline their individual purposes, interests and/or concerns. This allows us to distil a collective direction of travel – a theme we'll pick up in Chapter 12.

The discipline of starting every conversation by checking in can be hard to embrace, as the pull to quickly get into subject matter is sometimes strong. When a group is meeting for the first time, checking in with our purpose and what we'll do together has obvious value. However, we might need to dig a little deeper to see the value of revisiting this ground in each conversation.

To understand why it's important to check in every time we meet, we can begin with the recognition that the starting point of any follow-on conversation won't reflect where the last exchange ended. With the passing of time, circumstances may have changed, actions may have been taken (or not) and thinking may have evolved. We often overlook such things – especially if we're in a hurry to make

## Engaging with each other
### Third phase

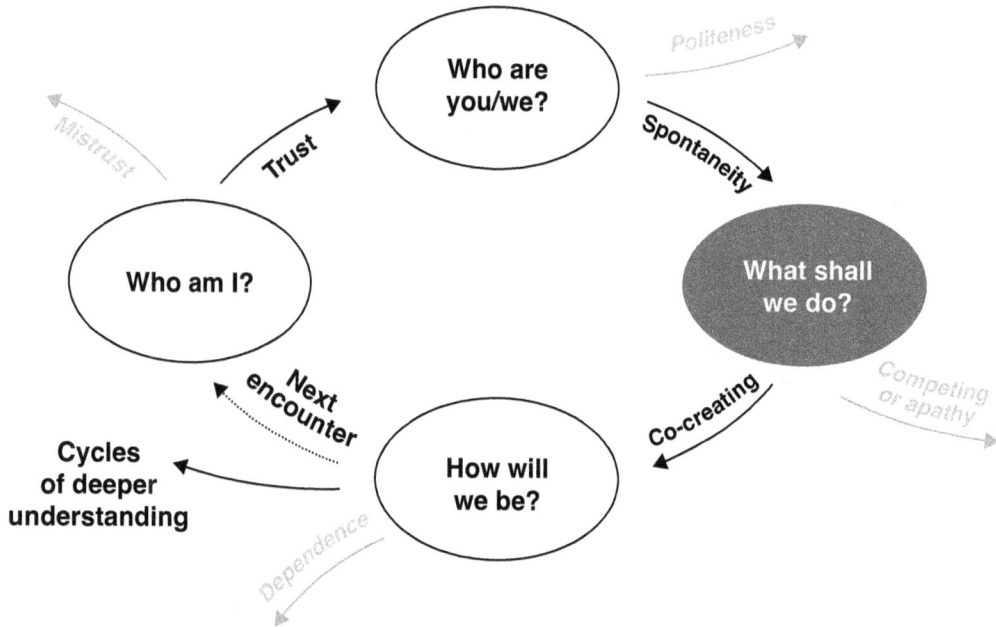

Based on the work of Jack Gibb

progress. Taking time to revisit 'what we'll do together' offers a way to update each other and ensure that today's conversation is rooted in what's current rather than what's past. The intention is to make sure we're on the same page or, as a minimum, using the same book. This makes it less likely that assumptions and misconceptions will gain traction and/or grow in stature.

In our book-based conversation, my aspiration for what we'll do together is that my writing will inspire you to embrace, explore and embody the practices of dialogue. I hope that what you discover will support you to more often recognise the energies of difference and to harness them in a creative way.

## Over to you ...

What are your aspirations for what we might do together?

How do you want to transform your leadership conversations? Perhaps you have a persistently troubling interaction that you'd like to change for the better. Perhaps you regularly participate in a conversation that leaves those involved frustrated and/or disengaged and you'd like to find a way to make these exchanges more satisfactory.

How would you like to change your practice in conversations such as these? How does this inform what we might do together?

So – what will we do together?

Since I can't know your response to this question, I'll take the liberty of assuming that we share the purpose of exploring practices for approaching difference differently. This assumption reflects the title of the book and probably played a part in your choice to read it, so I feel that I can place some reliance on it. You may also have other purposes – and, if you do, I hope that the ground we cover enables you to realise them.

To begin to be more specific about what we'll do together, I'll outline three tenets that have come to underpin my dialogue work. The tenets emerged because, over the years, I found myself repeating three themes, each drawn from a short passage in William Isaacs' book, *Dialogue and the Art of Thinking Together*.[2] From these themes, I distilled the tenets, which are:

- We are the method (pages 70 & 71 in Isaacs' book)

- Consciously holding a container (page 244)

- Entry is everything (page 293)

Later, we'll consider each tenet in depth. For now, I'll try to capture the essence of them. In doing so, I'm asserting each one as if it's true in its own right. However, the words are simply a guide to an element of practice that can support a conversation to go well. With this in mind, please treat each tenet as a hypothesis and test it against your own experience.

## Three tenets

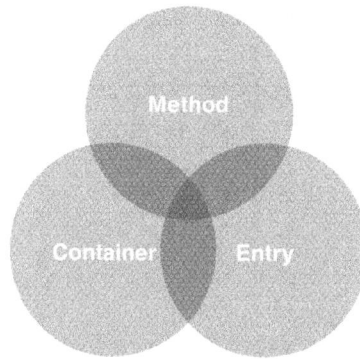

*Tenet 1: We are the method*

There is no separate, mysterious set of rules and techniques that guarantees that dialogue will occur. There's no 'method' that's distinct or separate from ourselves. Whether in a room, process or agreed virtual space, dialogue is co-created by the way that people carry themselves and relate to each other. We might say 'dialogue is us'.

*Tenet 2: Consciously holding a container*

The conditions, or container, for a conversation form collectively. In dialogue, we make this process conscious, so that the energies of difference can be held and the differences explored. Each of us is responsible for our own contribution to a conversation and, in dialogue, we also play a part in establishing and holding the shared space. When we grasp this, stewardship of the conditions for our conversation becomes as important as the subject matter.

*Tenet 3: Entry is everything*

The way a conversation begins disproportionately affects how it unfolds. The seeds of the whole conversation are sown in the very first moments and, in my view, even before we engage with others. Each of us brings assumptions, preoccupations and expectations into a conversation, and the way we begin has to cut through them so that we can all start afresh.

When taken together, the three tenets invite us to pay attention to the way we carry ourselves in our conversations. Everything we say and do sets something in motion and, as we begin to understand how we influence what unfolds in a conversation, it may prompt us to make changes in our practice. This will involve some examination of our inner world – the thoughts, feelings, beliefs and impulses that form the hinterland of what we say and do – and we may not like what we find there. However, this is part of the journey ahead – it's not for the fainthearted.

The three tenets will recur throughout this book, both structurally as later chapter headings, and more softly, woven in and out of other strands of the work we're doing together. The tenets are interdependent and I've been thoughtful about the order in which we'll explore them. In the end, I decided to set them out in a way that reflects my belief that it's *embodying* dialogue practices that makes the most difference, consciously inhabiting them, whatever's kicking off around us. When we begin with 'self', we realise that the way we show up influences the environment in which a conversation is held (the container). This invites us to be mindful of all that we say and do, since every contribution to, or entry into, a conversation sets something in motion. We'll explore this interdependence more fully when we've considered each tenet separately. In the meantime, I'll deliberately repeat the tenets and/or related themes, again and again, doing so because repetition is the bedrock of absorbing principles and putting them into practice.

A final note about the tenets and the themes they represent: I didn't consciously select them. I feel it's important to be transparent about this because the tenets are based on just 124 words taken from the 403 pages of *Dialogue and the Art of Thinking Together*. Clearly, I've omitted a great deal of the book's wisdom, and it's a risk to take such an obviously partial perspective. It's also human to be partial, in two respects: the information we take in and use is always both incomplete and subject to our preferences. Whilst I wonder how my practice would be different if other things had come to the fore, I believe these particular themes emerged because of my emphasis on embodying dialogue practices.

## Checking in – phase four

When we've considered what we might do together, we turn to the fourth phase of Gibb's approach: the conditions that will support this shared endeavour. Our attention shifts from 'what' to 'how' and we ask: how will we engage with each other? With this question, we begin to locate ourselves more fully in the way we intend to foster the conditions for our conversation. Having gained a sense of those present and our collective purpose, we consider how we'll conduct ourselves and what kind of energy we'll bring to our conversation. In doing so, we begin to consciously hold our container.

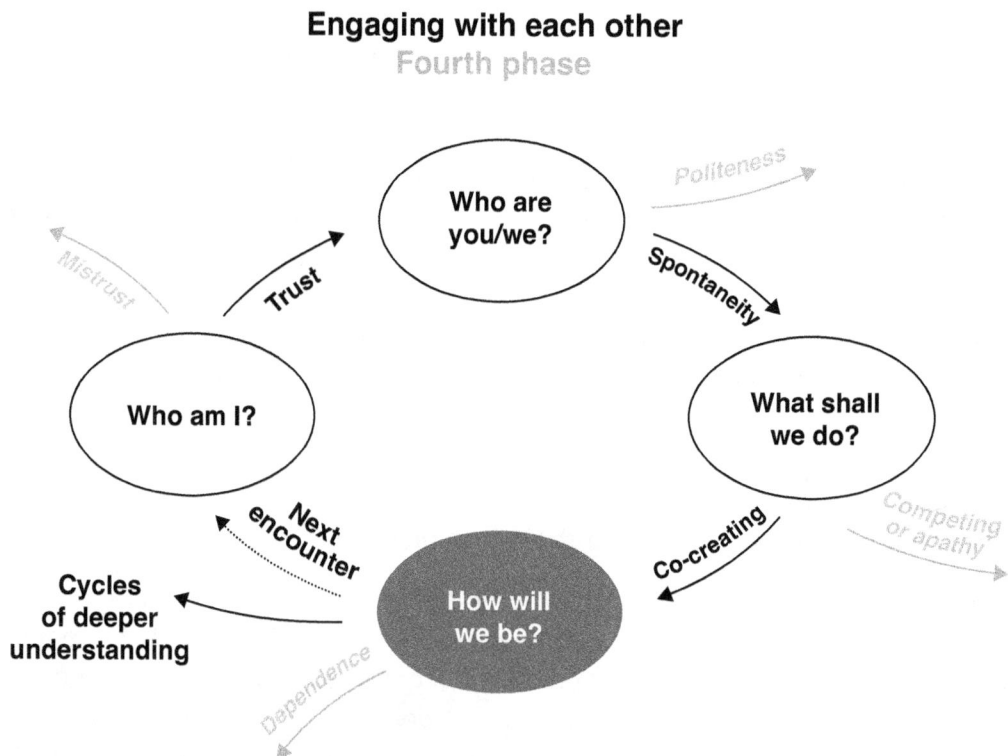

**Engaging with each other**
Fourth phase

Who are you/we?

Politeness

Mistrust

Trust

Spontaneity

Who am I?

What shall we do?

Competing or apathy

Next encounter

Co-creating

Cycles of deeper understanding

How will we be?

Dependence

Based on the work of Jack Gibb

34

The principle of this phase of Gibb's approach is that good engagement is underpinned by a qualitative climate that allows us to navigate the bumps and potholes of a conversation. When people are initially unknown to each other and need to build trust from scratch, this aspect of checking in clearly matters. And, when people know each other rather too well and come into a conversation with baggage, it may matter even more.

In my workshops, I tend to engage with 'how we'll be' by inviting those present to identify a really good conversation that they've been part of and reflect on what made it possible. This offers some pointers for the conditions that we'll need to cultivate if our own conversation is to go well. I then emphasise that the quality of our collective energy, the ambience of our environment, will depend on how well we each uphold the conditions we've described.

Of course, I'm assuming that we're able to shape the way a conversation is set up, and sometimes this isn't possible. When we're not in a position to influence the setting, the best we can do is see the circumstances clearly and act as well as we can within them. Much of the guidance offered in these pages can be used in such situations: the way we carry ourselves affects what unfolds in a conversation whether or not we've been involved in establishing the container for it.

Let's return to our book-based conversation and explore how we'll approach it. Through my intention to be in conversation with you, I've set the scene for the qualitative conditions that I hope we'll foster together. For my part, I'm aiming to be present to you, in my full humanness. I'm a work in progress, doing my best to share my experience. As I write, I'm immersed in our conversation, attending to you, my reader, even though I don't know you personally. You're present to me in that I try to imagine what it'll be like to read what I've written. You're also present as I wonder how to create space for your voice alongside mine.

Another aspect of how I'm approaching our conversation is to try to be clear that it's up to you whether and how you embrace what you find in these pages. Some things will feel more pertinent than others and I encourage you to work with what you find relevant. However, it can also be useful to examine the things we feel more inclined to reject. When we examine what we resist, we sometimes find valuable data that we've side-stepped or overlooked.

For example, many years ago, my coach supervisor suggested that I might be listening too intensely to my client and she wondered what impact this might have. At the time, I found the concept of 'over-listening' very strange and dismissed it. In truth, I didn't really understand what she was saying. Yet, because I found the moment odd, I didn't completely forget it.

Then, in a Leadership Embodiment workshop several years later, Wendy Palmer invited participants to explore the different energies of distracted listening, overly attentive listening and centred listening (which we'll meet in Chapter 11). As my practice partner embodied the kind of listening that hangs on to every word, I felt squirmy and stifled, and then annoyed. The penny dropped. It *is* possible to over-listen, and it doesn't create good conditions for a healthy conversation.

This insight provided the motivation to change my practice. One of my leadership values is listening well and I now had a deeper appreciation of how to embody this. I began to hold myself to account with greater rigour, and to fine-tune my listening energy so that, to those speaking, it feels open, receptive and spacious.

## Over to you …

What values do you aspire to embody in your leadership and in your conversations? How might they inform the way you approach the material in this book? What's your commitment to yourself as you engage with what's on offer?

And when, inevitably, you read something that you don't like or strongly disagree with, what will support you to examine your response for undiscovered insights?

To circle back to what we might do together, my aspiration for all my work, whether one-to-one conversations, workshops or writing, is that we each leave the encounter in better shape than we arrived. This sometimes means that a participant or reader has new resources to hand – but most often it means that they feel a little lighter of spirit and a little more able to re-enter the fray. This is a qualitative outcome that links 'how we'll be' with 'what we'll do together'.

So, as you read, I hope our book-based conversation replenishes your leadership spirit and supports you to reconnect with what matters to you. I also hope you'll feel energised enough to invest in changing your practice in your conversations.

## Making check-in a habit

We've come to the end of our check-in. We've checked in with ourselves and with each other, and we've anchored our book-based conversation in shared endeavour. We've also considered how we'll engage with each other and the book. Along the way, you may have realised that the Gibb approach reflects the three tenets that were introduced in this chapter. It supports us to begin a conversation well – entry is everything. It emphasises that the way we bring ourselves to a conversation, individually, shapes what's possible – we are the method. And it prompts us to pay attention to the conditions we're creating for our conversation – our container – and to consciously hold them.

This chapter began with the observation that, for dialogue, we use the practice of check-in each time we meet. Personally, I use the four phases of the Gibb approach to prepare for most of my conversations, whether in a group or a one-to-one conversation such as coaching. It's a powerful way to support the process of checking in and I encourage you to use it so that it becomes a habit.

For my part, it took time and effort to adopt this habit. I was introduced to Gibb's work in the 1990s by facilitators from The King's Fund.[11] At the time, I was a director of finance and had a strong predisposition to 'cut to the chase' and drive things forward. The Gibb approach gave me pause and helped me to understand that connecting at a human level before getting 'stuck in' might create a more robust foundation for collective work.

Later, in my consulting practice, one of my clients had the Gibb approach taped to her wall. We'd once been colleagues and had good rapport. Intellectually, we both saw the power of checking in. Did we do it? Of course not! I'd arrive in her office, already mid-sentence about our next steps and we'd both get drawn into the potentials of our project. Then, usually about twenty minutes later, one of us would say: 'oops, we forgot to check in'. Thankfully, we had the discipline to back-track, each of us clear that we wanted to embrace this process. Gradually, our commitment to taking remedial action seeped into our task-oriented brains and we more often remembered to check in at the beginning of a conversation. To borrow a phrase from a fellow coach supervisor, Monica Ross, the underlying principle is 'cont*act* before cont*ract*': we connect at a human level before we get down to work.

Like my client and me, your current habit might be to move straight to task and action, especially in conversations with colleagues. The benefits of checking in at a human level are easy to overlook and, if we're already in a trusting environment and/or we're addressing issues that are linear in nature and easily resolvable, this may not matter. However, in more complex dynamics, we may hinder progress if we don't make contact at a human level before engaging in collaborative effort.

## Transition to Part II

As we come to the end of our 'preparation and beginning', let's pause and reflect. Through the process of checking in, we've started to become more aware of, and prepared for, the factors that influence our conversations. When something important is at stake, the difference between a good outcome and an indifferent one might depend on the attention we pay to how we'll begin, how we'll carry ourselves and how we'll create good conditions for our conversation. The essence of working with dialogue practices is that we attend to the elusive nature of the 'how' of a conversation as well as the magnetic material of the 'what'. We kick the habit of 'content is king' and put energy into fostering the 'look and feel' of our conversations. The dialogue practice of check-in supports us to introduce this change.

## Over to you …

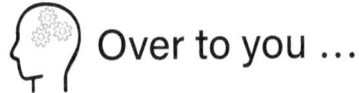

As you reflect on the ground that we've covered in Part I, what has caught your imagination? What has seemed less important?

What one thing might you adopt and begin to put into practice? How will you assess the impact of doing this?

In Part II, we'll continue to explore the factors that influence the way our conversations unfold. We'll start to use models and frameworks to describe the shape and quality of our interactions, building our capacity to 'zoom out' of a conversation to consider the interplay between individual contributions and emerging collective patterns.

The overall theme of Part II is the relationship between the elegance of ideas and messy human reality, and we'll take our time at this boundary between concepts and experience. We'll begin to work with an aspect of our embodied experience, a visceral reality that can quickly derail us when we find ourselves in the energies of difference. We'll also discover how to embody a centred state that can support us to engage skilfully with these energies. Part II will prepare us to work with body and mind when we engage deeply with the three tenets in Part III. This is our pathway to embodying dialogue practices and to approaching difference differently.

Let's embark on the next stage of our journey.

# Part II

## Ideas and realities

# Chapter 5 Ideas and realities: introduction

In Chapter 1, I observed that most leadership is conducted through the medium of conversation, adding that any preparation that we do tends to focus tends on *what* we want to say rather than *how* we'll say it. The collective parallel is a focus on agenda topics rather than the climate that will support the kind of conversation we hope to have.

## Our leadership development path

If we wish to nurture our capacity to pay attention to the 'how' of a conversation, there are two strands to the leadership development path ahead. The first is increasing our knowledge by adding material that can be used to describe the shape and quality of our conversations. This 'ideas' strand matters because it helps us to articulate both the way a conversational experience is unsatisfactory and our aspirations to stimulate something more worthwhile. When we're able to describe the nature of a conversation and how and/or why it might not be meeting the needs of those present, we can share these insights with others.

When we acknowledge that a conversation isn't fit for purpose, we're more likely to address the issue and to foster an environment that will support a better outcome. There are many frameworks that can help us in this. In the following chapters, we'll explore how we can use some of them to shed light on the relationship between the shape and quality of a conversation and its outcome.

The second strand of our developmental path is to increase our personal capacity to be poised, open and effective, even when an environment or conversation becomes unsettled, unwieldy, ineffective or toxic. One composed and skilful person, with the right knowledge, insight and presence, can bring a conversation back from a precipitous edge. By handling ourselves well, we can favourably affect the energy and tone of a conversation, and potentially neutralise any destructive momentum that might otherwise go unchecked. Becoming this kind of conversational superhero calls for a different development path, that of:

- cultivating awareness of the way physiology hijacks our good intentions; and

- conditioning our mind and body to regain perspective and equanimity, even in testing circumstances.

This is the focus of the realities strand of Part II. Broadly, we can learn how to handle ourselves in the way that an elite tennis player does. This involves being able to operate well under pressure and to regroup when things are going badly (or unexpectedly well). We know that this kind of mastery takes effort – dedication, repetition, stress-testing. Yet many of us expect to simply be able to emulate such feats without putting in the practice. This is the bad news: we can't replace unhelpful embodied habits and behaviours with more fruitful approaches just because we get the gist of the process.

It takes time and repetition to build the capacity to recover our equilibrium when we're knocked off balance or have retreated into a familiar, but unproductive, course of action. In Chapter 9, we'll meet a centring practice that we can use to support us to regroup – it's a practice of body and energy as well as mind. This means we have to put in the work to build a neural pathway for it and develop something like 'muscle memory'. We have to apply ourselves to this process.

There's also good news. Combining new knowledge and new practices increases both our leadership repertoire and our versatility. Like those elite tennis players, we have a greater range of strokes and can play them more readily, sometimes instinctively and with brilliance. Further, as we develop in our own leadership, we may inspire others, sowing seeds that can grow into increased collective capacity for skilful and productive conversations.

## Over to you …

What's your level of openness to new ideas? Are you willing to begin to look at the shape and quality of conversations alongside their content? How might you make a start on this?

What's your initial response to the reality that embodied learning will take time and effort? What outcome would make it worthwhile to invest in building a new practice? To begin, how might you pay more attention to your embodied experience?

## Daunting realities

In the chapters that follow, we'll explore ideas and frameworks that will offer ways to describe different aspects of our conversations. We'll also probe two rather daunting realities, one relating to individual experience and the other to collective experience. The first is that, inconveniently, the human body is wired with a powerful legacy system that can override our mind and derail our plans. This is a physiological process that gives rise to reactivity in the form of a tendency to flee, fight or freeze. When we understand the impact of this legacy system, we may be motivated to find ways to work skilfully with it. We'll feel the benefit … and so will everyone around us.

The collective reality is that human groups establish patterns of interaction that support their shared purpose. In a given context, this is initially useful. However, elements of a collective 'routine' may remain in place despite changes in purpose, group membership or the wider environment. An established collective habit can survive beyond its sell-by date.

These two aspects of our engagement with others are testing enough when we meet them in relatively bounded situations, such as in a team or organisation. However, in an era in which it seems that tolerance of difference is reducing, they also play out at a societal level. In these settings, our human reactivity and the tendency for groups to establish patterns of interaction can combine to silence those who don't subscribe to a preferred narrative. When this happens, voices are excluded, diversity is reduced and inequality increases. We'll consider these themes in Chapter 11.

First, we'll explore how we can describe the shape and quality of our conversations.

## Chapter 6    Ideas: the shape and quality of conversations

Conversation – in its broadest sense – is the medium in which difference is most obviously encountered. If we're to take an embodied approach to being in dialogue, it's important to understand what might influence the way a conversation plays out when differences arise.

To perceive what's unfolding in a conversation, especially when good intentions falter or dissolve into acrimony or a stand-off, it's useful to step back and examine what took place (or is taking place) with an attitude of kindness and fascination. As a general principle, an unexpected turn of events is unlikely to have its roots in subject matter. Instead, the *form* and *energy* of what's being said may be creating conditions that *squeeze* a conversation into a corner, reducing the available possibilities. Those present feel the squeeze, viscerally, and they tighten in response. Unless someone intervenes in a way that reverses the process and creates more room for manoeuvre, things get worse.

## Conversational patterns

When we lift ourselves out of the magnetic hold that words and opinions seem to have, we might notice that there are recurring patterns in our interactions. If we attend a regular gathering of the same people – a management team, for instance – we may notice that the same people tend to speak, possibly in a fairly predictable order. We may also notice that they repeat similar themes in what they say: certain people tend to speak of possibilities, or push for decisions or actions, while others habitually raise problems with proposals or want to spend more time considering all angles. These are all useful contributions – when they're made at the right time, in balance and with awareness. However, such recurring behaviours often give rise to a conversational 'routine', with one type of contribution, or a particular pattern of contributions, prevailing. Inadvertently, this can become encoded as 'the way we do things'. Then, when circumstances require a different kind of conversation, it can be challenging to break out of the routine.

For example, if a team prefers to explore perspectives in order to get a sense of things 'in the round', they may be less comfortable about making decisions, as there's always another angle to consider. This may lead to difficulties in situations that require a speedy assessment of options followed by swift and convincing action. The team have unconsciously developed a collective form and patterning of energy that holds them in seeking more information, even when they're trying to move to a conclusion at pace. A counter-example is a group whose conversational convention is to quickly find and implement solutions to problems. When they encounter a knotty, nuanced issue that requires more insight into interdependencies and uncertainties, their customary routine may generate a suboptimal choice, leading to problematic unintended consequences.

It's important to say that no pattern of conversation is universally good or bad – a routine that works well in one set of circumstances may be unsuitable in another. Energetic patterns arise and repeat without being consciously recognised because most people don't attend to the structures and forces at play in a conversation. There's a kind of blindness to the shape and quality of a conversation, which can be exacerbated by the collective nature of it. A pattern can become accepted and embedded without anyone noticing.

This is similar to what happens when an organisational culture develops. Its roots may go back decades and the culture remains alive, even as those who first established it move on. Conversational patterns can also carry prevailing behaviours into new settings, sometimes inappropriately. The patterns come about stealthily: in the words of one of my MBA lecturers, they *accrete*, like mould. Later, I'll call these patterns conversational 'operating systems', the background coding in which all conversational 'programmes' or 'apps' run (or not).

There's a corollary to the presence of an unnoticed conversational pattern. When a conversation derails, it's often the underlying form and energy that's the root cause, rather than a 'difficult' or 'obstructive' person or a particular idea or view. In essence, if a conversational form isn't fit for purpose, it's unlikely things will go well. When we understand how the shape and quality of the energy we bring to a conversation enables or limits it, we may begin to consider how to set things up to support a more fruitful outcome. This is the territory of containers, which we'll consider in depth in Chapters 24 to 29.

## Over to you ...

Think of a time when you've attended a regular meeting, whether at work or in a community or volunteering setting. When you reflect on things such as how people arrive at the meeting, where they sit, who speaks first, what do you notice?

What unspoken customs seem to 'hold' the meeting in a particular form, such as the role of chair, the style of agenda and factors such as seniority or tenure?

What types of conversation are productive in this setting? What types of conversation don't seem to gain any traction? What insights arise from this reflection?

When we grasp that the underlying energetic form of a conversation can disable our efforts to be effective, we can see the value of gaining insight into the currents that influence our exchanges. This, in turn, allows us to discern whether our own actions are reinforcing existing patterns or usefully disrupting them.

## The shape and quality of conversations

Over time, I've come to consider conversations as entities in their own right, arising from the dynamic complexity inherent in even the simplest human exchange. I invite you to adopt this perspective. With it, we start to expect that collective patterns of activity, words and energy will become established, and we actively look for them and consider their influence. Such patterns are influenced by all present, and aren't directly attributable to any one person or contribution. Simply by being human, everyone involved in a conversation affects the tone or vibe of it. We're energetic beings, and we often communicate more potently through our mood and disposition than through what we say.

So, how might we attend to the shape and quality of a conversation?

To gain insight into the 'shape' of a conversation, we can use theories, models and frameworks developed by thinkers and practitioners in the field of dialogue and related subjects. Such ideas support us to describe the form of a conversation and to identify things we might try to change. This is predominantly an activity of mind and is reasoned, analytical and/or diagnostic. In the next chapter, we'll use a short case study to explore how we might do this.

To tune in to the 'quality' of a conversation, we pay attention to the energies that different people bring into it and the way these combine. In essence, we ask: in this conversation, what's being embodied, individually and collectively?

We're now on ground that's experiential and qualitative, and draws on senses beyond words and language. We're picking up a mood, a tone, a feeling. We have two primary antennae for such energetic experiences:

- our ears pick up the pace, timbre and tenor of what's said (as well as the words themselves); and

- our body senses mood and ambience.

Our eyes may also play a part, by noticing posture, gestures and unconscious behavioural 'tells' such as micro-movements or changes in expression. Whilst not strictly energetic in nature, such observations are sometimes an indication of a change in energy.

The mind also has a role in discerning the vibe of a conversation in that it supports us to access and pay attention to the qualitative data that's available to our ears and body. When we try to articulate these energies, we often use metaphor, imagery or a memory. We're giving an *impression* of an experience. It's an art, not an analytical process and it brings richness into the way we describe a conversation.

## Over to you ...

Take some time to reflect on your response to these last few paragraphs. How much attention do you tend to pay to the 'feel' of a conversation, its ambience? How do you notice changes in this?

Can you identify an example of a situation when a phrase or question significantly changed the nature of a conversation? If so, how would you describe the *atmosphere* before and after this moment? What might have contributed to any change of mood?

In the next chapter, we'll begin to explore the way that tools and frameworks can help us articulate the shape of a conversation and offer insight into what unfolds as a consequence.

# Chapter 7  Ideas: using models

As we start to wonder why things turn out the way they do in our conversations, we can draw on the ideas of those who've already travelled this path and developed models to communicate their insights to others. In this chapter, I'll introduce a short case study based on a snippet of a real exchange, and we'll use a framework to examine its shape and quality.

When reflecting on a conversation, models and frameworks provide a *language* to help us describe what might be going on. No matter how well-researched, they don't define 'truths' and aren't predictive tools. In addition, most aren't valid in all circumstances. However, they can offer creative 'prompts' that shed light on what's taking place. They can also draw attention to things that are over-used or missing, which might suggest an alternative way of contributing. On a personal level, they can help us to see our own part in what's playing out, whether actively or through inactivity.

When applied thoughtfully, a good model or framework can offer a plausible and useful representation of events and dynamics – providing we hold what we surmise lightly. A good model or framework is any vehicle with the potential to lift us out of the 'content' of a conversation, so that we can reflect on:

- how well the shape and quality of the conversation supports our shared purpose;

- fresh perspectives, questions and insights, and what we might be missing; and

- different ways of contributing.

Let's use the simple, yet powerful, distinction between advocacy and inquiry to look at how we can apply the ideas of a model to the realities of a conversation.

## Advocacy and inquiry: a case study

The framework of advocacy and inquiry introduces two archetypal kinds of contribution to a conversation. They are:

*Advocacy:* Speaking what you think, outlining a point of view, position or opinion.

*Inquiry:* Looking into what you don't yet know or understand, seeking to discover what others see and how this differs from your perspective.

These definitions (which are advocacy in themselves) focus on the content and intent of what we're saying. Typically, advocacy might be a statement and inquiry a question. But it isn't quite as simple as this – we can use tone, timbre and inflection of voice to bring *inquiring energy* to a statement, while the feeling of a closed question resonates with *advocating energy*. It's the quality of energy we bring to what we say that most eloquently expresses whether we're advocating or inquiring. Let's take a brief look at the characteristics of these energies, then we'll explore them in greater depth later.

Inquiring energy tends to be exploratory, curious, inviting. I think of it as being circular and receptive in shape and nature. When it's skilfully used, I experience it as either:

- spiralling down into deeper discovery of what's being said; or

- soaring upwards, like an eagle catching a thermal to gain perspective.

In Chapter 11, we'll discover that our energy radiates out from us to form a personal space – we know this instinctively when someone 'invades' it. Then, in Chapter 21, we'll explore how we can consciously influence both the shape and extent of our personal space. For the moment, and from a bird's-eye perspective, we can imagine circular energy 'around' us, as shown in the diagram below.

## Bird's-eye view of energy
Inquiring

This balanced, circular energy is open and receptive, which supports skilful inquiry and communicates that we're interested in what others say. Much later, in Chapter 31, we'll look at what others might experience when this circle of energy contracts or expands unevenly.

In contrast, advocating energy tends to be directional, purposeful, clear. I think of it as being pointed in nature, a triangular shape, and we can see this when someone extends their hand or finger to 'make a point'. When advocating energy is skilfully used, I experience it as either:

- coursing towards something, like the bow of a boat moving through water (and perhaps creating waves); or

- probing a proposition or idea, seeking lucidity and coherence.

From a bird's-eye perspective, this triangular energy is depicted in the following diagram.

## Bird's-eye view of energy
Advocating

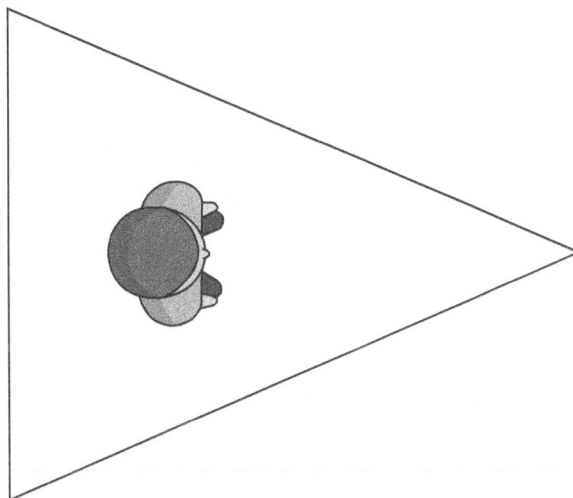

A key feature of advocating energy is that it can be more or less 'pointed' in nature, and this affects the impact of our words on those listening. In Chapter 31, we'll look at this in detail. For the moment, let's bear this in mind as we apply the framework of advocacy and inquiry to an exchange based on real events.

### Case Study 1

What follows is a summary of an exchange between a managing director (MD) and a chief operating officer (COO). It took place in the corner of a wider gathering and concerns a written report which identified a key objective that hadn't been met. The report recommended a significant financial investment to address the issue. The two people involved held different opinions about what to do next. This gives us an opportunity to look at the shape of a conversation where difference is expressed.

# Case Study 1

| 1. MD: | I don't want this report to go to the Board. |
|--------|---------------------------------------------|
| 2. COO: | I know you don't, but it's a governance requirement. |
| 3. MD: | I think you're wrong and I don't want the report to go. |
| 4. COO: | Why not? |
| 5. MD: | I don't think it needs to – we can sign this off ourselves. |
| 6. COO: | We can't. The total cost of the project exceeds our sign-off limits. |
| 7. MD: | Well, the limits are ridiculous, I want them changed. |
| 8. COO: | Perhaps, but for now we need to comply with what's in place. |

When we use the framework of advocacy and inquiry to examine this conversation, we see that the first three inputs are statements of position, of point and counterpoint. While the fourth input is a question – and an open question, potentially seeking to understand – it too seems quite pointed. This impression is reinforced by the reply – short and sharp. We can almost feel the rat-a-tat rhythm of this brief exchange between colleagues (who, for the record, had a strong and constructive relationship). We're getting a feel for the shape of the conversation.

The sixth input is more advocacy and you can almost feel the tension rising. The people concerned are in opposition, holding different views. In addition, one has greater position power. However, the other may be on higher moral and governance ground. Whilst we can't know this for sure, because we only have access to a snippet of their world, this observation is based on what the MD says next: 'Well, the limits are ridiculous ...'

Rather than continue back and forth, the MD sidesteps and condemns the basis of the COO's case. My guess is she knows that she'll lose a 'straight fight' and goes for a side swipe. She's on the weaker ground and changes tack. The COO doesn't fall for this diversion and sticks to the issue at hand. He prevails, but in an unsatisfactory way. He's defeated the MD's stance, rather than coming to an agreed position.

*After* the event, the COO reflected on the shape and quality of this conversation. In doing so, he realised that every contribution was advocatory and wondered what would have happened if he'd been more genuinely curious about the MD's reluctance to put the report in front of the Board. A few days later, over a coffee, he followed up on this and discovered that the MD was concerned about a potential media storm if the report was in the public domain. In this more informal setting, and after the dust had settled, he elicited more information from the MD.

To accomplish this, it's likely that the COO embodied inquiring energy and conveyed genuine interest about her stance. In fact, the COO had already discussed the media issue with the comms team, who were confident that they could handle the matter to the advantage of the organisation. He was able to share this with the MD. Through this follow-up conversation both the COO and the MD had a better understanding of what had taken place and their strong relationship was reaffirmed.

While the COO's reflection took place after the conversation, he then took the opportunity to practise a different kind of contribution by returning to the issue with the MD in more genial circumstances, thus reinforcing his mental reflection. In addition, having an embodied experience of inquiring energy acts as 'training' for the next time a similar energetic structure occurs – which, inevitably, it will. In taking the step of *trying out* a change, it's more likely that he'll be able to inquire in the moment when such circumstances arise again.

## Over to you …

How does the 'stuck' conversation described in the case feel familiar? What tends to happen when you experience this kind of impasse?

Now see if you can find an example of a different kind of 'stuckness', one in which the conversation seems to go round in circles – what tends to happen when you experience this kind of impasse?

Which of these two kinds of stuckness (there are others) is most prevalent in your conversations? How might you change your contribution and see how this affects the pattern?

## Embodying a change in practice

The case study offers the opportunity to begin to attend to the energetics of a conversation. We can take another look at it and consider the mood and atmosphere generated in the exchange: it feels like a strained, tightening energy that could have completely derailed things. This is an embodied aspect of what took place, rather than an intellectual one. Can you tune in to the qualitative 'feel' of the energy? Have you had a similar experience?

In personal or leadership development, using a model or tool to generate cognitive insight is the easy bit. The hard part comes when we try to put the insight into practice. When we attempt to change the way we're contributing to a conversational pattern, both our personal reactivity and the pattern tend to hold us in a familiar place. In one-to-one exchanges, patterns are often fairly clear, and they're tailored to our different familiars, whether friends, family or colleagues. When we attempt to make a change in what we say and/or do, the pattern acts as a homeostatic tendency that tries to return us to whatever 'steady state' has been established.

In the case study, we can see that the pattern of interaction between the COO and the MD is an advocatory 'to and fro'. If either of them becomes more strident or reactive, the energy of the conversation will rise while the focus narrows. If this happens, the energetic pattern is 'in charge', rather than the people. In this instance, the COO had enough awareness of the heightening tension to maintain his composure and not get sucked into an energetic endpoint of 'pistols at dawn'. However, in the moment, he wasn't able to change the way he was contributing to the pattern.

When we understand the role of patterns in what plays out, we can look for the signs that one is forming and take steps to mitigate its magnetic pull. How we do this will vary with the circumstances – but in a one-to-one conversation, a starting point is to recover our equilibrium and re-set our own energy and perspective. We'll look at a practice for doing this in Chapter 9 and, if you're curious in the meantime, you can find it at Appendix B.

This brings our initial scrutiny of the case to a close. In Chapter 10, we'll revisit the embodied element of it and further explore the challenge of putting what we know into action.

For now, let's summarise how we've approached the case so that we can apply the process to our own conversations. The first step is to examine what happened with curiosity. This creates space to draw on models and frameworks and apply them to the reality of our situation. With as much impartiality as possible, we wonder:

- what's happening for individuals, between individuals and collectively?

- what's my part in this?; and

- what might I change in the way I contribute?

Having done the mind work, we then enlist the support of the body to test the potential change of approach: we find an opportunity to try it in a follow-up situation.

In this chapter, we've begun to acknowledge that body and mind aren't separate – the mind is hosted by the body, a reflexive complex of chemicals, electrical signals and pre-verbal coding that is beyond direct 'management'. Both body and mind play a part in what we communicate. Sometimes, they appear to be at odds with one another – such as when we proclaim our support for a proposal (mind-based) whilst literally turning away with our body. When this happens, we're delivering a mixed message. As we start to understand how mind and body work together (or not), we can take steps to ensure they're synchronised so that we communicate with clarity and coherence.

When we give it some thought, we're likely to realise that there are many ways in which we can be misguided or mistaken in our mind, and this can cause difficulties in our conversation. What tends to be less well known is that, if we disregard the role of the body in our interactions, any difficulties are exacerbated, to the detriment of outcomes and relationships. It's time to focus on the body – we ignore it at our peril.

# Chapter 8    Realities: context

Whereas ideas tend towards what's possible and what might be changed, reality is often messy and problematic. So, in this chapter, we shift our focus away from the potentials of dialogue practices and towards an exploration of how and why our conversations blow up, get bogged down or simply bypass what matters.

When conversations go awry, the reasons are situational and nuanced. Many factors affect how someone shows up for a conversation, from the kind of day they've had to their history with the other people involved. We each bring a mind-set into the room (whether physical or virtual), with assumptions, preferences, preoccupations and insecurities. The stakes may be high and there may be many uncertainties and unknowns in the subject matter that's being explored. Everyone will be influenced by this. If we then add difference in to the mix – different views, values, aspirations, cultures and so on – the situation can quickly become intense. Any or all of these considerations might be in play – and many of them are outside our influence and control. In addition, they affect us energetically, whether we're aware of it or not – and this shapes how we react (or respond) to what others say.

Within this, there are two things we can influence, even if we expect to walk into a hostile and combative environment. One is the way *we carry ourselves* and the other is *the energy we bring* to a conversation. Our demeanour and presence materially impact what unfolds, yet we don't often take this into account. Let's pause so that you can get a sense of what I'm alluding to.

## Over to you ...

Recall a situation in which you faced mild adversity, such as dealing with a difficult issue or person, or being in a conversation that slightly threatened your aspirations, values or reputation. How did you feel? What thoughts ran through your mind? What did you experience in your body and breathing?

Take a short break to 'shake off' this recollection.

Now recall a situation in which you felt inspired, such as a successful collaboration, or being in a conversation full of possibilities and encouragement. How did you feel? What thoughts ran through your mind? What did you experience in your body and breathing?

Again, take a short break to let this example go.

Now take a few moments to compare these two situations – try to characterise their energy and notice how you were affected by each one. How did your inner experience affect what you said and did?

In tricky circumstances, the role the body plays in our conversations is often more apparent. It's also more important. Even in mild adversity, we're physically 'on alert' and have an increased sense of watchfulness. When facing a greater challenge, chemicals such as adrenalin and cortisol are released, flooding our body to ready us for fight or flight. We're at the mercy of our autonomic nervous system, a biochemical legacy of the eat-or-be-eaten days of our early ancestors. Before we know it, we've become 'jammed' as our physiology prioritises survival and closes down non-essential functions. Our focus narrows and our capacity to act or speak skilfully is reduced, if not entirely compromised. This affects how we show up.

In a group, the stakes may be high for everyone. If so, each body will be on alert, creating a collective tension that isn't located in any single person. Without awareness, stakes may be further raised by individual reactions to this communal energy. The energetic temperature rises – an escalation which is almost viral in nature – and this compromises individual and collective capacity to engage skilfully with difference. The good news is that this collective energetic heat can be reversed if we're able to re-set our personal energy. How might we do this?

## The role of the autonomic nervous system

A first step is to regard the energetics of a conversation to be as important as the subject matter and to take this into account. This supports us to recognise how we're affected by being in (or approaching) a conversation that's crucial, either personally or professionally. In my case, I experience a state of heightened vigilance – especially if I expect to encounter some opposition (or difference). Specifically, I tighten and hold myself more rigidly, becoming combative or defensive as if I'm preparing for battle. In contrast, others may become quiet and withdraw into themselves, or may take steps to try to smooth things over.

On an individual level, we each have a personal suite of physical 'early warnings' that signal that our ability to be skilful in what we say and do is compromised. These 'alerts' indicate that our autonomic nervous system is activated and, if we learn to spot the signs, we can regroup and return to presence.

Personally, when I'm caught up in my own preoccupations, I listen less. I'm quick to judge, disconnect, dismiss. Essentially, I lose contact with myself and any sense of good grace. If those around me become similarly focused on their immediate concerns, things don't tend to go well. Each of us is in survival mode, without access to warmth, humour, perspective and generosity. If this limiting energy goes unnoticed, we're likely to let it gather momentum or to inadvertently suppress it. We then become hostage to it. This is when a situation can become flammable.

If, instead, just one person is able to change their energetic state and become more composed and open, their lighter spirit acts as an 'antidote' to the rising intensity. The situation improves – sometimes dramatically. When one person recovers their presence, it can nudge others to do the same. People literally 'collect' themselves.

Channelling our personal energy in this way is an art, and it involves learning how to disentangle our energetic experience from the content of a conversation. To do this, we use the sense of heightened tension brought about by adrenalin and cortisol to prompt us to change our energetic state. We'll look at an effective way of making this embodied change in the next chapter. For now, I'm inviting you to consider that the root of reactivity is a survival pattern deeply ingrained in the legacy system of the human body. This means that, however good our intentions (located in the mind), they're susceptible to hijack by this primitive process (located in the body). To follow through on good intentions when the chips are down involves cultivating greater embodied intelligence. We're then more able to notice when physiology takes over and this allows us to take steps to recover presence.

All this is important for the way we approach difference because our legacy survival system (the autonomic nervous system) is specifically designed to alert us to it. In earlier times, some difference in our environment could indicate danger and we evolved a protection mechanism to prime our body to deal with it. This embodied mechanism can be activated by anything unfamiliar or unexpected – and we can't override it with our mind alone. To work with the reality of our tendency to fight, flee or freeze, we enlist the support of the body.

Over to you ...

To explore how the autonomic nervous system is activated in you, reflect on what happens when you're preoccupied by a recurring thought or impulse, almost a compulsion to say or do something. What do you notice about your posture, breathing and energy? How is this different to moments when you're at the top of your game?

What are you learning about your personal survival pattern?

When our composure is disturbed by the autonomic nervous system, we can draw on approaches from martial arts to guide us to return to embodied presence. As I've mentioned, from my earliest engagement with dialogue I saw a connection with my experience of T'ai Chuan. In particular, both disciplines look for constructive ways to work with opposition. In T'ai Chi, we learn to make soft contact with an incoming energy (usually in the form of a fist or foot), and skilfully redirect it. Realising that we can do something similar in our conversations, I began to wonder how I could bring this insight into my leadership development work.

I had an early opportunity to explore this when working with a divisional management team who were challenging the direction of travel of their new CEO. The team's language focused on overcoming the CEO's wrong-headedness and 'taking him down'. Their energy was combative. I suggested that, in a straight power struggle, the CEO had both organisational position and personal authority on his side. He would prevail – and was unlikely to regard them favourably in the aftermath. I asked the team what they thought was at stake for the CEO and for themselves and encouraged them to explore how they might *meet* his energy and harness it for the benefit of the wider system. Through this conversation, the team identified more constructive ways of engaging with the CEO and agreed to look for opportunities to work with, and influence, him rather than actively obstruct him.

More generally, I began to experiment with designing embodied activities to support others to explore the movements and flows within conversations. Then, in 2010, I met Wendy Palmer and adopted the Leadership Embodiment approach. I trained with Wendy and became accredited as an LE teacher. This 'short cut' served both me and my clients.

## Leadership Embodiment

The LE approach draws on principles and practices from the Japanese martial art of Aikido and from Buddhism. It's a suite of activities that reveal, viscerally, phenomena and potentials such as:

- what we say is often not aligned with our energetic message – if we're aware of this, we can learn to actively synchronise our energy with our words;

- we're often energetically 'closed' to receiving the views of others – if we're aware of this, we can learn to expand our energy to include other voices; and

- when we meet difference, we often get 'jammed' energetically – if we're aware of this, we can learn to change our energetic state to move beyond resistance in ourselves and others.

The central principle of LE is that we can build our capacity to recover our centre and presence when we're jammed, closed or misaligned. As we do this, we consciously expand our energetic presence, or personal field, to include others. This field is a personal container, a holding space for our physical body, and LE practices support us to be more aware of it. When we centre, we're more able to be poised and resourceful when things kick off – and this can contribute towards creating conditions in which differences can be explored. We'll look at this more fully in Chapter 24.

Personally, I use LE practices frequently – whether to be more skilful in my own challenging conversations or to coach others to handle the energies of their highly charged exchanges. Over time, I've come to understand the immense difference between mind-learning and body-learning: the former dances amongst concepts, perceptions, knowledge and ideas, whilst the latter grapples with the realities of bones, tissues, chemicals and energy pulses. To be skilful in the conversations that we find challenging, we have to develop both body and mind.

To make this practical, we might think of the body as a vessel for behaviours. It's the body that leans in, turns away, makes gestures and generally enacts what we sense and feel, often before a thought forms. Sometimes, such movements are aligned with what we're saying, and this supports our words to land well. At other times, what we embody doesn't align with what we're saying, and this can give a mixed message. The familiar saying that 'actions speak louder than words' encapsulates this relationship: what we communicate energetically is more powerful than our words.

We can use the relationship between mind and body in two ways – we can focus on behaving our way *into* our good intentions or aspirations and/or we can notice the problems caused by our current practice, and focus on behaving our way *out of* them. The key point is that we have to *behave* our way into good practices or out of undesirable ones – we can't talk ourselves into these changes. While we can grasp the potential of different conduct in our mind, it takes time to reliably embody a new attribute, skill or behaviour. In other words, we have to enact the change and keep doing it until it becomes a habit.

Then we hit another hurdle. It's hard enough to change our own practice – whether adopting a new approach or changing one that has passed its sell-by date – but changing *collective* practice is exponentially more difficult. This is because collective habits are almost always established gradually, making them easy to overlook – we touched on this in Chapter 6. In practice, this means that even when we realise that we're in the habit of operating in ways that frustrate our aspirations, our attempts to change can be derailed by the strength of established – and collectively embodied – customs. We'll get some insight into how we might approach this challenge when we explore the three tenets in Part III. For now, let's consider how we can recognise moments when body and mind are in alignment.

## Over to you …

Take some time to recall an embodied experience of being at your absolute best in a conversation – everything seemed to fall into place and you 'just knew' what to do and say, and did it with clarity and ease.

Linger in this memory for a moment – what do you notice about your posture, breathing and energy? How did you feel towards the other people present? How did they respond to what you said?

How does this glimpse of a centred experience differ from your more usual ways of being in conversation?

This chapter has set the context for the next two. In Chapter 9, we'll build on the reflection that you've just done to see that moments of clarity, alignment and ease characterise the centred state. We'll discover how we can access this state and then, in Chapter 10, we'll revisit Case Study 1 and look at it from an embodied perspective.

# Chapter 9    Realities: embodied learning

Making the shift from a conceptual insight to changing practice is a crucial step towards having more flexibility in challenging situations. To embody a different approach, we have to try it out, reflect on the impact, make adjustments and try again.

This kind of process is well understood for building a specific embodied skill such as training endurance in order to run a marathon or developing the dexterity to play a musical instrument. However, we're less accustomed to applying it to leadership skills. Short of time and long on confidence (at least superficially), we like to believe that reading about something or going on a short course will be sufficient to change how we operate. Usually, this isn't the case. In reality, we need to put a new skill to the test in the pressure of a 'live' situation and then refine it to suit our character, preferences, strengths and shortcomings. This begins to lay down a neural pathway for the skill, which is made more viable each time we reuse it. With repetition over time, we'll be able to use the new skill even when we're 'under fire'.

We may each have succumbed to some version of hoping for a quick fix or a silver bullet. For example, I'm inspired by the presence, equanimity and wisdom of many spiritual leaders, and I know that meditation is the foundation of this. To develop these qualities, the spiritual leaders will have spent years doing many hours of meditation practice a day. Despite knowing this, I seem to think that I can access these qualities by doing a bit of meditation on most days. I astonish myself with my naivety (or arrogance) – and laugh ruefully when I catch myself thinking this way. The bottom line is that I know what to do and how to do it – but I'm short on the will to put in the work required. And, as one of my wise friends commented, life gets in the way.

However, there's good news. We can work with a single embodied practice to build our capacity to recover centre when we're caught in the energetic patterns of a conversation. And, when we commit to doing this, we'll experience some fairly immediate benefits. In further good news, the Leadership Embodiment centring practice that's described in the next section will support us to respond to *all* circumstances in a more resourceful and constructive way. Let's understand its provenance and then look at the nuts and bolts of doing it.

## Foundation four-part centring practice

To recap: to carry ourselves well in the energies of difference, we have to work with a biochemical legacy system that's primed to regard anything different as a potential hazard. Basically, our autonomic nervous system causes us to react to 'sabre-toothed ideas' in the same way as we reacted to a sabre-toothed tiger in days gone by. This reactivity is designed to protect us – it narrows the field of our attention to focus on survival. Non-essential services are temporarily shut down, reducing our capacity to be open, curious, compassionate and creative. To navigate the energies of difference skilfully, we learn to recognise this 'shut-down' and adjust our 'energetic set' with the LE centring practice (Embodied Practice 1, which is set out later in this section and in Appendix B).

First, we become familiar with our personal version of the fight/flight mechanism – it's usually a pattern, which means we can learn to recognise it. If you engaged with the 'Over to you …' aspects of the previous chapter, you'll have begun this process. When we realise that we're caught in our reactive pattern, we apply an antidote – the LE centring practice. This practice harnesses our mind to re-set our body, which, in turn, reactivates the 'paused' parts of our mind. We're now more able to engage skilfully with whatever activated our reactive pattern.

Wendy Palmer based the LE centring practice on her experience in the martial art of Aikido, in which a practitioner aims to meet incoming energy with soft, poised strength. In doing so, they aim to include the incoming energy in their own 'universe', to blend with it and to redirect it in a way that, as a minimum, averts harm. There's great potential in this moment of blending as it creates a new energetic system, in which fresh possibilities arise. Centring benefits both parties – one avoids harm and the other avoids causing harm.

The energy of this martial arts interaction is similar to that of actively welcoming the incoming energy of verbal opposition or difference and harnessing it to create something new. If we're able to steady our physiology and mind when we hear something that we find unsettling, confusing, obstructive or threatening, we access greater perspective. When we centre, we create space to view testing circumstances with lightness, curiosity and even humour.

You'll already be familiar with the experience of centre – it occurs when we're 'in the zone', in flow or 'on form'. It's innate – those moments when something just seems to click into place and everything becomes easy. We're calm, adept and have a broad perspective. We experience clarity, efficiency and ease, and we're part of what's unfolding. It's a sharp contrast to the everyday effort of making things happen and having to do it all ourselves.

## Over to you ...

See if you can recall an example of a centred moment. Perhaps you were struggling to solve a problem, took a break and then everything fell into place? Perhaps you were out running and feeling every step, then became aware of a sense of spaciousness and running became effortless? Or perhaps you were trying to master a piece of music and, about to give up, found that the music was 'playing' you?

How might you describe the quality of your energy in this centred moment, the feel or vibe of it?

The foundation four-part centring practice that's described below underpins all the embodied practices in this book. When we use the centring practice, we're not trying to *create* a new experience. Instead, we're consciously accessing an underused aspect of ourselves. The centred state is an innate part of the human experience – we access it naturally, often without recognising it. When we embody this part of ourselves, we change our relationship to adversity, difference and/or unexpected events and create the potential for a good outcome. In this way, centring can help us to change our practice in our conversations.

The LE foundation centring practice has four main steps, which are summarised as Embodied Practice 1. Please note that the language used to describe all eight embodied practices has a different tone and is gently instructional. To get the most from this, imagine that each is a guided visualisation or mindfulness practice. You might record yourself reading the steps and then use this to coach yourself through them. To make the practices easy to find, they're also included as appendices. This one is at Appendix B.

## Embodied Practice 1

### Foundation four-part centring practice†

1. Posture and breath

> Become uplifted and aligned in your posture, with your spine easing to its natural length and curve. As you do this, exhale slowly and imagine the breath spiralling down through your body and into the ground.

> Inhale softly, imagining that the gentle inflow of air lifts each vertebra from the one below it, bringing a sense of lightness into the spine.

> Exhale slowly, imagining the breath flowing down, softening the front of the body and forming a root in the earth below.

2. Balancing and opening personal space

> Now become aware of the space you occupy – pay attention behind you as well as in front of you, to the left and right, below your feet and above your head. Notice if this space has a colour or texture associated with it, or even a sound …

… what would it be like if this personal energetic space was a little more equal and even, a little more balanced?

… what would it be like to consciously enlarge this personal container in all directions so that it includes those around you, whilst holding you gently at the centre?

## 3. Softening

Whilst maintaining an uplifted posture, soften your forehead, your jaw and your shoulders – imagine they're melting, like butter, and succumbing to gravity …

## 4. Cultivating beneficial energy*

Invite a little more ease* into your being – where do you experience it and what difference does it make?

*I've used 'ease' as a generic quality of energy – you can tailor the practice by choosing a different quality.
† Based on the work of Wendy Palmer.

The result of the centring practice is that we sit or stand (or walk) a little taller, our energetic presence expands and our leadership spirit shines more brightly. Let's briefly touch on some key aspects of the practice, then we'll revisit it in Chapters 11 and 12 to explore how we can apply it.

The essence of the first three parts of the LE centring practice is to come into alignment and expand our personal field or container to include whatever's 'incoming'. When we do this, the boundary between self and the incoming energy dissolves and we effectively create a new energetic system. We soften, and settle into this new system. When we open to include other people, events or issues whilst remaining aligned within ourselves, we model acceptance and respect. From this ground, new possibilities arise.

In the fourth step of the centring practice, we consciously flavour the expanded system with a beneficial *quality of energy*. I've used 'ease' as a generic quality, but you can tailor the practice by choosing a personal quality of energy, a feeling tone or vibe that reflects your personal experience of being centred. In doing this, we're not trying to correct a perceived shortcoming – we select a quality that we already recognise in ourselves, and would like to embody more frequently. Some examples to consider are openness, gentleness, assurance, calmness, lightness, courage, acceptance, wisdom, poise … the list is endless. You might ask: what beneficial quality of energy best reflects the leadership presence that I aspire to embody?

To experience the impact of the centring practice 'in action', we can apply it to the memory of a recent event that made us feel annoyed, dissatisfied or uneasy. The following steps allow us to map the experience of this event in our body and then notice what changes when we coach ourselves through the four-part centring practice. You can find this practice at Appendix C.

## Embodied Practice 2

### Centring in action[†]

1. Recall a recent event that was irritating, stressful or frustrating enough to cause tension and/or discomfort in your body – keep this proportionate and use an event such as getting a parking ticket or someone forgetting an appointment. Don't use a major life event.

2. Notice and acknowledge any specific areas of tension or discomfort, perhaps gritted teeth, fluttering in your belly, tightness in your chest or a sense of heat in some part of your body.

3. Do the four-part centring practice (Embodied Practice 1), taking twenty seconds or so for each step.

4. Once your system is settled and you have a sense of spaciousness, revisit the event – what's different in your body and mind? How do you experience the event now?

† *Based on the work of Wendy Palmer.*

In later chapters, we'll expand on the foundation centring practice and add new dimensions. At this stage, I've tried to keep it simple and include only the essential elements of the practice. I hope this makes it as easy as possible for you to try it out – which I strongly encourage you to do. The greater your experience with it, the more you'll get from later explorations.

## Why embodied learning matters

As we've discovered, it takes time and effort to embody a new practice in our conversations. It can be daunting to get started, and we might even wonder whether it's really necessary to engage with this aspect of what's set out in these pages. To counter this kind of reservation, it can help to recognise that both speaking and listening are physical activities.

When we speak, our mouth, lips and tongue create shapes to form words and our vocal chords vibrate to produce sound. More subtly, our whole body is involved – the tonal quality of what we say is affected by our breath, which is influenced by our posture. When we listen, the bones, fluids and hairs in our ears move in response to the vibration of sound waves. These delicate mechanisms allow us to pick up tiny qualitative variations in what we hear. We also listen with our eyes as we notice small movements and changes in expression, and with our bodies as we tune in to the 'vibe' of what's being said and how it's being said. The state of our body – tense or at ease – affects all these functions.

Further, most of us have habits of speech – tried and tested approaches that are our go-to recipes in certain situations. These well-worn words and phrases, facial expressions and gestures are encoded physically in our neural pathways. They're so familiar (to us and to others) that we no longer notice them. Some of them are almost verbal 'tics' that we use to punctuate what we say. For example, one of mine is 'does this make sense?'. I notice others using phrases such as 'one hundred per cent' and 'you know what I mean'. Perhaps you too have a 'go-to' filler or end-of-sentence phrase.

When we take account of the embodied, energetic aspects of speaking and listening, it seems logical that changing our practice in conversations will involve body-learning as well as mind-learning. We can begin simply, by more often paying attention to our leadership energy and presence, and noticing that of others. We can also develop greater awareness of the physicality of speaking and listening in ourselves and others. When we make these adjustments, we become more conscious of both what's being said and how it's being said. In addition, we become more aware of *how* we listen and *what* we're listening for, and we may begin to notice these things in others too.

## Over to you …

How might you increase your awareness of your energy and the energy of others in your conversations and in life and work more generally?

When you tune in to how you listen, what do you notice about your posture, your breathing, and what you experience in your body? How do others respond if you make deliberate changes to your posture or your breathing? What changes in your own experience?

When you tune in to how you speak, what do you notice about your posture, your breathing and what you experience in your body? What happens if you make deliberate changes to your posture or your breathing? How does your voice change? How does this affect those present?

When we set about embodying a change of practice in conversations, we'll always encounter some setbacks. How do we persevere when things go awry?

## Persevering with a change in practice

It's easy to become discouraged when we try something new and things don't go quite as we hope. Participants in my dialogue programmes regularly describe two experiences of this. In the first, they declare: 'things are getting worse'.

This apparent deterioration in experience is a consequence of *noticing* things we've previously been oblivious to – our radar is becoming more finely tuned. So, for instance, we might realise that others take our 'robust' questioning of a proposal as criticism and/or obstruction. Then we notice that their defence or resistance prompts even greater sharpness and persistence in us. Things do seem to get worse …

However, when invited to say more, a participant will often acknowledge that, even though they're experiencing more occasions of regret, discomfort, awkwardness or embarrassment in their conversations, they also feel they're being more skilful and human in them. While it may feel like things are getting worse, they're actually getting better. Something is changing.

The second way we can be discouraged is that, when we try to change our practice, we're on untested ground and can feel deskilled. We don't yet have confidence in what we're doing and, in the spotlight of a leadership role, this can be unnerving. We try something new, which may go well. However, if things take an unexpected turn in public view, it will probably feel uncomfortable. It might then be hard to try again.

Take heart. A similar process shows up in elite sports. For example, a cricketer changes his or her bowling action and sees their deliveries become more erratic for a time, or a golfer changes their putter and temporarily becomes more inconsistent on the green. They too are instigating change in a public setting. During the transition to a new 'form', it may be tempting to return to the more familiar way of doing things. It requires courage to weather a 'dip' in performance whilst feeling deskilled and whilst potential benefits remain unrealised. And yet, this is the nature of leadership development.

If you decide to take on the challenge of changing your practice, my role is to inspire confidence that the long-term benefits will outweigh any initial snags. Your part is to be clear about why you want to make changes, as this will strengthen your resolve when you encounter setbacks and/or feel discouraged. You might take inspiration from a director of finance on one of my dialogue programmes, who said: 'When something "doesn't work", I no longer think: I'm using the wrong technique. Instead, I think: I need more practice ...'

You can also support yourself by trying out a new approach in low-risk situations, by which I mean circumstances where the stakes are not too high. In my dialogue programmes, I always suggest this at an early stage and with strong advocating energy, almost capitalising the words. I then repeat the advice often. *Everyone* ignores it – which provides enriched learning material for the whole group. These experiences can also prompt a collective, rueful smile – the desire to fast-track runs deep in many of us.

The advice to begin in low-risk situations has parallels in many disciplines: cricketers learn to bat and bowl in the safety of the nets; martial artists learn to fall using padded mats; and actors and musicians rehearse many times before performing in public. Please take heed!

## Over to you ...

In what low-risk situations might you try out new approaches? What situations are real enough to test you, yet have limited consequences if they don't turn out as well as you expect? How will you pick yourself up after a setback, and then try again?

In the next chapter, we'll begin to explore the energy that arises when we meet difference and we'll look at how we can change our experience of it by using the LE centring practice. With this in mind, I encourage you to become familiar with the four parts of this practice and to actively try it out (in low-risk situations) so that you can readily access a centred state. The beauty of the practice is that we can use it in many situations. One leader, already familiar with dialogue practices, noticed that her conversations were transformed when she adopted the LE approach. She often refers to this, saying: 'when I started to practise Leadership Embodiment, I found I could access the tools of dialogue in a much more powerful and 'in the moment' way.'

# Chapter 10  Realities: an exploration

In this chapter, we'll revisit the case study from Chapter 7 and explore the energy of it. To support this, we'll use an embodied activity for changing our perspective and a framework that can help us untangle what's going on in our mind.

To briefly recap the case, a COO was pressing for a report on a particular issue to go to the Board of the organisation. The MD disagreed. They exchanged views in a fairly pointed way and the COO prevailed. He later reflected on what had taken place and wondered what he might have done differently.

Before revisiting the case, we'll explore an activity from Leadership Embodiment that, in workshops, often comes to be known as 'wall–window'. The activity is usually done in a group, but it works just as well with two people. In either case, it begins with a pair of people facing each other, about two arm-lengths apart: if they each extended a hand, their fingers would touch. They stand so that each person can see something different. Perhaps one is looking at *a wall*, with features such as pictures, an air-conditioning panel or a door. Their partner is looking in the opposite direction, perhaps towards *a window* and whatever they see through it – sky, trees, buildings.

Having set things up, the brief is for each person to say what they see and to stick to their guns.

## Exploring the energies of difference

The exchange starts with one person describing what they're looking at, including whatever details catch their eye. Then the other outlines their view. The first restates what they see, then their partner repeats their perspective. After (perhaps) three rounds, *even though* they know that this is an exercise about nothing much, a sense of wanting to convince or persuade usually kicks in for one or both parties. Essentially, if they follow the brief, they become attached to their position and the energy of difference takes hold. Each person feels this viscerally – reason has less traction and the conversation becomes stuck. Do you recognise this conversational pattern and energy?

The first stage of the wall–window activity is to notice how the dynamic of difference affects you. Even as you do what's asked, you may feel an impulse to disengage or move away or an impulse to explain, appease or soothe. Perhaps the requirement to stick to your guns suits you and you dig in, or perhaps you quickly lose confidence in restating your position. The activity allows us to notice the impact of difference at a primal level – the urge to fight, flee or freeze. If the activity continues, what usually happens next is that one party pushes their agenda or gives up. Neither party feels great about the outcome.

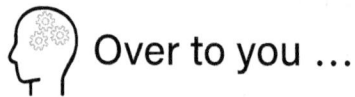

## Over to you …

Can you identify an exchange in which you traded point and counterpoint in the way described in the wall–window activity? How does this dynamic tend to affect you? Do you dig in and try to convince or persuade? Do you disengage and start second-guessing yourself? Do you quite enjoy the tussle? Or another option entirely?

Take a few moments to reflect on how this tendency shows up more generally in your conversations – what are the consequences for you and others?

In the LE wall–window activity, the next stage is that one partner – let's say the person looking at the wall – uses the four-part centring practice (Appendix B) to come to their senses. They then step slightly to the side, representing a willingness to 'get off their position' or to park their opinion *for a moment*. They walk towards the wall, passing their partner, and then *turn around*. Settling into this new place, and centring again, they look: Oh! What I see now is ... a window!

It may take a moment to acclimatise to the reality that their partner is quite literally coming at things from a different direction. This realisation changes the energy of the situation from either/or to both/and.

The person who suspended their opinion for a moment – which doesn't signal agreement – now returns to their original position. Energetically, their stance is more inclusive, representing something like: I disagree, I see a wall – and I appreciate that you see something different. This shift in *energy* is felt by the person looking at the window and, even though they may not quite understand what's happened, they're less likely to press their own point.

In a real situation, we can't predict how this shift in energy will affect what then plays out. It's possible that an appreciation of legitimate differences will prompt more general curiosity about how they've arisen, introducing more inquiry into the conversation. This creates the potential for dialogue. Equally, it's possible that one or both parties will quickly reattach to their position, and the exchange will get stuck again. In general, I've found that what unfolds depends on the sincerity of my willingness to understand what someone else sees.

In summary, the wall–window activity allows us to experience the energy of disagreement and explore how that energy shifts if we centre, become respectful in our opposition, then set aside our view in order to create space for centred inquiry. You can try this activity yourself – a summary is set out below and also appears as Appendix D.

## Embodied Practice 3

### *Centred inquiry with a practice partner[†]*

To explore the 'wall–window' activity, work with a partner. Stand facing one another in a place where you can see obviously different things such as a blank wall and a window, or walls of two different colours. You should be about two arm-lengths apart. Decide which of you will choose to approach difference differently.

1. The first step is to create an energetic experience of difference – an argument, if you like. To do this, each person picks a feature of what they can see and briefly describes it as a fact, with the energy of being right. For example: 'it's a red wall' – 'no! it's a window and a tree'.

2. Repeat this exchange – insisting on your chosen details – until you feel some discord and intensity, perhaps some exasperation, frustration, tension or judgement.

3. To approach difference differently, do a four-part centring practice (Appendix B): uplifting, exhaling, opening your sense of space to include your partner, calling up a beneficial quality of energy. This is respectful opposition. Notice what changes.

4. Having centred, step slightly to the side (suspending your position for a moment) and walk past your partner. Once you're past them, turn to look at what they can see.

5. Do another centring practice: uplifting, exhaling, opening your sense of space to include your partner, calling up a beneficial quality of energy. Stand in this experience for a moment – you're willing to see the world the way your partner sees it. Notice what changes.

6. Finally, return to your starting place and reiterate your original words. You still disagree and … notice how the energy of difference has changed.

7. Debrief with your partner – what happened for them as you tried out this activity? What do you conclude from this?

8. Now change roles and repeat …

*† Based on the work of Wendy Palmer.*

☆

In a real situation, enacting the principles of this embodied activity might involve centring to be respectful of someone holding a different view, and becoming curious about what underpins it, asking them to outline their thinking more fully. What's informing their view? What do they see differently? What matters to them? Asking these kinds of questions introduces inquiring energy into an exchange of advocating energy. This brings curiosity to a tussle between one opinion and another.

The trivial content of the wall–window exchange and the embodied experience of getting quickly drawn into the energy of 'being right' demonstrates the importance of tuning in to the forces in play when disagreement arises. When we feel ourselves being drawn into a narrow trading of positions, we can zoom out and see that the root of this experience is the energy of two (or more) people who are each attached to their view. The energetic experience is independent of the subject matter. If we can loosen our sense of certainty about what's right, we create room for exploration. We can ask questions of ourselves such as: what if there's something I'm not seeing? What if I'm misinformed or I've made a mistake in my reasoning? What if the other person has a different cultural perspective or holds different values?

Having explored this energetic ground, let's return to the case study from Chapter 7.

## Case study revisited – energies

For ease, Case Study 1 is repeated below. Take the time to revisit the exchange of views and see if you can tune in to the energy of the conversation.

# Case Study 1

| 1. MD: | I don't want this report to go to the Board. |
|---|---|
| 2. COO: | I know you don't, but it's a governance requirement. |
| 3. MD: | I think you're wrong and I don't want the report to go. |
| 4. COO: | Why not? |
| 5. MD: | I don't think it needs to – we can sign this off ourselves. |
| 6. COO: | We can't. The total cost of the project exceeds our sign-off limits. |
| 7. MD: | Well, the limits are ridiculous, I want them changed. |
| 8. COO: | Perhaps, but for now we need to comply with what's in place. |

With the wall–window activity in mind, can you feel the rising energy present in this clash of opinions? You may recall that, after this exchange, the COO reflected on its shape and quality. He then set up a conversation with the MD so he could better understand her perspective. He was primed to do this because he'd experienced the wall–window activity and, even though he was practising inquiry *after* the event, he was building his capacity to use it 'in the heat of the moment'. With this embodied experience under his belt, he'll be better equipped to recognise the energy of difference when it arises, whatever the topic and whoever is involved. He'll also be a little more able to handle his own energy in a way that doesn't escalate the disagreement. He might even be able to intervene in the limiting pattern in the moment, allowing the conversation to expand into more fruitful territory.

This is the return on the investment of practice. Embodied skills take time to build up, which can be a difficult pill to swallow. There's no short cut. However, each time we realise that a pattern is (or was) playing out and there could be (or could have been) an alternative, we've made progress. And each time we *try out* an alternative approach, turning the idea to reality, we build capacity to deploy it in more testing conditions.

## Over to you …

Find an example of a conversation in which the ground seemed to narrow and the energy became more intense – what was your part in the conversation? How did the conversation conclude, and how did you feel about it?

What might have changed – for you and others – if you'd practised centred inquiry? How might you prepare to practise centred inquiry during a similar experience?

The willingness to look at someone else's point of view and to discover what we don't yet know about it is the essence of centred inquiry. To use this approach in 'real life', alongside the centring practice, we work with our mind and the way we think. To prepare our mind for inquiry so that we can explore difference, it's useful to remember that the views we hold are often informed and influenced by many events and experiences. They tend to be headlines, snapshots or summaries of the things we've been exposed to, filtered through a jumble of personal factors and preferences that affect what we perceive and the sense we make of it. In summary, what we say is rarely unquestionable fact.

Let's explore the implications of this, for ourselves and others.

## Untangling our thinking

Most opinions (our own and those of others) have a long heritage and are a mixture of our values, experiences and inclinations towards some things and away from others. We often forget this. While it may be based on evidence that bears collective scrutiny, what we believe to be fact is usually flavoured with the unique seasoning of the way an individual mind processes the (partial) information available. In a landscape, what we see is largely determined by where we're standing and the direction we're facing. The same is true for how we perceive the important issues of our times and the day-to-day matters we have to navigate.

In overlooking the way that human knowledge and experience are acquired, processed and stored, we've let a key skill fall into disuse: the kind of inquiry that uncovers the provenance of an assertion and examines its coherence in a constructive way. This form of inquiry is crucial to exploring the views of others. It's also essential to getting our own story straight.

One of my touchstones for this ground is Edward de Bono's book, *Six Thinking Hats*.[12] The hats offer a framework for untangling the many influences that, often unnoticed, shape our thinking, orientation and attitude. For example, red hat thinking is specifically for airing emotions, feelings and instincts. We can use yellow hat thinking to explore possibilities without having to consider whether they're feasible or not, while black hat thinking allows us to give full rein to the potential downsides of a situation or obstacles to a proposal. Our focus is on white hat thinking: the domain of getting facts out into the open.

White hat thinking sits in the context of five other aspects of thinking that encompass possibilities, upsides, downsides, reflective process and new growth. Each of the five non-white strands is flavoured by being somewhat subjective, perceptual, uncertain and/or speculative. Each has a place in dialogue, as does white hat thinking, which is concerned with data, information, facts. The aim is to use the hats to clarify our stance on an issue by distinguishing between aspects that we may otherwise conflate. As we do so, we may find that our opinions are not quite as lucid as we imagine. We may find that we have to handle differences *within* ourselves, as well as differences with others.

I find the Thinking Hats useful. However, in the climate of the 2020s, it's worth remembering that it's a framework of its time. It was devised in the 1980s and,

86

naturally, there are different sensitivities in a changed social context forty years later. To consider these would divert me from my purpose, which is to outline how the framework can be applied to help us understand one of the ways in which our capacity to handle difference is eroding. So, we'll use it as de Bono set it out.

Let's explore how white hat thinking can help us to explore contested ground. What I particularly love about white hat thinking is that de Bono differentiates between 'checkable facts' and beliefs, which seems prescient in an era of disinformation and fake news. In making this distinction, de Bono invites us to be more precise in the way we use language and present facts. In reality, most 'facts' are qualified by a range within which they're true – some are true for all circumstances, but most only apply subject to certain conditions and caveats. In order to determine the legitimacy of a particular fact in a given situation, we may need some context about the likelihood that it will occur. So, it may be useful to know if a fact is always true, generally true, sometimes true, anecdotally true and so on. Then we can ask: does it apply in this setting?

De Bono asserts, 'Truth and facts are not as closely related as most people imagine.' This is an opinion or belief, and so we can agree with it or not, as we choose. Better still, we can talk about *the extent to which* it may be true (or not). For the moment, I want to use the statement as a working hypothesis, because it begins to engage with the delicate matter of a world in which 'my truth' and 'my lived experience' have great currency.

A person's truth is, of course, true for them and is to be respected in that context. However, it seems to me (opinion – you may not agree) that there's an evolving cultural trend in which such personal truths carry an assumption that something 'true for me' is true more generally. If I begin to insist that my truth must also be your truth, I deny you the freedom I'm taking for myself – the freedom to make sense of my experience in my own way. If I hold 'my truth' to be legitimate, it's principled and fair to hold your truth to be legitimate too, even if it contradicts mine. If I'm able to do this, we can agree to disagree. Or, more generatively, we might wonder how and why we have such different 'truths' and become curious about the circumstances that give rise to them.

To work constructively with the spectrum of realities inherent in the human condition, we have to find ways to include both very personal ways of interpreting our experience and matters which can be externally verified. These are not mutually exclusive arenas. A personal view might be based on checkable facts and yet be flavoured with experiences, values and emotions. Even an expert interpretation of the most robust data will be shaped by the hinterland of the person creating the narrative. We all have biases, preferences, outlooks … and, subtly, these show up in the language we use. To riff on de Bono, the relationship between what we *believe* to be true and any underlying facts may be more nuanced than we imagine.

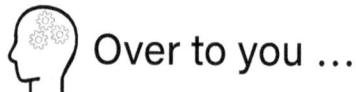

## Over to you …

How do these ideas land with you? What resonates? What do you question? Can you think of a situation when the discipline of white hat thinking may have supported greater clarity of thinking and broadened the scope of a conversation?

In a complex, nuanced world, de Bono's white hat thinking invites us to inquire (gently, with curiosity) into the provenance of what we're hearing. What we can be sure of is this: whatever is being expressed will only be a sliver of a speaker's experience. If we take a sliver of someone's thinking at face value, we tend to limit our response to agreeing or disagreeing. This limits the potential of a conversation and, perhaps, does a disservice to all. Instead, we wonder … where is someone standing? In which direction are they looking? What's in their hinterland? What's framing and informing their view?

And then we ask them about these things.

This is the essence of the wall–window activity. In the spirit of more fully understanding how someone is perceiving and experiencing the world, we step into an exploration of their terrain and what might be shaping their thinking. As we seek to discover what we don't yet know, we express interest in their view and, as they respond to this interest, they 'think aloud' with us. In doing so, they may recall things they've forgotten, or refresh some aspects of their thinking. They may find new connections and/or avenues to explore – as might we. Together, we gain an enriched and layered sense of the ground we're on, which places their thinking and ours in a wider context.

On my own account, I know that hearing myself actually express something to a good listener sometimes leads me to question what I'm saying: what 'sounded' OK in the closed world of my mind doesn't bear too much scrutiny when it's liberated into a more public space. Or, as I search for words to convey something complex or something I discern within myself but haven't fully examined or articulated, I deepen my awareness of what I really think. I go beyond my habitual words and phrases and unearth more rounded thinking. In habitual talk, I tend to recycle familiar thoughts. When I'm more mindful of, and deliberate about, what I'm trying to communicate, I'm thinking in the present, and am more open to change. This process is playing out as I write: I'm discovering new ways to express what I'm trying to say.

Until now, we've focused our exploration on conversations between two people. With white hat thinking and centred inquiry in mind, it's time to start looking at larger groups. With greater numbers of people, we can still apply the principles and practices that we've covered so far. However, as group size increases, we meet a broader range of perspectives and things become messier. This calls us to consider the shape and quality of conversation that will be able to hold the energies of diverse views, and to explore how we can 'hold our own' in the fray. We'll look into this in Chapter 12.

First, in Chapter 11, we'll look at the way difference is handled in the conversational forms of debate and dialogue, and take a brief look at the implications of this in a societal context. This offers some insight into the public paradigm in which all other conversations take place.

# Chapter 11 Diverse ideas, diverse realities

As mentioned in the Preface, I'm increasingly troubled by an apparent decrease in both the skills for handling different views and the will to engage fruitfully with those who hold them. Of course, I see this through my own limited perspective – from a relatively comfortable existence in a small country that sits, geographically, on the edge of Europe. I haven't travelled extensively and I have no true sense of whether the patterns that I perceive are relevant to other cultures. Anecdotally, they seem to apply in the USA, where friends are also disturbed by greater polarisation and intolerance in society.

Do similar circumstances arise in other places? I can't know. I mention the narrowness of my experience to offer a context for what follows. I invite you to explore what I describe and to form your own view about its relevance to your setting.

In my terrain, the UK, I'm aware that many columnists and commentators are describing concerns similar to those that disturb me. Their appraisals often reflect a sense of frustration, and even exasperation, towards the limited nature of debate about contentious issues. For example, ahead of an election, the writer of a political column in *The Sunday Times*[13] noted that a number of politicians were appealing for unity. Regarding unity as both unattainable and undesirable, he championed healthy diversity of thought, urging politicians to work through their differences rather than supposing them to be damaging. He added that 'we don't have a good vocabulary to describe political disagreement' and that 'we could all do with a crash course in how to disagree better'. He concluded that we need to engage in 'vigorous debate about what divides us'.

Whilst I support the desire to learn how to 'disagree better', I have a different view about 'good vocabulary' for describing disagreement (whether political or not). It exists in the field of dialogue, where we find frameworks that allow us to describe the nature and structure of disagreement and to explore what might be changed. Sadly, these frameworks and their language aren't widely known.

Further, I question the conclusion that we need to engage in vigorous debate about what divides us – it may, I think, rest on an untested assumption that most of us know *how* to debate skilfully and *how* to handle ourselves well in the cross-fire. More significantly, I believe that it misconstrues the nature of debate, which doesn't lend itself to better understanding 'what divides us'. This is a common misconception.

To develop a theme from Chapter 6, conversations have a form, a distinguishing shape and quality which influences their suitability for different purposes. In what follows, I'm proposing (advocating) that the most appropriate conversational form for engaging skilfully with passionately held differences is dialogue, not debate. And, if this is so, it's a compelling reason to build capability and capacity for dialogue. To consider my proposition, let's explore the nature of debate and dialogue.

## The nature of debate

In terms of structural form, debate is an exchange of point and counterpoint to determine which best stands up to scrutiny. It tends to *emphasise* difference, becoming focused on claim and rebuttal. This, in turn tends to narrow the potential for broader thinking. Opinion is divided and there's an assumption that one stance will triumph by being argued more cogently than another. Skilful debate is therefore an ideal conversational form when you want to compare and contrast the benefits and drawbacks of different proposals or courses of action. However, it's less appropriate for some purposes. For example, when used in the complex process of disentangling a union, debate emphasises polarity and becomes a choice between 'remain' or 'leave' (for the UK in relation to the EU), and 'yes' or 'no' (for Scotland in relation to the UK).

We can see some of the constraints of debate in social and societal contexts, where the form and tone of conversations develop in informal and consensual ways. In such settings, there are few (if any) means for reducing the dominance of a particular shape and quality of conversation once it's taken hold.

For example, when a conversation is based on advocacy and statements of what someone believes to be true, any attempt to raise questions and seek understanding (to inquire) is likely to be met with more advocacy. This hinders inquiry and, perhaps, eventually deters it. And, when alternatives and dissent are also expressed as statements, we have the structure of debate. When opposing positions are repeated with increasing fervour, the energy of difference becomes divisive. Let's explore this through a recent example of public discourse.

In the global pandemic of the early 2020s, a key narrative developed: vaccination would be the principal means of mitigating the spread of SARS-CoV-2 and reducing the severity of the illness it caused. In countries such as the UK, significant pressure was applied to encourage the population to be vaccinated. This is an example of advocating – speaking for a point of view – and this 'pro-vax' position was delivered with a confident energy imbued with both political and scientific authority. For some, this policy and the energy with which it was delivered was just right; for others, it was too much or too little. Regardless of how it was received, it was a well-defined direction of travel, an example of clear advocacy.

However, the pressure to be vaccinated could be seen as an infringement of existing freedoms to make personal healthcare choices. An opposing narrative took shape, articulated most loudly by those who stood against *all* vaccination, as a matter of principle. This is also an example of advocacy. The dissenting voices attracted the soubriquet 'anti-vax'. All who preferred not to be vaccinated were dubbed 'anti-vax', whether they were generally against vaccination or had personal reasons for opting out of this particular vaccine.

The act of not being vaccinated is, in itself, an example of advocacy. Declining to participate expresses an opposing view: it's a way of saying 'no' to what's on offer. During the pandemic, this enacted dissent was the strongest form of advocacy in the disparate group of people choosing not to be vaccinated. Their verbal advocacy was less clear and coherent, and carried less authority, because it lacked the substance of a shared principle.

As the weight of the governmental stance met the stubborn refusal of some citizens, simplistic battle lines were drawn between those who'd been vaccinated and those who hadn't. The exchange became squeezed into the corner of whether someone had a vaccination certificate or not. This gave rise to a really disturbing development: an anti-anti-vax narrative, which persecuted those who hadn't been jabbed. In short, it became personal, which is an example of unskilful advocacy. It was no longer about speaking for the advantages and disadvantages of vaccination. Instead, it focused on speaking against the people declining to be vaccinated.

And if we pause, and replace pro-vax, anti-vax and anti-anti-vax with the topics of trans rights, race, climate change, gender, nationalism or a myriad other contentious subjects, we'll see a similar pattern of exchange. A strongly held view of what's right (advocacy) gives rise to an equally unshakeable assertion of an alternative view (also advocacy). In a belief that there's only one truth, nuance and tolerance are disregarded. Strident repetition of a position only serves to increase the volume of those who disagree and, eventually, one camp or another is likely to start to 'play the player, rather than the ball'. The exchange becomes personal, rather than issue-based, and this spirals into intolerance and verbal violence. Each time this happens, we're all diminished. And with each repetition, the pattern gets more entrenched – and is transferred to other topics.

This is difficult territory that you may be inclined to avoid. However, in terms of conversational form, the example given is simply an extreme version of what happens (sometimes, but not always) more politely in organisations. Factions arise and positions get entrenched. Reputations are undermined. Those who feel disempowered 'play the player not the ball'.

Broadly, I'm suggesting that the rise of conversational customs based largely on affirming or negating a prevailing narrative makes it difficult to inquire into our differences and to better understand them. When we understand the conversational trap that we're in, we may be inspired to regain our appreciation for diverse ideas and to equip ourselves to lessen the risk that we'll be ensnared by such patterns. Imagine what might be possible if enough of us make this choice.

When we use the framework of advocacy and inquiry to reflect on the pro-vax and anti-vax exchange, we can see that a *widening* of the divide between opinions might be a key indicator that a conversation is likely to erupt into anger or collapse into resentment. When a divide widens, the disputed ground is usually *narrowing* and becoming less nuanced. Advocacy-led, the conversation is squeezed into a series of pointed exchanges which limit room for manoeuvre. In an unregulated setting, this rarely ends well.

When this kind of pattern arises in an organisation, there are ways to contain it, and we'll explore this ground in later chapters. However, in societal settings, we have no real means to moderate destructive and divisive exchanges. What we *can* do is to resolve that we won't engage in personal vilification or contribute to widening a divide.

## Over to you …

Find a personal example of an occasion when opposing points of view were passionately held and expressed. How might you describe the look and feel of this conversation? How did it play out in terms of widening or narrowing differences? What was the outcome, and how did people feel about it?

What insights arise from your exploration?

If debate tends to emphasise what divides us, what kind of conversation will highlight what connects us? It will be a conversation that focuses on shared ground, finding a centre rather than taking sides. It will balance advocacy and inquiry, supporting those present to voice disparate beliefs, views, preferences and interests and to raise wide-ranging questions about the provenance and meaning of what's being expressed. In other words, the conversational form will be dialogue – let's explore its nature.

## The nature of dialogue

In terms of shape and quality, dialogue is a holding space for both advocacy and inquiry. In dialogue, we pool diverse ideas, experiences and realities and seek to more fully understand how individuals are *framing* their perspective. If we're skilful in this, we'll uncover some of the interdependencies, uncertainties and ambiguities inherent in any statement of position in a complex world. In the spaciousness of dialogue, we may find shared ground in apparently disparate views, and/or realise that opinions and beliefs are underpinned by a multiplicity of values, priorities and concerns. In this territory, the energy of inquiry, which is circular and spiralling, acts as an antidote to the pointed energy of advocacy. The energy of difference is redirected into curiosity and the adventure of discovery.

When the layers and nuances of the hinterland of someone's advocacy are surfaced, the richness, potentials and contradictions in them can be collectively explored. In this process, difference is *included* as a natural facet of being human. Held in the energy of inquiry, differences are simply differences. Shorn of their energetic charge, we're more able to probe them and to deliberate on the consequences of them. In dialogue there's no aspiration to reach agreement, which means that disagreement has less traction. Instead, we're seeking better understanding of the complexities of an issue. In such an environment, new insights can arise.

In essence, dialogue is an exploration of the different ways that human beings perceive the world and come to hold their views. Dialogue asks us to listen to ourselves and to one another in light of the possibility that, if we dig deeply enough, we'll find common ground in point and counterpoint. As we listen receptively to the views of others, we have the opportunity to unpick our own certainties – and, perhaps, change our minds.

These potentials were realised in a moment in a leadership development workshop. In an organisation responsible for paying suppliers on behalf of a large network of institutions, a colleague and I were introducing the concepts and practices of dialogue. Significant developments in technology meant that working methods had to adapt, and the managing director had initiated a process of change. This gave rise to tensions between the management team, those delivering day-to-day operations, and union representatives.

In one workshop session, we were using an approach called a 'fishbowl' to support conversations between these different constituencies. In a fishbowl there are (typically) two concentric circles of chairs and people with one outlook sit in one circle, while those with alternative perspectives sit in the other. The session is structured so that those in one circle talk together, while those in the other circle listen. Then the activities are reversed. The cycle can be repeated several times. In the process, each conversation is influenced by the other. In this way, differences can be carefully and spaciously aired.

In this case, the senior team were sitting in the inner circle and everyone else was in the outer circle. As the two circles took turns to talk it seemed that, for the first time, people were really listening to each other and acknowledging the legitimacy of different views. All those present began to realise that they wanted the best for their services, clients and colleagues – they simply had different ideas about how to go about this.

And then, quite spontaneously, a member of the outer circle noticed his response to two opposing perspectives, one offered by a senior manager (Joanna) in the inner circle and the other offered by an operational manager (Bob) in the outer circle. He said: 'As Joanna spoke, I found myself nodding along … then as Bob spoke, I found myself nodding along. And I have to conclude that I agree with both of them, even though they seem to disagree with each other.'

This insight changed the nature of the conversation – it became more collaborative, a shared exploration of varied perceptions of what was and wasn't working. Those present were seeking understanding rather than agreement, and were engaging more dialogically. It's not that all issues were resolved, but everyone now grasped that their shared experiences and concerns might support them to find a way forward.

## Over to you …

What does this example evoke in you? Can you identify a similar moment from your personal experience, a moment when you could see merit in two opposing statements? What flowed from that realisation?

For me, this example clearly shows that we can create conditions in which even entrenched differences can be heard, held and honoured so that those present can reorganise their thinking. When we feel heard, we often loosen our grip on our strongly held views, and this makes room for curiosity about what others think. When we don't feel heard, we often simply reiterate what we feel needs to be said – and get more insistent. When this happens, it's easy to lose our bearings and forget the value that a different perspective might offer.

When we recognise that feeling heard supports people to hold their positions a little less tightly and make room for difference, an important question arises: what might make it possible to really listen? Also, in the context of dialogue, we aspire to approach difference differently by including a variety of views and perspectives, whether we like them or not. This raises a second question: how might we create space in which to hold our differences so that we can explore them?

On an individual basis, the practice of centred listening offers a response to both these questions.

## Centred listening

The embodied element of making room for difference begins with noticing how we're reacting to what's been said – perhaps we have a strong sense of agreement, disbelief or outrage. Or perhaps we experience confusion or self-doubt. We can use this reaction as a prompt to use the four-part centring practice outlined in Chapter 9 (Appendix B). When we use the practice, we collect ourselves and step back from the immediate narratives – both our own and those of others – whilst remaining present to them. Let's look at each part of the practice in more detail.

We first consciously align our posture. We sit or stand (or walk) a little taller and, in doing so, we inhabit our personal space with confidence and lightness of spirit. We're signalling that we're present, paying attention and available to others. It's a small movement – just lengthening the spine slightly and balancing the left and right sides of the body. I think of lengthening the spine as a process of each vertebra lifting slightly from the one below it – so I put my attention at the base of my spine and slowly move it upwards, feeling my way into a slight increase in spaciousness. You can get the same feeling by imagining someone running their fingers lightly up your spine. The spine is loosened, lengthened, uplifted – all of which tend to lighten our spirits.

In the next instant (or even in the same moment) we exhale, deliberately pacing this breath to be long and slow. Physiologically, breathing out is a release and it's connected with the soothing aspect of our autonomic nervous system, the aspect which resettles us after an alert. Consciously exhaling counterbalances the tendency to have a sharp intake of breath when the fight/flight system is triggered. This kind of 'gasp', whether audible or not, often brings some tension to the area of the neck and shoulders. As we deliberately make our outbreath long and slow, it acts as an antidote to this tension – so that, even if we're not at ease, we don't add to (or escalate) the state of being 'ready for danger'.

Physically, breathing out might seem to be at odds with the uplift associated with aligning our posture, because an exhale can sometimes feel a bit like deflating a balloon. In fact, in combining these activities, we emphasise the benefits of each, which results in a beautiful balance of poise and ease.

It's probably taken you a couple of minutes to read the preceding three paragraphs. However, aligning our posture and lengthening our outbreath only takes a second or two. We might slow the process down a little at first to clarify the component parts and to practise them. However, once we're familiar with the feeling of being 'loosely tall' (rather than sitting or standing 'up straight'), we'll be able to access it in a moment, exhaling as a natural part of the adjustment.

Having regrouped physiologically, the second part of the practice is to pay attention to the energetic space that we're occupying, our presence beyond the physical container of our skin. We're accustomed to using the phrase 'personal space' and we're usually familiar with the feeling we get when someone 'invades' this space, even when they're behind us. However, we don't often give much thought to this experience and the implications of it. It's an aspect of ourselves that we tend to overlook or ignore.

In Chapter 7, when we looked at advocating and inquiring energy, we briefly touched on this part of the practice, the reality that what I consider to be 'me' and 'my body' extends beyond my skin. If we had a heat sensitive camera, it would show that we occupy a larger energetic space than our eyes see – perhaps as much as a couple of feet. When we bring our attention to this holding space, front and back, left and right, above our heads and below our feet, we can sense into it and discern its shape and quality. It pays to become familiar with this space, this personal container, so do take a few moments to explore it.

## Over to you …

Sit quietly, with your spine loosely straight – aligned, uplifted. For a few moments, pay attention to your breath, noticing the length and quality of each inhale and exhale.

Now tune in to the space around you, noticing that it's possible to be aware of the space outside your field of vision – you can sense into the space behind you, to each side, above your head and below your feet.

What shape is this space? Perhaps it's circular/spherical – if so, is it evenly so or irregularly so? Are there segments missing? Perhaps it's a different shape – trust your sense of this – and then notice if it has a texture, a colour, or a sound or vibration associated with it?

What have you learned about the nature of your personal space or container?

Just as we can simply notice our breath or consciously change it, we can also simply notice our personal space or consciously change it. We can coach ourselves to make this energetic container a little bigger and more evenly balanced. We do this by asking a question and observing what happens: what would it be like if our personal space was a little more equal and even? You might try this, and see what happens.

The third part of the centring practice is to settle into this expanded space, to soften and feel held by it. And, in the fourth part, we strengthen our presence by inviting a beneficial quality of energy into our being. This is the feeling tone, the vibe, that we want to bring to our actions and interactions in the world. To cultivate this quality, we wonder what would change if we had a little more of it in our presence.

## Bird's-eye view of energy
### Centred listening

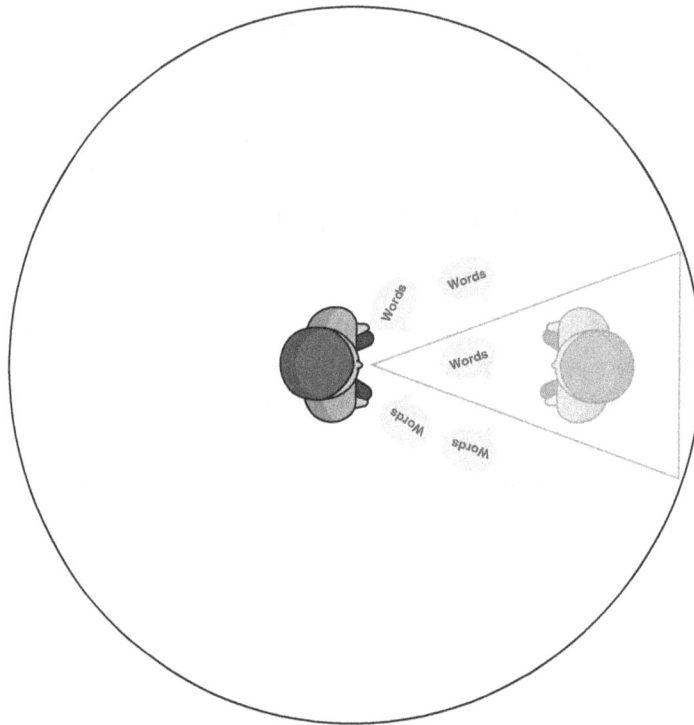

**Key:**

Centred listening, energetic space is expanded evenly to include speaker and their words

Speaking, advocating energy, words may feel pointed and/or personal

We can use the expansive aspect of the four-part centring practice to really listen and to hold a space in which differences can land and be explored. We start by imagining our personal space to be circular, representing listening (or inquiring) energy. We're open and receptive. Then, we use our imagination to expand our personal space or energy to include a person (or people) with an alternative point of view. We then allow their words to float or fall into the space between us, as represented in the diagram above. We include what they say but don't 'take it on'. We receive what's said with respectful interest: the words are true for whoever said them, and are valid from that perspective, even if this clashes with what we think or feel.

In the expanded space of centred listening, we can recall the wall–window activity and practise centred inquiry (Appendix D), becoming curious about how someone came to see the world the way they do.

When we access the embodied element of 'creating space' for differences, it's important to expand our sense of circular space equally all around us, so that it remains balanced. If we're sitting across from someone and extend the space in front of us to include them, we also extend the space behind us, to the left and right, above our heads and below our feet. This means that we remain poised and at the centre of a balanced energetic space that includes another person (or other people). Then when they speak, we visualise their words landing in the space between us, where we can choose whether to leave them to rest or to 'pick them up' and explore them in preparation for responding. If we do respond, and if we're able to do so from a centred state, our words will come from a deeper place and be imbued with the quality of energy we've invited into our presence. This makes it more likely that our words will be received well. If we speak without centring, our words are more likely to come from a reactive place of persuasion or rebuttal.

The centred listening practice is summarised below and is included as Appendix E.

## ✴ Embodied Practice 4

### Centred listening, 'letting land'†

1. Do a four-part centring practice (Appendix B)

Become uplifted and aligned in your posture and exhale slowly, imagining the breath spiralling down through your body and into the ground, forming a root.

Become aware of the space you occupy – pay attention behind you as well as in front of you, to the left and right, below your feet and above your head. What would it be like if this space was a little more equal and even, a little more balanced, holding you gently at the centre?

Whilst maintaining an uplifted posture, soften your forehead, jaw and shoulders – imagine they're melting, like butter, and succumbing to gravity.

Invite a little more ease (or your chosen quality) into your being – where do you experience it, and what difference does it make?

2. Expanding and including

From this more centred place, allow your sense of space to be circular/spherical and expand it to include whoever is present. Balance the expansion back and front, left and right, above your head and below your feet.

As someone speaks, allow their words to float or fall into the space between you. Simply hear the words, don't take them into yourself. Let them rest in the shared space, whilst wondering what, if anything, you might respond to …

## 3. Responding

> If you decide to respond, do the four-part centring practice and connect with what matters – repeat this step until you feel ready to speak.

> Expand your personal space to include those present, and then say your words into the shared space, rather than delivering them to (or at) someone.

† *Based on the work of Wendy Palmer.*

☆

The centred listening practice is based on a Leadership Embodiment activity called 'letting land'. The essence of the activity is to work with a partner, who says something we find difficult to hear. This can be feedback, a passing comment or joke, or a view that you oppose or disagree with. It can relate to being given some difficult news, such as not getting a job or the funding for a key project. It's wise to choose something that's mildly difficult to hear, rather than something that's life-changing.

It can be helpful to explore the impact of centred listening and letting land by working with a partner. If you can call on a trusted friend or colleague, you can use the following guidance to try out the practice with them. The guidelines are also shown at Appendix F.

## ☆ Embodied Practice 5

### *Letting land with a practice partner†*

To explore the impact of centred listening and letting land, work with a partner. Brief your partner to say something that you find difficult to hear (go for something mild, not a personal criticism or a major life event). You can now compare and contrast the experience of receiving these words in an uncentred state and in a centred state.

1. In the first step, your partner delivers the words that you find difficult to hear before you've made any effort to centre or collect yourself. Notice the impact the words have on you and your reaction to them. Perhaps there's a physical sensation such as tightening or shrinking; perhaps there's a feeling such as annoyance or concern; perhaps there's an impulse to speak, to put someone right, to explain, to apologise, to hit back. Or perhaps all of these things. Simply notice and accept whatever occurs – does it represent a pattern?

2. Next, ask your partner to wait a moment or two, saying you'll nod when you're ready for them to speak. Do the four-part centring practice (Appendix B), and then expand your personal space to include your practice partner, remembering to expand it evenly in all dimensions. Nod when you're ready and, as your partner speaks, imagine the words falling or floating softly onto the table/ground between you. Notice the impact of the words when you listen in this way.

3. When your partner has delivered the words, connect with what really matters – do you need to respond? If so, what is it important to say? Centre again and speak.

4. Debrief with your partner – what did each of you experience in steps 1 and 2? If you responded in step 3, how did your partner experience your words? What insights arise?

5. Now change roles and repeat ...

† *Based on the work of Wendy Palmer.*

If you've been able to try this partner practice, I hope you found it useful. If you're curious about the inverse and using the centring practice when you're *giving* someone a message you know they'll find difficult to hear, we'll explore this in Chapter 18. In the meantime, you can find practices for centred speaking and giving unwelcome news at Appendices G and H.

In this chapter, we've had quite a detailed foray into the way our body and presence can support us to really listen. I hope you've experienced how the energy of a conversation changes when we listen from a centred, inclusive place. I also hope that this visceral evidence inspires you to try this in your life – at work or at home – so that you build confidence in the Leadership Embodiment practices.

A really good practice ground for centred listening and 'letting land' is public discourse. You can read an article, listen to a podcast or watch a film clip that relates to something you find difficult to deal with – a view you find disagreeable or a topic you find distasteful or disturbing. The practice is to centre before you begin, and repeat regularly as you proceed. Can you find a sense of interest and curiosity about the subject matter? Can you receive it neutrally and explore it? Once again, it's wise to choose something that you find mildly difficult rather than something you feel strongly about.

## Three steps towards approaching difference differently

We explored the centred listening practice as a response to two questions:

- what might make it possible to really listen?; and

- how might we create space in which to hold our differences so that we can explore them?

Once we've listened, and created a landing space, we can also ask: how might we engage with what's been said with respect and wonder? In this context, what I mean by respect is acknowledging the legitimacy of what's being said in the context of the speaker's personal reality, which is unique to them. This is where wonder comes in handy – we might wonder *at* the profusion of ways of looking at the world and *about* what's shaping the view that's being expressed.

If we summarise these three questions and consider what they invite us to pay attention to, we can formulate three steps towards approaching difference differently.

### *Three steps towards approaching difference differently*

#### ◉ Step 1

*Inquiring:* What might make it possible to really listen?

*Advocating:* Listen, receive, truly pay attention to … self and other.

#### ◉ Step 2

*Inquiring:* How might we create space in which to hold our differences so that we can explore them?

*Advocating:* Collectively create and hold a space in which a variety of views can be considered.

#### ◉ Step 3

*Inquiring:* How might we engage with what's being said with respect and wonder?

*Advocating:* Wonder … wonder at the diversity and richness of the views offered, wonder about how someone came to see the world this way … then inquire.

The three steps reflect the essence of the three tenets outlined in Chapter 4 in that they touch on how we handle ourselves, how we begin and how we create a holding space, or container, for our conversation. We'll add to these steps in Chapter 13 and later, in Part III, we'll explore how we can bring them to life by embodying dialogue practices.

First, we'll turn our attention to the greater complexity of the energies and patterns that arise when groups of people meet to talk together.

# Chapter 12  Realities: the energy of groups

In our journey so far, we've explored approaches that can offer insight into what's happening in an exchange between a couple of people. We've gained an appreciation of the difference between debate and dialogue and begun to explore how we can be more present to what's being said. We've also touched on the way difference can become divisive when public discourse relies on exchanging headlines. We'll now turn our attention to looking at collective energy in the size of group that might be common in the workplace, such as a management team or project team.

We can apply some of the approaches we've already met to these situations. For example, just as we looked at the shape and quality of the exchange between the MD and the COO in Case Study 1, we can pay attention to the interplay of advocacy and inquiry in a group. In doing so, we might discern that a conversation has an overall shape, such as directional and focused (advocacy-led) or circular and exploratory (inquiry-led). When we become aware of this, we create an opportunity to add different energy – perhaps we can introduce some advocacy to create traction in a diffuse or meandering conversation, or bring some inquiry to an exchange that's on a single track or becoming polarised.

## Collective energy and patterns

When we're in a group, we can use any of the embodied practices that we've encountered – however, our capacity to do this will be affected by the overall tone or vibe of a conversation. This collective energy will be influenced by several factors, such as the patterns and norms of the societal environment in which an organisation is located, sector-specific attributes, customs and language, and departmental influences such as the different priorities of finance and marketing.

In addition, collective energy will be affected by the size of the group. Broadly, as the number of people involved in a conversation grows, their interactions and the associated energies increase in both complexity and intensity.

To explain this, let's start with two people. There's a relationship between them, which means there are three energies to navigate: two individuals and the dynamic they create (or have created) between them. Add a third person and there are three relationships to attend to – essentially three pairs, A and B, B and C, and A and C. Three people and three relationships give us six energies to consider. With four people, the number of relationships increases to six because each person relates to three others. This means there are ten energies in play. So, in a conversation, increasing the number of people involved from two (one relationship) to four people (six relationships) doesn't double the energetic complexity, it more than triples it. The complexity of energy in a group escalates from here. In addition, the larger a group, the more views will be in play, which brings a potential increase in the energy of our differences.

Further, the relationships and interactions in a conversation give rise to a unique entity that isn't attributable to any individual person, contribution or cause. A conversation is an *emergent property* of a group and the context within which it's meeting. An emergent property is one that manifests in a whole system, rather than in individual members of the system. For example, a beehive is an emergent property of a community of bees – it develops through collective activity without any single bee having a plan. In the same way, a conversation quite literally has a life of its own, emerging from the overt and subtle interactions between those present – and, sometimes, significant people who aren't actually present.

A conversation is therefore an entity in its own right, a living system that's more than the sum of its parts. If we try to attend to each of the parts, we're likely to become overwhelmed. Instead, we can pay attention to the shape and quality of the whole conversation and notice its effect on those present. We may then be able to see a way to positively influence what's unfolding. In addition, if we have a role in setting the conversation up, we can create conditions that encourage a group to surface and explore differences in a generative way. If we're not able to influence this, we can aim to handle ourselves skilfully in charged situations so that we don't widen any divides or add to any turbulence.

## Over to you ...

What's your response to the possibility that a conversation has a life of its own? Can you think of an experience when a collective mood seemed to take hold and colour proceedings? Perhaps a sense of doom infected everyone, even those who are usually positive, or a sense of possibility carried along even those who are usually pessimistic. How do you describe such experiences? What do you attribute them to?

The nature, level and intensity of energy in a conversation affects all present, whether consciously or not. When this energy is warm, attentive and/or exploratory, individual energies are more likely to be at ease. When collective energy is unwelcoming, unreceptive and/or combative, the autonomic nervous system of those present will be 'on alert', primed to react in accordance with their tendency to fight or flight. This is where embodied practices become important – the way we handle our own energetic presence affects the energy of the whole conversation.

Within a conversation, working with our own thinking and physiology to change our practice is only the beginning. The collective patterns embedded in the living system of a conversational entity can help or hinder our efforts. This is true for all 'collectives', whether two friends, a project team, an organisation or a public discourse. In any given setting, there are likely to be established patterns of conversation which determine the conversational 'style' in all circumstances. For example, in an organisation, a team of creatives with a dominant discourse of possibilities and innovation may find it hard to talk about tough financial realities. Similarly, it may not be easy to set up a conversation about strategic thinking in a business where the primary focus is on near-term targets and performance.

This sense that there's often an underlying pattern to conversations, specific to a particular collective context, gave me the idea of a conversational 'operating system'. I introduced this in *Weekly Leadership Contemplations*,[14] writing:

In a working alliance of several people, individual energies and tendencies combine to configure a collective operating system, a received way of going about things. While this patterning may be influenced by factors such as an organisation's purpose, customs, practices and culture, it becomes tangible in the way people talk and listen to each other.

The premise is that, in any collective, a preferred communication pattern evolves, encompassing tone, idiom, what it's OK to say, what it's not OK to say, and so on. Essentially, human interactions take on a particular 'look and feel' and become encoded as an 'operating system' (OS), which often endures, even as people come and go.

In technology, an OS runs largely in the background and its configuration determines whether or not a program or app will work. Similarly, a conversational OS will favour some types of exchange and be incompatible with others. Framing unnoticed patterns of conversation in this way invites us to think about how and why some crucial conversations get derailed. If we don't understand the forces that can hijack our intentions, we'll be at their mercy as we try to change our practice, whether individually or collectively.

Typically, a conversational OS reflects the matters an organisation or collective holds dear, or the ways in which people are held to account, or both. Depending on the context, certain themes will arise, such as meeting sales targets, reducing costs, improving performance, communicating more effectively, using capacity efficiently, nurturing innovation, or minimising the impact of disruption. There may also be an innate template for the prevalent *style* of conversation – such as 'doing a deal', 'making a case', 'increasing engagement' or 'highlighting problems'. If we're able to recognise the characteristics of the kinds of conversation that predominate in our setting, we may begin to see their limitations. Then, by comparing means and ends, we can begin to assess whether a particular conversation is fit for purpose. For example, we can meet transactional ends with an everyday exchange. However, to handle complex adaptive challenges (known as 'wicked issues') and the differences that arise within them, dialogue is a better fit. We'll expand on the theme of 'fit' in Chapter 34, when we consider the types of conversation that might benefit from the additional effort required to create the conditions for dialogue.

A conversational OS may also have a characteristic qualitative feel, a tendency towards a particular vibe or tone. This will be linked to the nature of the typical themes, topics, purposes and style of regular exchanges. It may also be influenced by prominent individuals or subgroups, particular dynamics between key players and/or the culture of the organisation or team. It can be helpful to identify and describe this collective energetic mood because it will affect the way people approach a conversation. For example, many of us dread meetings that we know are likely to be downbeat or hostile, and look forward to those we expect to be lively and warm. In addition, if we start to pay attention to the qualitative feel of our conversations, we're more likely to notice shifts in energy and the way they affect what plays out.

In summary, everyone in a conversation is influenced by its collective energy, as well as by what's being said (or not). For example, if we arrive at a meeting feeling upbeat, only to find that the general tone is fractious and quarrelsome, what impact does this have on us? Are we able to stay connected to our own outlook, or do we get drawn into the prevailing mood? We'll have more options for the way we respond to such situations if we're aware of the energetic patterns in play and have developed our capacity to sustain (or recover) the quality of our embodied presence.

## Over to you …

Before moving on, think of a specific conversational setting – a team you're in, a regular social gathering, a committee – and test out the idea that it has an 'operating system', a tacit agreement about what you talk about and how you do this. What is it OK to talk about and what is off-limits? How does this affect what's possible?

As you reflect on this setting, how might you describe its feeling tone, the typical 'vibe' of it? How does this influence what unfolds?

Let's turn to the personal agency we have within the collective energy of a conversation. There are two broad scenarios to explore. The first is that we're in a conversation that someone else is hosting and we have to work within the conditions that they establish. The second is that we have the opportunity to play a part in the way a conversation is set up and to influence the way that collective energy is fostered.

The first scenario is most common and, in it, our only real agency is to pay attention to how the conversation is playing out alongside its content, and to be aware of how we're personally contributing to the patterns in play. Even when we have no formal standing in a group, the way we carry ourselves will uphold or modify the prevailing shape and energetic quality of the conversation. We can be mindful of this, and be selective in what we say and do. We'll explore this ground more fully in Part III. For now, a first step is to tune in to the energies and patterns of a conversation and to recognise that we're part of them ('we are the method', Tenet 1).

As we develop our capacity to describe what we're noticing, we might wonder what we can do with these insights. One option is to bring them to the attention of others and ask whether or how they're serving the collective purpose. A conversation that feels harmonious and pleasant may be prohibiting useful opposition or scrutiny. A conversation that feels fractious may be detracting from potential collaboration. Bringing the attention of a group to such things offers an opportunity to change tack. It's an interruption to the usual course of things, and may create a 'pause' in which some regrouping is possible.

In the second scenario, where we have the opportunity to play a part in how a conversation is set up, we can actively influence the initial conditions ('entry is everything', Tenet 3). This offers the potential for creating, and consciously holding, a space in which differences can be held and explored ('consciously holding a container', Tenet 2), and encouraging those present to play their part in the way a conversation unfolds ('we are the method', Tenet 1). If we have this opportunity, how might we influence the shape and quality of the conversation so that the energies of difference can be channelled towards something new?

112

## Influencing the shape of a conversation

To consider how we can influence the shape of a conversation, we'll briefly revisit the Gibb[6] approach to fostering trust, shown in the diagram below.

**Engaging with each other**

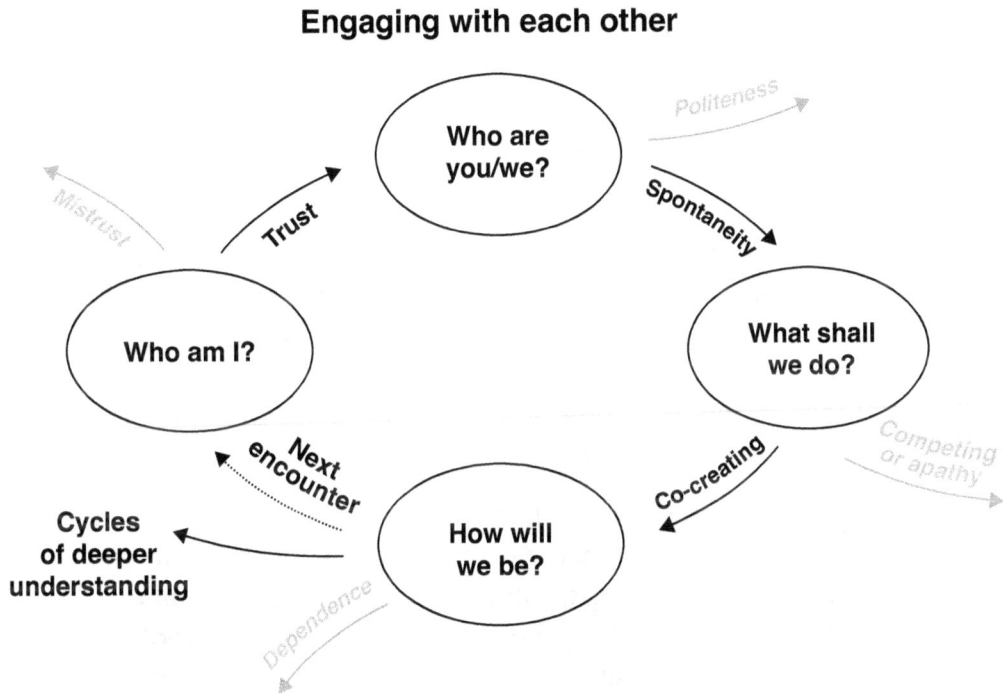

Based on the work of Jack Gibb

We met this in Chapters 3 and 4 to when we explored the dialogue practice of check-in. At its core is a premise that, whenever any of us enters a new process, group or conversation, we hold questions about how we fit in and whether the encounter will be useful or relevant. The questions fall into four broad arenas:

- Who am I in this setting?

- Who are you in this setting – and who are we?

- What shall we do together?

- How will we be together?

If we're bringing together a group for any kind of non-routine conversation, it's important to spend time establishing who's present and gaining some sense of why they've come. This is why we check in. Once we've connected to ourselves and with each other, we can turn our attention to what we want to do together. While the main focus in this section is the 'what' of a conversation, we'll briefly reprise the two phases of making contact at a human level.

To begin to establish trust, Gibb's work proposes that we first seek a sense of our 'place' in a group. If we remain unsure of our value, we'll tend to be mistrustful. Once we're at ease with our place, we begin to wonder about others – what will they bring to the group? If we can see the merit in what others offer, we have a strong foundation for collaborative working. Without this, we'll probably be limited to polite exchanges. When these questions are resolved for those involved, we clear the ground for collective endeavour.

In setting up a non-routine conversation, we ask 'what shall we talk about?' rather than 'what shall we do?'. When we gather to talk and listen to each other, there's usually a reason and, perhaps, some aspirations and expectations. When I'm working with a group, I explore this ground by inviting those present to consider three aspects of intention, using an embodied metaphor of head, heart and core (or 'gut'). These archetypal centres of energy and presence represent three 'voices' within us, and each has a different emphasis:

- purpose/head – what do each of us want from this conversation? What initial questions do we have? What does that mean for us collectively?

- relational/heart – how do we want to affect relationships within the group and beyond?

- systemic/core – what are our aspirations for the wider system? What impact do we hope to have on others? What really matters here?

The questions within this light framing invite group members to attend to relational and systemic matters as well as an immediate purpose or concern. When we layer 'task' with human factors and wider consequences, we support a more panoramic exploration of the ground. In addition, by clarifying our intentions in this way, we blend advocacy and inquiry, balancing directional and exploratory energy. We start as we mean to continue, which sets the scene for dialogue.

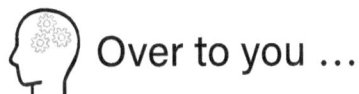

## Over to you …

Can you identify a non-routine conversation where you might 'road-test' this approach to clarifying the purpose of it? How might you 'recruit' people to give it a try? How will you assess what works and what doesn't work?

When we clarify both our intentions and what we hope to explore together, we create the means to 'stay on track'. If a conversation seems to be diverging from a shared purpose, we can pause and check whether the detour is useful in the context of the agreed terrain. If it isn't, we can refocus. We also begin to create the conditions for handling difference because it's unlikely that we'll find a single straightforward goal or aim for the conversation. In addition, when we hear the aims and aspirations of those present, we may uncover some of the assumptions being made. When we successfully navigate the differences in what we want to talk about, we build confidence in our collective capacity to navigate difference more generally.

When we use the framing of head-heart-core to include relational and systemic considerations alongside immediate purpose, we also to sow some seeds of coherence. If we give it some thought, most of us don't want to get our way at the expense of a fractured relationship. If a group agrees that they want their conversation to strengthen relationships (or at least not harm them), they give permission to pause and regroup if things get heated. If relational intentions haven't been expressed, it can be much harder to speak up if the conversational climate deteriorates.

Finally, it's easy to forget the bigger picture when we're pursuing a personal agenda, and so bringing systemic considerations into the field from the beginning helps everyone maintain a broad horizon. In my experience, cultivating greater clarity about what really matters creates room for people to change their minds. Personally, I'm more prepared to give ground on something if I can see that it will bring benefits more widely. Without this perspective, it's easy to remain blinkered and focused on immediate concerns and/or pressing issues.

We'll now explore some of the influences on the quality of a conversation.

## Influencing the quality of a conversation

When we consider the shape of a conversation in terms of shared ground in which to balance advocacy and inquiry, we're already attending to the quality of energy we want to foster. Indirectly, we've touched on how we'll conduct ourselves. This is the essence of the fourth question of the Gibb approach. We've expanded our intentions to include relational and systemic aspirations, which sets the scene for *how* we'll talk and listen together. We can now ask: what conditions will best support our intentions?

To explore this in a group, I usually ask those present to recall a really good conversation and to talk in pairs about the *qualities* that made it possible. This approach eases people into describing the conditions that might support meaningful and/or fruitful engagement. We then share our observations and reflections. The qualities we identify are usually many and varied, and include words and phrases like: time and space; being OK to disagree; genuine interest and listening; respect; openness; playfulness; being safe to share unformed thoughts; candour; trust; warmth and acceptance; breathing space; time to reflect; curiosity …

Next, we spend time getting a feel for what the named qualities mean in practice. For example, how do we know when others are genuinely interested, and what's the impact of their interest? What do we mean by trust, and how do we know that others trust us? In this exploration, we're aiming to get below the surface of (often familiar) words and gain insight into how we'll know when these qualities are present. We're looking into the difference between an aspirational idea and messy reality. We're also clarifying the implications of each word in terms of personal conduct. And ... as we explore the nature of the qualities that make good conversation possible, we begin to experience and embody them in our energetic field.

## Over to you ...

Recall a personal experience of a really good conversation – what supported it and made it possible? Try to think about this in terms of the quality of energy, the feel of the conversation, rather than practical things ...

For your next important conversation, how might you go about fostering this kind of energy amongst those present?

When considering the qualities that support good conversations with a group, my final step is to ask them to organise their selected words and phrases around four themes – the dialogue practices of listening, respecting, suspending judgement and authentic voicing (Chapter 1). When we embody these four practices, their energy permeates our shared environment. The vibe of the practices becomes the energetic tone of the field. For example, when we listen deeply – both to others and to our inner experience – it seems to me that we settle into ourselves and into a connection with others. This settling is an energetic experience, a quality of being together, and it brings a feeling of acceptance, spaciousness and connection. At least, that's how it is for me – how is it for you? We'll explore the embodied experience of all four dialogue practices in more depth in Chapter 20.

To bring this chapter to a close, let's return to the theme of the relationship between collective energy and group size. In my experience, the qualities of listening, respecting, suspending judgement and being authentic in what we say are more often present in smaller groups. I've been in many conversations that encompass, and fruitfully delve into, quite diverse views – and they've been amongst two, three or four people. The conversations were intense, light of spirit or somewhere in between, but were always engaging, wide-ranging and thought-provoking. Differences were aired, considered, expanded upon and absorbed. I was enriched by the conversation, whether or not I agreed with what others said. I expect you've been in this kind of conversation too. So, we know how it feels to be in a good conversation. The challenge is 'scaling up' this kind of experience.

In the context of dialogue, the bigger the group, the greater the need to consciously invest in good set-up and a check-in process (Tenet 3). A natural consequence of the reality that each person makes sense of the world in a unique way is that differences in view will arise – if we allow them to. This presents an invitation to approach important conversations in a way that expects and accommodates difference. To do this, we prepare to handle ourselves well in the accompanying disturbance: we are the method for dialogue (Tenet 1), and the way we carry ourselves and relate to others contributes to the collective container. In addition, if we expect differences to arise, we're more likely to consciously explore *how* we'll talk together and create conditions in which we can engage with them fruitfully (Tenet 2).

When we don't talk about how we'll engage with each other, we're much less able to accommodate our differences. When a group is large, open and changing, such as on social media platforms and in similar settings, there's no spoken or psychological contract in place. Therefore, when we share thoughts and feelings about societal concerns in such settings, the factors that support respectful treatment of our differences are likely to be absent. It's an extreme version of participating in a conversation of unknown provenance. It can feel like 'the Wild West' – because it is. In these public exchanges, the driving force is often the inherent human reaction to difference – fight, flight or freeze – and only the fight element is visible. Our fundamental choice is whether we add to the prevailing pattern or not.

This matters because each container that we consciously foster sits within a nest of larger and larger containers. We can create a container for great conversations in our team – and this sits within an organisational 'container', which may have different influences and concerns, and where we may have less agency. Any business, enterprise or institution sits within a wider sector and societal setting, each of which has a container established by custom and practice. At some point in the 'nest' of containers, we reach a place where our only real agency lies in how we handle ourselves within the conditions that are present.

## Over to you …

Take a few moments to reflect on the idea that each setting for a conversation sits within a bigger context, and so any local 'container' or holding space that we try to consciously create will be flavoured by these wider influences.

How might you take account of this when approaching your next important conversation?

Let's pick up the theme of expecting difference to arise in our conversations, and begin to think about how we accommodate the diversity that's inherent in being human. This brings us to the thorny matter of inclusion.

# Chapter 13 Realities: including diverse views

I think there are two aspects to inclusion – and each is 'thorny' in its own way. I use the word thorny because it evokes something that we have to handle carefully if we're to avoid harm. In the context of dialogue and handling difference skilfully, the aspect of inclusion that matters most is that we create space to encompass and explore diverse views, and that we consciously encourage expression of these views. This is can be thorny because of the way we're wired to react to difference (Chapter 9).

Bringing a variety of perspectives into a conversation raises a second aspect of inclusion – inviting people who are dissimilar in background and outlook to take part. This can be thorny if we're unclear about what we mean by inclusion in the context of the conversation we're aiming to have.

## Over to you …

Take a moment to consider what shapes your sense of what it means to include? What's your stance on the emphasis that's placed on inclusion in current times?

Now reflect on personal experience – how do you feel when you're included? What does inclusion mean to you? In contrast, how do you feel when you're excluded? What does exclusion mean to you?

To explore inclusion, let's look first at a potential challenge of inviting a wide range of beliefs, opinions, interests and stances into a conversation. Deliberately bringing difference into the room means that we have to find skilful ways of handling the thinking, reactions and impulses we experience when others speak – we'll like some of the things we hear and dislike others. We may find we're strongly moved to chip in, to challenge, to affirm, to question or to build. The desire to contribute may feel pressing – which, in itself, may be an indicator that we're about to act habitually and/or to recycle some preconceived thoughts. When this kind of urge to speak arises, it can be helpful to ask: what might be the benefit of continuing to listen rather saying my piece?

This isn't to say we remain silent. The question we ask ourselves is simply a prompt to stay present and to seek a balance between expressing our own view, more fully understanding what others are trying to say and sensing what collective circumstances might be calling for. I'm suggesting this balance because, while I believe that every point of view is valid and has worth, I also believe that any view will have greater or lesser relevance in a given context. This is as true for anything I might say as it is for others and so I try to sift through my thoughts and reactions to see what they might add (if anything) to the conversation. When I experience the urge to speak, particularly if I find myself being drawn into a narrowing narrative in my mind, I use embodied practices to regain my poise and perspective. The practices of centred listening (Appendix E) and centred inquiry (Appendix D) support me in the delicate matter of deciding if/when to speak and what to say.

Whilst potentially challenging to enact, navigating the dynamic balance between self and collective is, I think, crucial to dialogue and to approaching difference differently. If we can hold individual views *in parity* and *be discerning* about what's in service to the whole, we might find a form of inclusion that serves collective endeavour, whether in conversation or in collaborative action. This involves including differences and skilfully handling the way we're affected by them.

Let's look at the attributes of parity and discernment in more detail, whilst remembering that our context is creating space for different views to be aired and explored.

## Holding diverse views in parity

What I mean by holding diverse views in parity is that we consciously try to regard every contribution as being of value, and neither more nor less important than any other. Applying this principle to both self and others helps me to attend properly to what others say, regardless of my immediate reaction to it. It also encourages me to be thoughtful about whether I speak up or stay quiet. To emphasise that I see the act of holding different views in parity as a practice or discipline, I'm deliberately framing it as an aspect of how we perceive others. In dialogue, we try to adopt a state of mind and/or heart that gives equal weight to whatever's being said, regardless of who says it and whether we agree with it or not. The embodied practice of centred listening (Appendix E) supports us in this.

In essence, I'm suggesting that the responsibility for holding what we hear in parity lies with those receiving the words – it isn't an attribute of those who speak. This may be stating the obvious – and yet I think it's worth being explicit. A speaker may be articulate or not, well-informed or not, biased or not, privileged or not – there are many ways in which speakers will be 'unequal' (or unique) – and may express themselves well or clumsily. Those listening may be tempted to dismiss or discount what's being said.

However, in dialogue we work with trying to set aside such human tendencies so that we can receive and hold what's said in an impartial way. This allows us to explore the perspectives being offered; to probe them in order to understand their implications and relevance; to consider the questions they provoke; and (possibly) to adjust our thinking. If we're able to include different ideas and hold them all as being of value, we enrich our conversation. If, instead, we close down or skirt around differences, we lose the potential inherent in them.

All this can be challenging because the greater the range of perspectives in a conversation, the more we need to attend to treating them even-handedly. This particularly applies when opinions are strongly held, whether for or against a point of view. Fervour heightens the energy of a conversation and, on a personal level, it affects our capacity to receive and hold different views in parity. We'll look at the effects of this heightened energy in the next chapter.

Before we go on, I'll explain why I'm using the word parity in this section, rather than (perhaps) more familiar or widely used words such as equality or equity. First, when a word is frequently used in a particular context, it can be unconsciously linked with that context. So, for example, equality becomes equality-diversity-inclusion, rather than simply meaning 'being equivalent'. Second, I want to emphasise the conscious activity of receiving and holding what's said in an equitable way.

The essential point is that, in dialogue, we seek to hold views in equity (or parity, or as equal), and I'm drawn to using the word parity because equity has a greater range of meaning. In addition, when a word is less familiar, less prevalent, we may examine its meaning more carefully – perhaps by wondering: 'what does she mean by that?'. Broadly, we make more assumptions about the meaning of familiar words, and fewer about words we're less accustomed to. This reflects an important characteristic of dialogue: we're curious about meaning, so that we more fully understand what's being said.

## Over to you …

On a personal basis, what most gets in the way of holding different views in parity? What question might you ask yourself when you notice that you're dismissing or discounting a view, or when you strongly agree with it? What might give you 'pause'?

More generally, what might support you to foster curiosity about how and why others think the way they do? How might you inquire into what they say? How might you encourage others to do the same?

If the practices of dialogue ask us to hold diverse views in parity, how do we gauge the range of views that will enrich a conversation?

## Discerning inclusion – views

When we think about the possibility of including a wide variety of views in a conversation, we may be concerned that some will be tangential to the matter at hand. It takes time to hear many voices and, to echo the words of several participants in my dialogue programmes, we may feel that we 'don't have time for this'. By 'this', a participant often means the whole process of setting up a conversation in a way that supports wider exploration of different views.

In response, I usually observe that many of us seem to have endless time to address the consequences of not having the right kind of conversation in the right kind of way. I accept that it does take time to seek out and hear those who think differently, and that it's easy to feel that this impedes progress. And it can be hard to 'spend' what seems like a limited resource (time) to mitigate the risks of future fallout. And yet, for important matters, what's the alternative?

If time is short, what will support us to spend it well? This is where the quality of discernment comes into play. The invitation to include diverse views is not unbounded – we can be thoughtful about the degree of diversity that will enrich our conversation and collective endeavour. We can be discerning about what (and who) we include.

I often compare discernment to judgement in order to distinguish between one kind of selective 'assessing' and another. I do this because judgements form, naturally, as we listen to others. We appraise what we hear, sorting it into what seems relevant (or not), useful (or not) and/or interesting (or not). Judgements aren't problematic in themselves. They become unhelpful when we think we're right, to the exclusion of other views. When we become attached to a position, our certainty constrains what we're able to hear.

If, instead, we see our judgement as it really is – an opinion based on a current assessment of the value of something – we're less likely to place undue reliance on it. When we experience a sense of certainty, of being right, we can use it as a prompt to wonder … what's shaping my view? What if it's inaccurate, out-of-date or otherwise mistaken? In holding it, what might I be missing?

This kind of discerning inquiry loosens our attachment to a single way of looking at things, which creates room to include different perspectives. This isn't to say we simply accept other views – we're discerning about their provenance and their relevance to the wider conversation. To be discerning, we use our natural tendency to assess, appraise, evaluate – but we do it consciously and with care.

When a judgement forms, we can use it as a prompt to be discerning. If we think a view is wrong-headed, unpalatable, problematic or difficult to comprehend, we can choose to examine it. We already have an approach for doing this – the centred inquiry activity known as wall–window (Appendix D). A key principle of centred inquiry is that a willingness to look into someone's view doesn't mean that we agree with it (or them). We're simply acknowledging the presence of difference and seeking greater understanding of it. We wonder: what's shaping what they see?

As we build our capacity to work skilfully with the way we assess what others say, this might lead us to consider the degree of diversity of view that will be useful to a conversation. This will always depend on context. Too little variation in outlook is likely to impoverish a conversation, diminishing the potential for creativity, innovation and change. However, when the range of contribution is too broad, a conversation may lose energy and become diffuse, making it more difficult for those present to remain engaged. Finding an appropriate balance is an art rather than a science – we're discerning about the range of views we include.

When we deliberately include a wide range of perspectives in a conversation, another aspect of discernment applies. While inclusion can be positive, we sometimes forget or fail to notice that including one view may inadvertently exclude another. This applies both to the process of deciding which perspectives to invite into a conversation and to how we attend to differences as they're voiced. If we subscribe to a 'right way' of thinking about the world, we may sideline views which diverge from it. In doing so, we both limit the scope of a conversation and increase the risk that it'll remain on well-trodden paths: there's little chance that we'll create something new.

## Over to you …

Take a few moments to reflect on the benefits and drawbacks of including diverse views. Can you find an example of a conversation where the range of contribution was so narrow that it limited what was possible? Can you find an example of a conversation where the range of contribution was so varied that the central purpose became lost and it ended inconclusively? What insights arise from these reflections?

For your next important conversation, what range of views might best support your purpose?

Seeking out difference and bringing genuine diversity into a conversation usually involves including a broad range of people, with a variety of life experiences, credentials, values, roles, beliefs and ways of viewing the world. To foster this, we'll be discerning about who we invite and what they might contribute.

## Discerning inclusion – people

There's usually a reason for bringing people together to talk, and it can offer a basis for being discerning about who we include. We can consider the scope of the conversation by drawing lightly on the head-heart-core framework that we used to clarify intentions in Chapter 12. What do we hope for in terms of outcome? What are our aspirations for relationships and for the bigger picture? What kind of conversation will best support these ends, an exploratory one or a focused one? How might these considerations influence who we include?

The responsibility for deciding who to invite into a conversation usually falls to the convenor(s) of it, the person or group responsible for setting things in motion. The process of convening is an opportunity to do things differently and to be thoughtful about who to invite into a conversation, rather than reaching for a list of the usual suspects. In addition, we don't attempt to involve every voice, because we then risk diminishing the value of each voice. So, we pause, and think a little more deeply about who to include and why. We make a conscious change in the way we approach the conversation. This permeates what follows, reflecting the essence of the third tenet: entry is everything. There's a strong element of leadership in convening: the fundamental choice is to perpetuate existing ways of doing things or to work at introducing change.

When we take into account the purpose of a conversation, we may begin to shed light on what we're expecting from those we invite. It can be helpful to set this out in the invitation to join a conversation. Inclusion isn't a free pass – it's an opportunity to be present in exchange for a commitment to actively engage with whatever unfolds.

If we include this kind of signal in an invitation to participate, we indicate that this isn't a conventional conversation. Many meetings are called through an administrative function with the barest of practical details given – time, location, a topic (perhaps). These details may be inserted into electronic diaries without reference to feasibility. There's no meaningful agreement to participate – and it's easy to decline to attend, to cancel later or to 'attend' passively. It's also easy to misunderstand the purpose of the conversation. The unintended consequences of this kind of efficiency can be crossed wires, confusion and slow progress. Some of these consequences can be alleviated by being a little more thoughtful about how we convene any non-routine conversation.

To return to who we include in our conversation: we can forget or fail to notice that an invitation to a particular person or constituency may inadvertently discount or exclude others. Even when inclusion is rooted in a principle that seems universal, such as ensuring that those in an under-served group have an opportunity to participate, the consequences for others may be overlooked. If this happens, we're not holding different constituencies in parity – emphasising the value of certain voices can be perceived as regarding other voices to be less important. This isn't what we intended – we simply didn't appreciate how others might interpret our good intentions. Finding an appropriate level of inclusion is a complex balancing act.

## Over to you ...

Can you identify a situation, process or event that might benefit from including a greater range of people? What would constitute appropriate (and/or healthy and/or relevant) inclusion in this context?

Now identify a situation, process or event that might benefit from being less inclusive – what prompts you to choose this example, and what can you learn from it?

How is your sense of the meaning of 'inclusion' changing (or not)?

The way we approach inclusion as we set a conversation in motion will ripple through what follows – and we'll explore this further in Part III. In the meantime, the principles of discerning inclusion and holding diverse views in parity bring us to an exploration of the importance of holding each other in parity.

## Holding people in parity

When we encounter people who hold views that we find difficult and challenging, what will support us to include, accept and respect them so that we can hear what they have to say?

In dialogue, we seek to hold all those present in parity, as equal in terms of their participation and voice. This means working with the limitations of our humanness and our propensity to react to difference – and so to react to otherness in those around us. If we can acknowledge this inherent difficulty, we can work with it. If we pretend it isn't present within us to some degree, we'll gloss over it, ignore it or inadvertently enact it.

In parallel with the practice of holding diverse views in parity, the practice of holding other people in parity is about how we receive them – it isn't a condition of their nature or circumstances. Every conversation will take place on an uneven playing field in that there'll be a mix of fortunes amongst those present. Each person will have different advantages and disadvantages, and will see the world in a way that's influenced by their own make-up and experience. Difference is natural and present: no two people are the same, and inequalities exist. In this reality, we can only be even-handed in the way we regard our fellow human beings and strive to offer each of them equal attention, respect, curiosity and acceptance.

Whilst always important, the practice of holding others in parity is particularly pertinent to conversations in organisations, where there are often assumptions that some people have greater standing, weight and validity than others. In such settings, the words of those with position power, expertise and/or longevity may be preferred over the words of those who lack these attributes. This may be such a settled state of affairs that it's overlooked – by recognising it, we create an opportunity to foster change. To create the conditions of parity that allow for dialogue, we invite everyone to show up as human beings with equal standing. This can be profoundly challenging for those bound by the priorities, structures, hierarchies, privileges and customs of organisational life. In dialogue, we seek to include those offering a relevant perspective, regardless of their role and status. We do this to broaden shared understanding and, perhaps, catalyse fresh thinking.

Let's pick up the theme of our propensity to react to difference and to otherness in those around us. By definition, someone else is 'other' – so how can we work skilfully with the reality of a room (or virtual space) filled with others? How might we hold them in parity? I don't have a framework or 'lens' through which to explore this, although I'm sure that many exist. However, our focus is on the *embodied* experience of other, and so we can gain some insight from situations in which we've felt 'other'.

In my case, I've generally found it difficult to navigate social situations. I worry about how I'm supposed to behave, what others expect and what the 'form' is here – and these concerns are exacerbated in unfamiliar settings, including different cultures and contexts. I'm therefore slightly self-conscious and uncomfortable – in other words, my fight/flight system is on alert, if not fully activated. In this state, my tendency is to stand back initially, to see if I can work out what's going on. And then I'll probably try too hard to fit in – which may mean I'm clumsy and inadvertently cause offence to others. This is deeply ingrained, a personal reactive pattern provoked by difference.

A more general starting point is that, in being human, we're each unique – we're 'other' by definition. Since we're different to one another, we naturally tend to be slightly on alert or watchful in the presence of others, especially if we don't know them. This is the legacy of our autonomic nervous system, which may cause us to be wary of someone even before we've heard what they have to say. This is the embodied element of our experience of other – and it presents a challenge to holding them in parity.

Your response to being amongst unfamiliar others will be unique to you and, even if you're the epitome of confidence and social grace, there are probably some situations in which you feel slightly more self-conscious. Take a moment to explore this.

## Over to you …

Find an example of a situation in which you felt uncomfortable because people and/or circumstances were unfamiliar and you weren't sure how or whether you fitted in. Feel your way back into the situation and linger in it for a moment – how does your discomfort show up in your body? How does it affect your thinking and actions? What do you tend to do and/or say?

What does this reveal about your embodied experience of 'otherness'?

In general, in moments or situations when we're self-conscious and have less than our usual assurance, we may try to override our lack of ease cognitively, and coax or cajole ourselves into a better place. For example, my embodied experience in unfamiliar settings includes a tendency to flush, a slightly increased heart rate and a sense of caution or even apprehension. This begins in advance of an event and is accompanied by a pre-emptive version of standing back and then trying too hard – I toggle between thinking 'I won't go' and 'get a grip'. This is my mind's unskilful attempt to deal with an embodied experience of mild anxiety. Paradoxically, it tends to increase my unease.

If, instead, I recognise the embodied nature of my discomfort, I can respond in the same modality and use the Leadership Embodiment centring practice (Appendix B) to settle my system. As a minimum, this ensures that my unease doesn't increase. It may even alleviate it. In recognising my unresourceful state (mild anxiety and resistance) and choosing to change it by centring, I acknowledge and accept myself in all my humanness. In effect, I include myself and my experience, and this creates space within me to include and accept others in *their* humanness.

In addition, the LE centring practice offers a basis for an embodied approach to holding others in parity. Over time, as we build our capacity to centre, we also become more able to expand our sense of space and include others. We began to explore this with the centred listening practice (Appendix E). When we practise centred listening, we communicate inclusion and acceptance without words. We don't need to do anything more. However, there's a catch – most of us can't maintain a centred state for very long: we quickly fall back into our more familiar, habitual self, which tends to be either unhelpfully entangled with others or separated from them. When we recognise this natural limit, we can see it as an invitation to centre again, and again, and again …

To include others (and self), as they/we are, is so deeply challenging that it's unlikely that we'll ever master it. And yet we must do what we can – and embody an including and accepting presence whenever possible. There's no downside to making this a lifelong practice.

On a personal basis, I've used the LE practices to make progress towards being more comfortable with others. It's a slow process and I often fall short of the ideal I'm setting out in these pages. I'm being explicit about this because it too is part of being human. The good news is that I'm more able to be open and accepting of others, even though I trip up fairly often. I can only recommend that you work with these practices and judge their value by what happens when you apply them.

To bring this exploration of holding people in parity to a close, we can draw on the wisdom of Pat Parker, a Black American poet and activist. In her poem, 'For the white person who wants to know how to be my friend',[15] she summarises the paradox of genuine inclusion with elegance. The poem begins:

> The first thing you do is to forget that i'm Black.

> Second, you must never forget that i'm Black.

This succinctly and eloquently captures the dilemma we each face – we want our identity and uniqueness to be appreciated and yet don't want to be seen as different. To honour this in others, we try to see them as both who they are *and* no different to us. We seek to hold both self and other in parity. This is a tough ask.

## Over to you ...

What does this exploration of holding people in parity evoke in you? What questions does it raise? What might support you to see others as both who they are and no different to you?

In our exploration of diversity and inclusion in the context of dialogue, we've covered some complex ground. Let's draw these themes together.

## Reflecting and distilling

Inclusion and its corollary, exclusion, is a complex and nuanced domain – for me, at least – which is why I describe it as a thorny matter. In a messy, multifaceted world, we see some confused attempts to be more inclusive as leaders of institutions try to adjust to new social mores. While this adaptability is welcome, their efforts sometimes seem to focus on being *seen* to do the 'right thing' rather than finding a coherent response to the changing societal landscape. We can reflect on public examples of such situations to see what we might learn for our own leadership and conversations.

In a relatively recent example, an artist's work was removed from a gallery shop because the artist was reported to have expressed views that challenge today's moral code. In explaining their actions, the leadership of the gallery said that they were 'committed to equality, diversity and inclusion and [do] not knowingly support artists who act in conflict with these values'. However, by excluding the artist's work, those in leadership gave unequal weight to opposing views and, in doing so, reduced diversity. They had to reverse their decision. To me, this seemed like a hasty volte-face – bounced into unfamiliar terrain, leadership seemed to have lost touch with the wider purpose of the gallery.

This example reveals a difficult aspect of any attempt to challenge a pattern of behaviour: we inadvertently exhibit that unwanted behaviour in our own actions. We can use the gallery example to reflect on this risk and wonder: how might the leadership of the organisation have responded differently when they realised that the removal of the artist's work was ill-judged? By simply reversing the decision, they succumbed to an either/or dichotomy – to ban or not ban the artist – and, in doing so, lost sight of their espoused commitment to equality, diversity and inclusion. How might they have better honoured these principles and sought a way to make their point, whilst continuing to include the artist's work in the gallery shop? With thoughtfulness and skill, it's possible to acknowledge different views in a way that makes it clear that we don't agree with, or endorse, them.

In general, when we exclude a person and their voice, we also exclude those who share their view (or have some sympathy with it). This tends to exacerbate fragmentation and intolerance, in direct opposition to the greater principle that's often being sought: inclusion and acceptance. We see this when a speaker is no-platformed or cancelled because they're believed to hold views contrary to those currently seen to be desirable: their view is being treated as less legitimate than that of those denying them an opportunity to speak.

In an organisation, this paradox may appear when we try to address exclusion by including under-represented groups of people in our teams or conversations. When we do so, we may unintentionally disregard another cohort of people and devalue their contribution and concerns. We emphasise that we're being inclusive by paying attention to a particular group – which is likely to be a positive thing – without ensuring that those now being given less attention also feel included. We signal the importance of one group of people and, unless we're very skilful in the way we do this, we inadvertently lessen the standing of others.

To address exclusion skilfully, we must be clearer about inclusion and what it means to different constituencies within an organisation. To come to a sound conclusion in this sensitive territory, it may be helpful to explore a wide range of perspectives and concerns so that the means for developing an approach to inclusion reflects the ends. Skilfully handled, this kind of process allows for some of the potential unintended consequences to be surfaced – which means we can attend to them.

## Three steps become five

At the end of Chapter 11, we formulated three steps towards approaching difference differently. Taken together, the steps encourage us to foster our capacity to listen, to create space for differences to be held and explored, and to engage with what's said with respect and wonder. We can expand these steps to encompass inclusion and parity by adding a step at the start of the process and another at the end.

As a new first step, we bring discernment to the question of who and what to include. We might ask: what are we assuming about who to include and what's relevant collectively? How might we hold our assumptions lightly?

And then, as a fifth step, we seek to hold people and their views in parity. Whilst debate emphasises our differences, in dialogue we wonder how they're connected. We ask: how might we hold different views in parity and explore the connections between them? What connects us, as people? The principle is that, if we listen to one another and dig deeply enough, there may be common ground amongst our apparent differences (Chapter 12). For example, in a growing number of ways to describe gender, we might remember that each of us shares the experience of being human.

### Five steps towards approaching difference differently

#### Step 1

*Inquiring:* What are we assuming about who to include and what's relevant collectively? How might we hold our assumptions lightly?

*Advocating:* Be discerning about the diversity of view that's relevant to our conversation and, based on this, be discerning about who to include.

#### Step 2

*Inquiring:* What might make it possible to really listen?

*Advocating:* Listen, receive, truly pay attention to … self and other.

#### Step 3

*Inquiring:* How might we create space in which to hold our differences so that we can explore them?

*Advocating:* Collectively create and hold a space in which a variety of views can be considered.

#### Step 4

*Inquiring:* How might we engage with what's being said with respect and wonder?

*Advocating:* Wonder … wonder at the diversity and richness of the views offered, wonder about how someone came to see the world this way … then inquire.

#### Step 5

*Inquiring:* How might we hold different views in parity and explore the connections between them? What connects us, as people?

*Advocating:* Find common ground by asking questions to draw out more of what each person is seeing, so that others can also see some of it.

The five steps towards approaching difference differently are most useful if they're introduced in the early stages of a conversation. When we share the steps with others, we invite them to actively engage in creating the conditions for a different kind of conversation. Any one of the steps will change the tenor of a conversation and, when taken together, they create conditions in which something deeply meaningful might unfold. I invite you to play with them and to use them to focus attention on the 'how' of conversations.

In our quest to handle our differences in a creative way, these five steps are a kind of 'warm-up' for turning more explicitly and formally to explore some of the practices of dialogue. When differences arise, dialogue is the means by which we can harness the associated energy to generate new possibilities. Let's begin to explore the richness of this field.

# Chapter 14 Ideas: interplay of individual and collective voices

As we begin to focus explicitly on dialogue and its practices, we might wonder how we can cultivate *interest* in our differences rather than trying to resolve them. Being genuinely curious about the way differences arise offers a way to be respectful of both our own view and the perspectives that are true for others. This orientation is especially important if one or two narratives have gained acceptance with a number of people and become a form of 'received wisdom'.

When one or more groups of people feel they're on certain ground and/or are attached to their view, energy may begin to gather around polarised positions. It's then easy to get caught up in one side or another, even if we're trying to hold different perspectives in parity. The exchange then becomes a conversation of 'sides', of what divides us rather than what connects us. How do we hold ourselves well as this energy takes hold? This is where the embodied practices of centred listening and centred inquiry become important.

In dialogue, when we have a 'side', we try to be aware of how this influences our thinking. We aim to suspend our view for a moment, setting aside our attachment to it. This is the movement of 'stepping off our position' in the wall–window activity (Appendix D). When in dialogue, we aim to hold all views in parity, including our own. This creates the potential to explore all 'sides', which may lead to a change of mind and/or heart. As Isaacs says in *Dialogue and the Art of Thinking Together*,[2] dialogue is:

> a conversation with a center, not sides

I slightly amended these words for the corollary in Chapter 1, writing that dialogue is:

a conversation with centre, not sides

I made this amendment because, when Isaacs refers to dialogue having a centre, I take it to refer to a shared focus or some collective ground or purpose at the heart of a conversation. When a conversation has a centre, attention is drawn towards it, which helps to counterbalance any pull to take sides. This, in turn, supports those present to be more tolerant of, and curious about, their differences. My experience reflects this …

… and … since we're working with the premise of harnessing the energies of difference to create new possibilities, I believe dialogue to be a conversation 'with centre'. By this I mean a collective energetic state that settles on those present and shifts their attention from personal concerns to universal concerns. In this energetic state there are no sides. It's a collective version of the individual centred state that we began to explore in Chapter 9.

In truth, dialogue is a conversation with centre *and* a centre. My preference, with my profound interest in embodied practices, is to emphasise the energetic state. I also believe that some sense of a centre, a shared focus or intention, is important.

## Over to you …

Take a few moments to find your own words for the distinction between the focus of a conversation and the quality of energy in which it's being held. How do you prefer to describe a conversation where, instead of sides, there's a shared sense of what matters? And how do you describe the energy of a conversation when that shared sense of what matters seems to be palpable – perhaps when it feels like a conversation is holding those present rather than being held by them?

When energy gathers around polarised positions, it can be useful to have a sense of what might be going on collectively. To explore this ground, we'll use a framework from the field of dialogue that provides a language to describe and examine the collective energies that subtly induce and hold in place patterns of conversation (and behaviour). The framework is the Four Fields of Conversation, developed by Otto Scharmer. You can find it in *Dialogue and the Art of Thinking Together* and in Scharmer's book, *Theory U*.[16] It's also described in *Pause for Breath*,[1] in greater detail than offered here.

## Four Fields of Conversation

I was introduced to this framework over twenty years ago and, over time, I've tinkered with it. It's important to be transparent about this because my rendering of it may now be significantly different to both the original framing and the way Scharmer has continued to develop it. To introduce the framework, I'll outline its structure. Then, in Part III, we'll explore it in greater depth.

Broadly, Scharmer proposes four distinct conversational spaces delineated by two axes. My current descriptions of the poles of these axes are:

- primacy of collective voice (belonging) and primacy of individual voice (differentiation); and

- engaging habitually and engaging mindfully.

The four conversational spaces, or fields, created by these axes are:

*Field I:* Primacy of collective voice, engaging habitually

*Field II:* Primacy of individual voice, engaging habitually

*Field III:* Primacy of individual voice, engaging mindfully

*Field IV:* Primacy of collective voice, engaging mindfully

The following diagram shows the two axes delineating the four fields. Before looking at the nature of the fields, let's consider what each axis represents.

139

## Fields of conversation
Axes

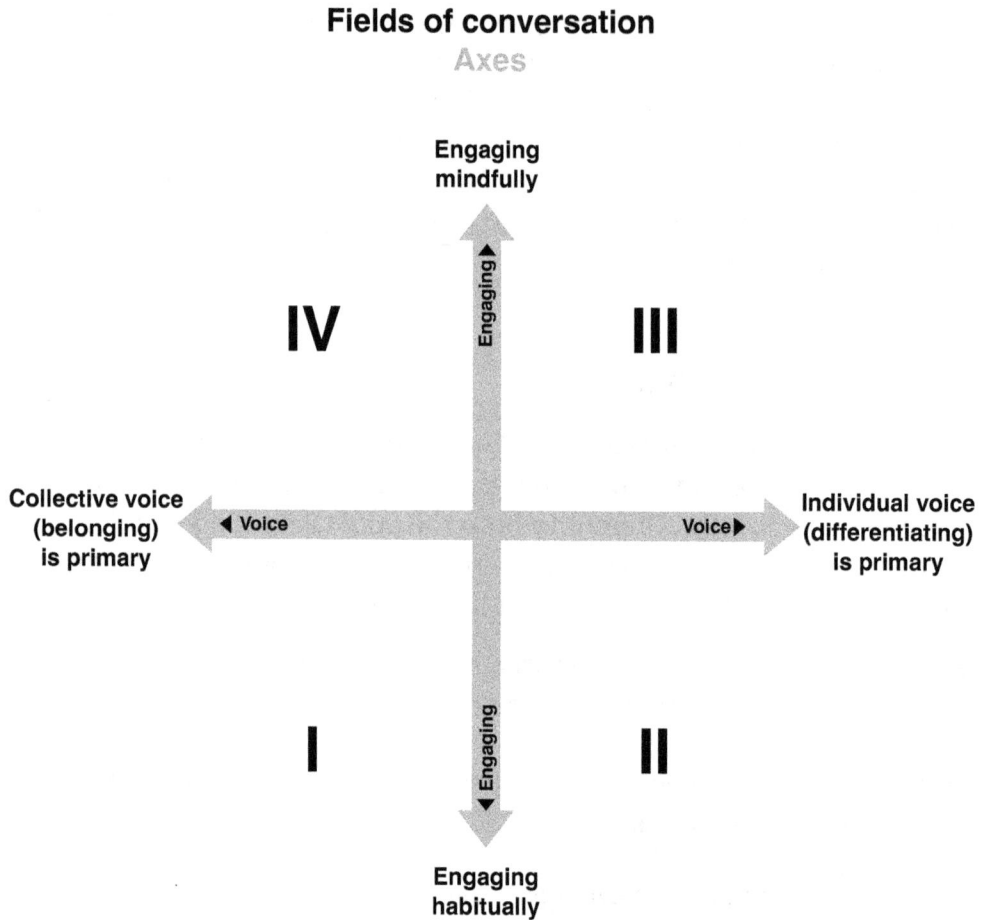

**Engaging
mindfully**

IV

Engaging ▲
Engaging

III

**Collective voice
(belonging)
is primary** ◄ Voice

Voice ► **Individual voice
(differentiating)
is primary**

I

Engaging
Engaging ▼

II

**Engaging
habitually**

Drawing on the work of Otto Scharmer

### The primacy of voice axis

In the diagram above, the *primacy of voice* axis is shown as horizontal. One pole represents a tendency to want to fit in and belong to a group – whether in a social setting or in a team at work. What we say and do therefore tends to conform to the collective norms of the setting, which include a sense of what it's generally acceptable to express. This reflects a kind of collective voice. At this end of the axis, we surrender some of our individuality to give precedence to belonging. We'll tend to be polite and accommodating – up to a point. This moderated behaviour brings benefits such as cooperation and fellow-feeling. We understand what's expected and know where we stand. We don't need to invest too much energy in wondering how to conduct ourselves.

The other pole of this axis represents individual voice taking precedence – we speak more candidly and with less concern about the impact on others or how well we fit in or belong. With greater or lesser skill, we speak our mind (or heart) and may raise uncomfortable issues, differentiating our view from that of the 'collective voice'. We may 'say the unsaid' which, in the moment, we feel to be more important than observing established customs.

It's essential to say that neither end of this axis is inherently better or more important than the other. Both collective voice and individual voice have a part to play in a healthy conversation – the key is to make sound choices about which will contribute most at a particular time. This can involve noting when either element is being overplayed. When collective voice is very strong, both dissent and challenge may be discouraged, as there's an emphasis on not rocking the boat. When individual voices speak in a way that pays scant attention to the effect of their words, this can inflame or stifle others, to the detriment of the wider conversation. The aim is to find a skilful balance between individual and collective voice

## Over to you …

What are your first impressions of this axis? In what circumstances do you tend to speak and listen in ways that fit in? In what circumstances is it more important to express your individual voice? How does the need to speak more frankly begin to establish itself within you?

### The engaging axis

In the diagram on page 140, the *engaging* axis is shown as vertical. One pole represents a tendency to engage habitually, operating on autopilot and contributing in familiar ways – which can be very efficient. It can also be effective. In using tried and tested means, we quickly accomplish what needs to be done. In this mode, we tend to be focused on immediate concerns and our words and actions can feel instinctive and be accompanied by a sense of competence and satisfaction. Such feelings endorse our choices, which can give us a sense of confidence that outreaches current circumstances.

The other pole of this axis represents mindful engagement, when we're present and responsive to what's unfolding. With this awareness, we tend to be more conscious of interdependencies, uncertainties, ambiguities and the multiplicity of factors that influence a situation. This makes us more circumspect about applying a familiar template. If needed, we can be decisive and focused, but more generally we may have greater bandwidth for picking up quieter voices and nuances such as shifts in relationships.

Again, neither a habitual nor a mindful way of engaging is inherently better or more important than the other. We may inhabit both states during a fruitful conversation. The key is to notice when habitual conduct limits what's possible or actively causes frustration in others. And then make the effort to be more present and deliberate in what we say and do.

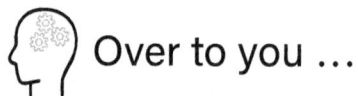

Over to you …

What are your first impressions of this axis? In your own conversations, what do you notice about the balance between being on autopilot and being present? When are you most likely to speak and listen in habitual ways? When do you pay closer attention to what's unfolding in the moment?

Before describing the four spaces delineated by the axes, I have one further observation about the axes themselves: something important connects them. Although one is essentially about being aware of the balance between expression of individual voices and the cohesive effect of a shared voice, and the other is essentially about how consciously we attend to our energy and presence, both are influenced by our motivations and mind-set. An important aspect of being skilful in our conversations is to be aware of our intentions, and to use this to guide our participation.

As we become aware of the factors described by the axes, we can look for them in our personal experiences. Then, as we begin to recognise the type of conversational spaces they delineate, we have a framework for understanding some of the influences that can hold a conversation 'in place'. This can offer useful insight into what we might do to change our practice in our conversations, which may prove thornier than we imagine. However, the alternative is that things remain exactly as they are.

## Four conversational spaces

Let's look at the four spaces delineated by the axes described above. In the diagram overleaf, you'll see them set out in a positive frame that summarises what each space supports, at its best.

First, a note about the way my practice continues to change. The names I currently attribute to the fields are slightly different to those used in my earlier book, *Pause for Breath.* As my sense of the nature of each field has evolved, my descriptions have become:

> *Field I:* Routines – primacy of collective voice, engaging habitually
>
> *Field II:* Breaking open – primacy of individual voice, engaging habitually
>
> *Field III:* Exploration – primacy of individual voice, engaging mindfully
>
> *Field IV:* Dialogue – primacy of collective voice, engaging mindfully

Let's explore the nature of each field.

## Fields of conversation
### Spaces

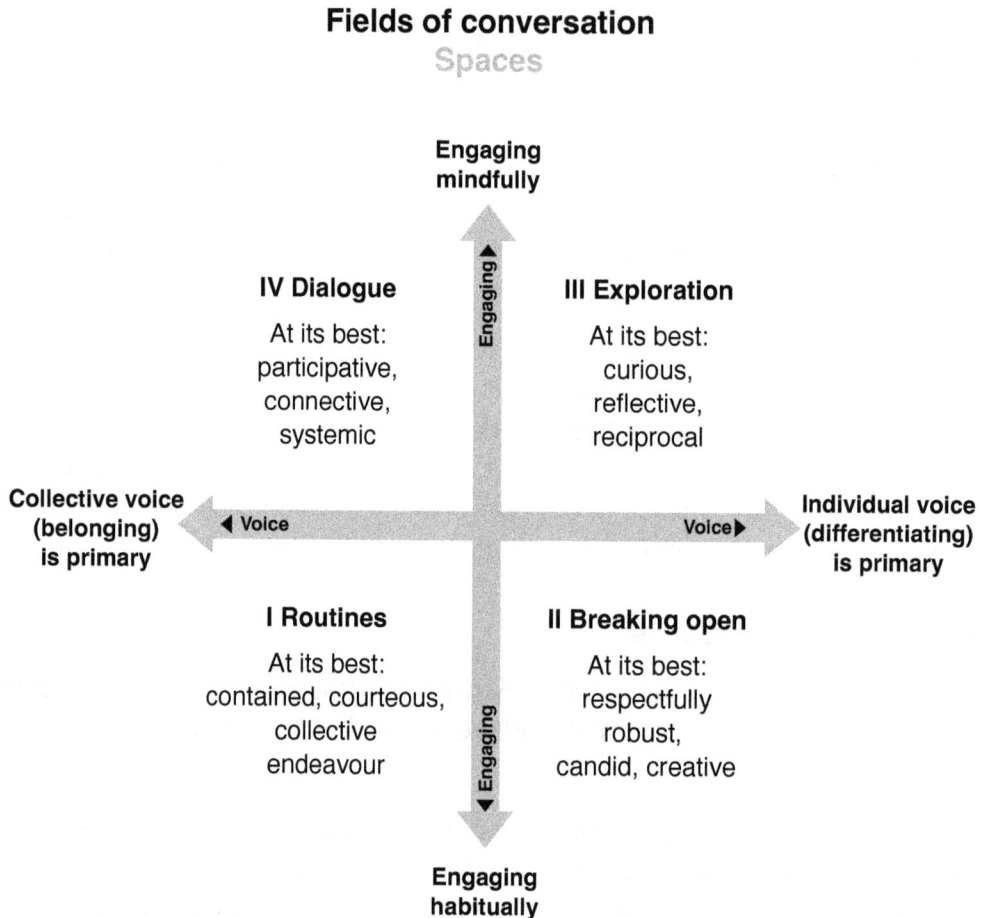

Engaging
mindfully

**IV Dialogue**

At its best:
participative,
connective,
systemic

**III Exploration**

At its best:
curious,
reflective,
reciprocal

Engaging

Collective voice
(belonging)
is primary

◀ Voice

Voice ▶

Individual voice
(differentiating)
is primary

**I Routines**

At its best:
contained, courteous,
collective
endeavour

**II Breaking open**

At its best:
respectfully
robust,
candid, creative

Engaging

Engaging
habitually

Drawing on the work of Otto Scharmer

Field I is bounded by primacy of collective voice and engaging habitually and is labelled 'routines' as it's characterised by habitual patterns such as: the order in which people arrive (or log on) and where they sit; a familiar agenda; and exchanges of a fairly predictable nature. Conversations in this space are known entities and are useful for everyday matters or formal processes. They're less useful for resolving complex issues, strategic thinking and creativity. The collective 'habit' is founded on individual habits and each tends to reinforce the other. The contained quality of conversations in Field I can feel limiting and frustrating and, because people tend to react to this in habitual ways, they may nudge (or catapult) the conversational energy into an unskilful version of Field II.

Field II is bounded by primacy of individual voice and engaging habitually and was originally labelled 'breakdown' by Scharmer. I found that this phrase had negative connotations for some people, and I wanted to emphasise the creative potential of this space. The unsettled nature of this field is essential to escaping the routines of Field I and so I call it 'breaking open'. Conversations in Field II can be respectfully robust, candid and creative. However, they can also be uncomfortable, as individual voices and concerns predominate and the habitual reactions of fight/flight/freeze arise. Energy is often heightened and things can become fractious. However, if we're able to skilfully navigate this turbulence by hearing and acknowledging different views and holding them in parity, we reach the calmer waters of Field III.

Field III is bounded by primacy of individual voice and engaging mindfully and was originally labelled 'reflective dialogue' by Scharmer. I'm calling it 'exploration' to reflect the energy of the field, which is characterised by people loosening their attachment to their positions and creating some space to hear what others have to say. As we listen, we become curious about what others think and feel and what's informing their view. We adopt the essence of the centred inquiry practice (Appendix D) and are willing to look into the way others see the world. While individual voices and concerns still prevail, those present begin to engage mindfully with each other and with the matter at hand. The conversation becomes reflective and reciprocal. However, it's hard to sustain mindful engagement indefinitely and the conversation can return to the heightened energy of 'breaking open'. Alternatively, when Field III is inhabited, embodied, there's a possibility that Field IV will occur.

Field IV is bounded by primacy of collective voice and engaging mindfully, giving rise to generative dialogue of the kind described in Isaacs' definition (Chapter 1):

> … taking the energy of our differences and channeling it toward
> something that has never been created before.

This field arises from a collective mindfulness that's established independently of individuals; it's an emergent property of their collective presence. Energetically, it feels like a collective experience of a centred state, in which boundaries between self and other dissolve and individual concerns evaporate. This is why I prefer to say that dialogue is a conversation with centre rather than with *a* centre. In this collective state, something new can surface.

This energetic state (and, by implication, Field IV) can't be 'made to happen' – but we can create conditions in which it's more likely to occur. The nature of collective voice now present is concerned with the universal. It's the voice of the conversation being expressed by whoever happens to speak. However, even in this field, we can become less mindful. If engagement becomes habitual, a conversation returns to Field I, albeit with a new routine.

Whilst a Field IV conversation can't be engineered, we can foster the conditions for a Field III conversation which, in my experience, is often sufficient for organisational needs. The nature of a Field III conversation is significantly different to most everyday exchanges, and this creates possibilities.

## Over to you …

Take some time to identify a repeating and unresolved conversation in your life or work. What comes to light if you use the framework of the four fields and their axes to reflect on what might be holding the conversation in this pattern? What would motivate you to change the way you contribute to this pattern? What approaches might you try?

The four fields represent four 'containers', four archetypal holding spaces for the way we talk and listen to each other. Having got a sense of them, let's look at how we might use this framework. We can start, lightly, with our own book-based conversation. It's likely that you have a standard way of reading a book, and there are also 'norms' about how books are supposed to be written. This has the makings of an established 'routine' – the usual expectations that are in play. This represents our Field I.

In aiming to be 'in conversation' with you, I'm trying to change the conventional container – and so we spent time checking in and setting the scene. Somewhere along the way, you may have experienced some frustration about the pace ... and somewhere along the way, I began to introduce more 'individual voice'. This may have provoked some reaction in you – either as challenge or support for my view. In essence, we've ventured into Field II.

We're now approaching Field III – and Part III – where we'll explore ways of embodying dialogue practices. Whilst I can't affirm that I hear you, I can acknowledge that what you're reading may or may not be to your liking, and accept this. As I introduce a deeper inquiry into the three tenets, I invite you to set aside your current view. This will support us to be in the reflective and reciprocal experience of Field III at its best.

For now, let's look at how we might use the fields of conversation more generally.

## Using the four fields to discern patterns

As with the framework that distinguishes between advocating energy and inquiring energy, the fields can be used to unhook us from the magnetic pull of the subject matter of a conversation. Let's use it as a medium to consider patterns that might be playing out in the public exchanges that turn to animosity (or worse). What follows could refer to any societal issue, such as gender, ethnicity, gun control or nationhood.

In my view, public exchanges about such issues are exaggerated versions of conversational patterns that occur in workplaces, homes and communities. Because they're more visible, we can use them to gain insight into the way divides widen and, potentially, become acrimonious.

Regardless of subject matter, public exchanges of different views represent (largely unskilful) versions of Field II conversations. Individual voice has primacy ('what I believe to be true') and engagement is habitual, in that it's dominated by adherence to, and reiteration of, strongly held opinions.

Generally, respect for others and their views tends to be in short supply in unskilful Field II exchanges: they become conversations with sides. How this plays out depends on the way we handle ourselves within the associated advocating energy. For example, in a meeting, we might experience a stand-off between those proposing different courses of action, each speaker confident that they have right and reason on their side. If the matter can't be resolved, or is resolved in a way that seems unjust, ill-feeling can develop, infecting future conversations with a negative vibe. This reflects a corollary of a belief that we're right: anyone with a different perspective is wrong. When a Field II conversation becomes combative, our survival pattern kicks in and we react to difference by defending our position or attacking the positions of others. Reason is no longer a player – we're being run by our physiology, not our heart and/or mind.

In such circumstances, while each party might claim to be listening, they tend to be listening _for_ things they can criticise, trivialise or challenge. They're not listening to consider what's being said. Further, if someone is unable to gain ground, then they may resort to personal attacks as a way to undermine or see off opposing views.

This kind of pattern plays out in public Field II battles, and divisions can widen because protagonists seek support from those who have a high level of agreement with their position. While it's easy to dismiss this as an echo chamber, it's simply an example of a human tendency to connect with those we have something in common with.

As we find consensus with others, a collective voice emerges – and a bond is formed. This can be rewarding and enjoyable. However, there may be a shadow side of seeking out like-minded people: it deepens our conviction that we're right, decreasing our tolerance for alternative views. This, in turn, makes it more likely that we'll be confrontational towards others, which creates conditions that may descend into hostility and aggression.

When collective voice is primary within a community, and the course of a conversation is fairly predictable, we're in the terrain of Field I. In exchanges within the community, dissent and questioning are generally not welcomed and different views are likely to be discouraged. In such conditions, those who wish to express disagreement might remain silent – they want to belong more than they want the freedom to express themselves. Others, for whom candour is important, may leave a community when they discover that challenge isn't valued. In both situations, the predominant community voice strengthens.

It's tempting to see such patterning within a community or group as benign. However, when these 'norms' are transferred into a more public domain, they're counterproductive – anyone outside the community or group has less desire to belong. If they're silent, it's probably because they don't care sufficiently about the issue at hand. If they do care, having spoken up (which requires courage), they're more likely to stick to their position. They may have their own community of like minds in the background. Or their stance may inspire other voices to join them. If an exchange between opposing communities polarises, it's likely that most contributions will be made from a place of reactivity, prompted by the physiology of our human survival system. The energy of battle prevails. In this unskilful expression of Field II, those who try to offer a nuanced and well-reasoned intervention can become a casualty of the currents and tides of the combat zone.

Reactivity is, by its very nature, habitual – and Fields I and II are governed by habitual engagement. On an individual basis, we know how difficult it can be to change an ingrained habit, such as not exercising enough or drinking too much. Collective habits, once established, have even greater traction and are therefore even harder to modify.

When a pattern of exchange is firmly ensconced in Field II, it requires both *skill* and *will* to nudge it into the more inquiring ground of Field III. It also takes commitment and persistent application. It's a big ask even in a setting with some regulatory capacity, like an organisation. It's a big ask even when a group has both the skill and the will.

In the public domain, these factors are often lacking – there's always someone ready to reignite an argument, even when others are intervening in more constructive and exploratory ways. Sadly, I have no remedy for this. We can, however, learn from it and take steps to ensure that we don't re-create these destructive patterns in our own important conversations.

## Over to you …

As you digest the idea that there may be a structural underpinning to acrimonious public exchanges, what comes to mind? To what extent do you support or question my view that there's a common architecture to these clashes, independent of subject matter?

When you feel drawn into such exchanges, or similar patterns at home or at work, what will support you to pause and make conscious choices about what you say and do?

In this chapter, we've taken a first look at Scharmer's Four Fields of Conversation. When we find ourselves in a conversation that seems unsatisfactory, we can begin to use the principles of this framework to gain insight into what's happening. We might ask ourselves:

- to what extent do those present feel a need to fit in? How is this influencing what's playing out? How might I encourage individual differences to be aired and received?; and

- to what extent are those present distracted, disengaged or on autopilot? How might I encourage more engagement or presence?

As we move into a deeper exploration of the three tenets and how they can support us to approach difference differently, the four fields offer something akin to a map of conversational terrains. They represent four distinct types of holding space or container and, if we use the framework to help us recognise which one we're in, it may guide the way we contribute.

The theme of Part II has been 'minding the gap' between ideas – how we think things *should* be – and the messy realities of human experience. As we learn to pay more attention to the 'how' of a conversation, we may see such gaps more clearly. Each gap represents a moment of opportunity to enter into a conversation in a different way.

# Part III
## Embodying dialogue practices

# Chapter 15  Embodying dialogue practices: three tenets

It's time to get into the heart of the three tenets that support us to embody dialogue practices and to approach difference differently. As I explained in Chapter 4, the tenets emerged when I found myself repeating them in my dialogue work. They're based on words taken from *Dialogue and the Art of Thinking Together*[2] and are:

- We are the method

- Consciously holding a container

- Entry is everything

## Three tenets

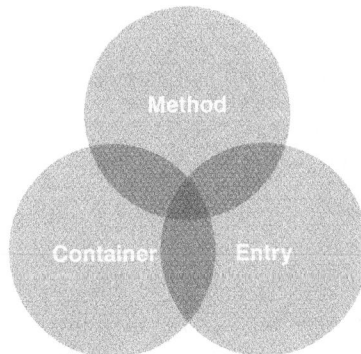

You may recall that the tenets are interdependent and so we could explore them in any order. I've chosen to start with self and the way we affect a conversation by the energy we bring to it – we're part of the method. This leads us naturally to invite others to be part of the method and to share in consciously holding the energetic space, or container, for a conversation. Together, these two tenets begin to build individual and collective capacity for dialogue and for navigating difference skilfully. We can then refine our practice by paying attention to each moment of 'entry' into a conversation – everything we do sets something in motion. This brings us back to self, and being part of the method. It's important not to see the tenets as sequential or linear. Once we've explored them individually, we'll see that they're essentially three facets of a single principle.

For now, let's revisit the essence of each tenet. Then we'll look more deeply into their role in creating conditions in which we can channel the energies of difference into new thinking.

## We are the method

The phrase 'we are the method' is distilled from three sentences in *Dialogue and the Art of Thinking Together* (pages 70 & 71):

> In dialogue, you yourself are part of the method. You cannot be separated from it. To engage in dialogue is to engage with yourself in a profoundly new way.

There's a lot of complexity to unpick in these sentences. In essence, there's no 'method' for dialogue. There's no agenda, no chair or facilitator, no defining procedures or techniques. Dialogue is a way of being, rather than something we do. It involves a shift in orientation from 'going to' or 'attending' a meeting or conversational event to being an integral part of what unfolds, of fully participating in it. We become more aware of the quality of our embodied energy and how it's impacting others. Communal energy will be amplified, dampened or changed by the way each of us carries ourselves and the contributions we make. If we show up well, we positively influence the environment. If we show up gracelessly, get derailed during a conversation or allow our physiology to have the upper hand, we play a part in limiting what's possible.

Showing up well might include taking time to prepare by clarifying our personal 'take' on an issue and recognising the anomalies and nuances within it. For example, we may be 'in two minds' about something and, if we don't acknowledge these internal differences, what we say may seem inconsistent or confused. Alternatively, we may know that our heart-response to a particular situation is different to our head-response and, if so, it will be helpful get our stance straight before a conversation so that we don't baffle others during it.

There's an additional benefit to doing this kind of preparation and exploration. As we see that our thinking, feelings and inferences about a subject might not be quite as coherent as we believe, we create room to hear the views of others. We find some tolerance for difference within ourselves, and this allows us to accommodate difference in others.

Another way we can be more receptive to difference is to become more aware of our own reactivity and preconceptions. For example, we may be intolerant of individuals or groups of people, making us more likely to dismiss or discount what they say. Or we may hold some of our beliefs to be right in absolute terms, limiting our capacity to work with alternatives. To work skilfully with the way our inner landscape affects what we say and what we're able to hear involves changing our relationship with our accepted version of 'self'. We begin to engage with ourselves in a new way, identifying factors that might reduce our capacity to appreciate difference, especially when someone challenges one of our own dearly held views. The greater our clarity about any gaps or misalignment in our own perspective, the greater our ability to receive the ideas of others, even when we find them confusing or disjointed.

Over to you …

To reflect on this overview of 'we are the method', take a moment to think of a conversation that went really well – how did you show up in it? How did this influence others? How did this affect what was possible?

157

Now think of a time when you showed up less well in a conversation – how did this influence others? How did the conversation play out? What might you have done differently in light of what you're reading in these pages?

What might you conclude about the relationship between how we show up and what unfolds in a conversation?

We first met the concept of a 'container' or holding space in Chapters 3 and 4. In some ways, 'we are the method' invites us to consciously hold our *personal* container and to be aware of our internal environment and the energy we bring to a conversation. As we appreciate how this affects the way a conversation unfolds, we naturally want to encourage others to share in creating a *collective* container.

## Consciously holding a container

The phrase 'consciously holding a container' is distilled from two sentences in *Dialogue and the Art of Thinking Together* (page 244):

> The premise I work with is 'no container, no dialogue'. More precisely, no consciously held container, no dialogue

For me, these words emphasise the *conscious* holding of a container. This is because I believe that a container forms, whether consciously or not, whenever people talk together. In any given setting, we're working out what's OK and what's not OK, and we're building a sense of the 'norms' of engagement – what's acceptable and what's not. And the next time we meet, we usually carry a sense of this with us, whether consciously or not. For dialogue, we pay attention to our conversational environment and, rather than leaving it to chance, we bring deliberate stewardship to it. We actively consider the energetic tone, quality of engagement, freedoms and responsibilities that we want to foster in our shared holding space. And then those present agree to collectively uphold them. This

158

marks a shift away from 'content' (*what* we're talking about) as the main (or even sole) focus of a conversation.

When we begin to build collective capacity to welcome and entertain our differences, we're often working against the grain of the established patterns and conventions of a conversational operating system (Chapter 12). Each conversational OS is largely situational and is shaped by societal norms and our setting and context. For example, in any organisation (or any system, including families) there are likely to be received ways of behaving, topics that are off-limits, and assumptions about power and status. Such factors ensure that conversations are contained in well-worn grooves.

If we want to navigate our differences in a way that creates fresh thinking, existing conversational habits are unlikely to be fit for purpose. If they were, we'd already be experiencing benefits in terms of creativity, collaboration and innovation. To foster a conversational space in which diverse views can be aired, held and explored calls for a shared commitment to establishing new practices in order to counter the gravitational pull of custom and habit.

As with our personal intentions and aspirations, we can focus on behaving our way *into* a new conversational OS and/or behaving our way *out of* the limitations of the current one. The key point is that we have to *behave* our way into new habits or out of undesirable ones – we can't talk ourselves into making these changes. For example, saying we'll listen respectfully is easy – what's not easy is doing this when the temperature rises, or when we strongly disagree with what's being said. It then takes presence, intention, commitment and humility to receive and consider what's being said. These qualities can leave us in the heat of a moment.

In groups, it makes sense to work collectively towards adopting and inhabiting new practices because the 'pull' of existing patterns can be very strong. We can loosen the hold of legacy conditions by clearly articulating the kind of container we want to establish and setting a path towards it. The optimum time to do this, and to bring our intentions for a conversation into consciousness, is during, or immediately after, a check-in. This requires some discipline because it defers engagement with the subject matter, which can be quite frustrating for those who are impatient to 'get stuck in'. However, without a deliberate effort to create the conditions for dialogue, existing conversational patterns will prevail.

We can bring our aspirations for a container to life with sustained effort over time. This, in my view, means revisiting the nature of the container each time a group meets. When we do this, we bring the quality of the shared holding space back into collective consciousness. This allows us to review and refine the container, which renews our commitment to it.

However, revisiting the aspirations for a container can be even more frustrating than setting them out. It can be tempting to think 'we've already done this'. This misunderstands the nature of a container: the work of consciously creating the conditions for a conversation is never 'done'. A container is a living thing enmeshed in the conversation itself: its evolution is inseparable from the people present and the way they talk and listen to each other (we are the method). Each time a group gathers, the container changes – for good or ill. By actively paying attention to it, we can nurture and reinforce positive change.

When a container is explicitly and consciously held, we're actively inviting all present to support each other to show up and contribute in ways that reflect what's been agreed. Over time, confidence in the container grows, and the breadth and depth of the conversation grows too.

## Over to you …

To reflect on this overview of 'consciously holding a container', think of a conversation that went really well – how was this conversation set up? What kind of attention was given to things like ground rules, expectations, conduct and the climate for the conversation? How do you think this influenced what unfolded?

In your experience, when little or no attention is paid to the way a conversation is set up, what tends to happen?

As we attend to the interplay between individual and collective energies in our container, we can refine our practice by bringing moments of 'entry' into sharper focus.

## Entry is everything

The phrase 'entry is everything' begins a paragraph in *Dialogue and the Art of Thinking Together* (page 293):

> Entry is everything. The way you approach a situation will determine a great deal about how it will unfold.

The essence of this assertion is that the way we begin has a disproportionate effect on what follows. This reflects one of the Buddhist principles outlined in Chapter 3: each moment conditions the next. Each choice we make sets in motion what follows for ourselves, our conversation and, perhaps, the wider system. This principle invites us to have clear intentions – both individually and collectively – and to be thoughtful about how we begin. It gives weight to the dialogue practice of check-in, and invites us to adopt it.

When we recognise the importance of 'entry', we may lean in to the habit of making time to prepare for our important encounters. We can prepare personally, clarifying what matters to us and identifying what we're curious about and the questions we might ask. We can also consider how we'll support ourselves to show up well, perhaps by using the Leadership Embodiment practices set out in these pages. I think of this kind of preparation as 'convening self', of gathering the disparate parts of ourselves and bringing them into some sort of order.

We may also be able to contribute to convening collectively, shaping how people are brought together and how a conversation begins. This too might involve clarifying what matters and the questions we might ask – for the conversation as a whole, rather than from an individual perspective.

We might also consider entry in a broader way. Each contribution we make to a conversation is an act of entering, of intervening, and each is a moment that conditions the next. Thinking in this way invites us to pay attention how we 'enter' a conversation once it's underway, as well as being thoughtful about how we begin. This means becoming aware of the ways our habits of body or mind distract us from being present and then using the foundation centring practice (Appendix B) to return to presence. Essentially, we intervene in ourselves as we fall into habitual patterns of engagement and/or feel an impulse to speak or act. When we notice these moments, we pause to check our motivation and consider what we intend to contribute. This reflects 'we are the method' – we engage with our 'self' in a new way.

When we intervene in a conversation, the energy we bring to what we say affects how our words land with others. We've already worked with centred listening (Appendix E) and centred inquiry (Appendix D) and, when we explore 'entry is everything' more fully, we'll bring centred speaking into our repertoire. This will support us to align our energy and intention when we intervene in a conversation.

Over to you …

To reflect on this overview of 'entry is everything', think of a conversation that went really well – how did you prepare for the conversation? How did you decide when and how to contribute? What was your part in supporting the conversation to go well?

When you pay little or no attention to preparing for a conversation, how do you tend to contribute? How do your contributions tend to land with others?

In this chapter, we've been working with a premise we can foster the conditions for dialogue if we attend to:

- our relationship with our 'self' and the way we carry ourselves as we engage with others (we are the method);

- articulating the conversational climate that we intend to foster together and doing our best to inhabit it (consciously holding the container); and

- the way we begin, individually and collectively, and the energy we bring to each intervention, each moment of 'entering into' our conversation (entry is everything).

Fundamentally, the three tenets are all ways of being, ways of living our way into a different kind of conversation. They're interdependent and represent a suite of ongoing practices that call for our attention again and again.

When we consider them together, the three tenets coalesce to invite us, individually and collectively, to pay attention to our motivation, the energy we bring to a conversation and the energy we create together. If everything we do sets something in motion, it's wise to take responsibility for this and do what we can to generate positive, beneficial consequences. In essence, we actively participate in whatever is happening around us, through what we do or don't do and what we say or don't say. If we sign up to this premise, it provides a compelling reason to make all our choices as conscious as possible.

In the remainder of Part III, we'll look at each tenet in more depth. We'll start with the principle that, in dialogue, self and method aren't separate. This offers immediate ground for changing our personal practice, and we'll explore this in Chapters 16 to 21.

As we gain insight into the way our personal presence and energy affect a conversation, it's a short step to recognise the benefits of co-creating a container. This is the art of consciously fostering conditions that support dialogue, and it's the territory for Chapters 22 to 26.

Finally, and somewhat counter-intuitively, we examine how beginnings influence what follows and we consider how we can refine our contribution in each moment of entry. In Chapters 27 to 31, we'll look into the relationship between our intention, embodied presence and the impact we have when we contribute to a conversation. This brings us full circle to being part of the method.

When we've explored each tenet, we'll consider the possibility that they're essentially three facets of a single practice.

# Chapter 16 We are the method: introduction

**Three tenets**
We are the method

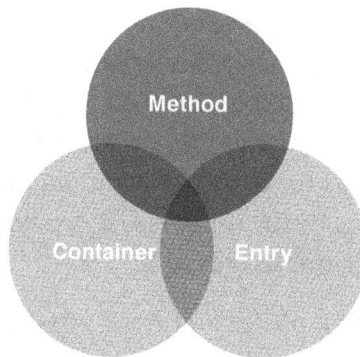

*In dialogue, you yourself are part of the method. You cannot be separated from it. To engage in dialogue is to engage with yourself in a profoundly new way.*

– William Isaacs, *Dialogue and the Art of Thinking Together*,[2] pages 70 & 71

We're starting our exploration with this tenet because, as we discovered in Part II, the way we work with our personal energy and physiology has a huge influence on how our conversations unfold. This is especially true when we're navigating difference and fostering the conditions for dialogue. In addition, being in dialogue asks us to show up in all our humanness – with the doubts, desires, feelings and insights that we carry within. This usually means making ourselves a little more available to others than we prefer, which can feel a bit uncomfortable. Being in dialogue also asks us to welcome all the warts, wisdoms, strengths and shortcomings of others. This usually means being aware of, and setting aside, our preconceptions.

These two measures – revealing aspects of ourselves that we typically keep under wraps and being more accepting of the idiosyncrasies of others – begin the process of engaging with our experience of 'self' in a profoundly new way. As we change our relationship with self, we change our relationship with others and begin to experience them in a profoundly new way too. This supports us to engage in dialogue and to hold others and their views in parity (Chapter 13). In dialogue, we're equal in our human experience and each voice has equal weight.

This is a high ideal – and most of us aren't this saintly. However, we can seek to be a little more open in both what we offer and what we receive. If we apply ourselves to this, our conversations will improve in terms of outcomes and relationships. At least, this is my personal experience. I don't pretend that all my conversations go well, but when I take time to embody what I know, there's usually a positive change in their quality.

When we appreciate that there isn't a separate 'method' for dialogue, we realise that we can prepare for dialogue by being more aware of the way we engage with ourselves. When we begin to study ourselves, we may notice that the energy we bring to a conversation plays a part in the way it unfolds. We may gain insight into our individual preferences and insecurities, and into other aspects of our humanness. This allows us to set aside those that don't serve us. Overall, we seek to become aware of our habitual tendencies so that we can be thoughtful about their role in our conversations.

As we engage with ourselves in this way, we recognise that we're shaped by our experiences in life and have developed habits of thinking and communicating that suit us in some way. For example, we might quite like a fight or we might prefer harmony in our interactions with others. Perhaps we tend to rise to, or back down from, a challenge. Perhaps we like to speak up early in a conversation, or are more inclined to listen first. Perhaps we sift through what we think and feel by talking with others, or perhaps we prefer to sort through our inner experience in solitude before we speak. Whatever our habits, when we recognise them, we equip ourselves to discern whether they're relevant and/or useful in our current conversation.

As we become more aware of our personal tendencies, we prepare to be part of the method for dialogue. And, when dialogue occurs, it deepens the change in our relationship with 'self'. It's a virtuous developmental cycle. We can also prepare to play our part in dialogue by adding to our conversational repertoire. To do this, and to embody new ways of working with difference, we have to navigate two inconvenient human realities – one of body and one of mind.

## Two realities of changing practice

When we're inspired to change the way we approach difference, the first reality we face is that we're hard-wired to react viscerally to it (Chapters 8 and 9). Our autonomic nervous system is an embodied legacy of our early ancestors – it alerts us to any difference in our environment in order to protect us from potential danger. Therefore, when we encounter difference, this warning system generates a physical impulse to overcome it or to run from it – and, sometimes, we get stuck between these two reactions.

In our conversations, the difference that we want to defeat or sidestep comes in the form of words, opinions, assertions or beliefs. These tend to threaten our identity rather than our life, but our legacy software hasn't been updated to reflect this, and so, when we're in the presence of different views, our survival pattern is activated. Non-essential functions are briefly shut down and we lose access to our creativity, compassion, generosity and sense of justice. Our focus narrows and is dominated by whatever has disturbed us, which means we lose access to the bigger picture and to wider information. In general, our options become limited. If we're able to recognise that this legacy system has taken hold, we can reorganise our energy by using the centring practice that we've become familiar with (Appendix B). When we access a centred state, we don't speak or act from the imperatives of survival.

The second human reality of changing the way we approach difference is that what we see and hear is partial, in terms of being both incomplete and subject to personal preferences. This means that our view (stance, belief, opinion) is partial, as is our understanding of what we hear. What we *think* we hear is a personal interpretation of what's being said. We make assumptions and inferences based on our experience and often forget to check that we've got the right end of the stick.

In my case, I know I tend to jump to conclusions, and so I work hard to inquire and to clarify what someone means. This *always* enriches my understanding.

In terms of our view, there'll always be things that we don't (and can't) know, see, sense and understand. This means that, however well-informed, clever, insightful or wise we are, our perspective will be bounded. In my case, I know I tend to assume I'm infallible, and so I work hard at remembering that I'm not. This *always* gives rise to new possibilities.

In summary, one of the human realities of changing practice is a limitation of perception and mind, and the other is a physiological process that closes down options to concentrate on survival. So, to engage with ourselves in a profoundly new way, we have to become aware of, and work with, our limiting patterns in both body and mind.

## Over to you ...

Take some time to reflect on the way your embodied survival pattern affects your conversations. How does your tendency towards fight or flight affect what you say and how you say it? How does it affect how you listen and what you listen for? How do these tendencies limit your options in your conversations?

Now reflect on how your habits of thinking affect your conversations. How do your personal preferences, interests and concerns affect what you pay attention to and what you overlook? How does your level of confidence in your own view affect how you respond to the views of others? What other habits of thinking and communicating might limit your options in your conversations?

How might these reflections support you to engage with yourself and others in a new way?

The most useful vehicles for studying our internal landscape and our habits of speaking and listening are conversations between two people. When working with others, I always advise them to start with these exchanges because there are fewer variables to consider, which makes it easier to identify our own part in them. The patterns we discover and the insights we gain will also be present in more complex group dynamics, but in such settings, it can be harder to recognise them.

In addition, in one-to-one situations, we get clearer feedback when we try out a new approach. When we consciously change something, we can regard it as an experiment: if I do this, what happens? Generally, the best way to learn is to keep things simple and low key. I caution against trying a new approach in a high-stakes situation or in a large group for two reasons: it complicates matters and it increases the risks involved.

As we become more conscious of our individual part in how a conversation unfolds, we naturally become more aware of the dynamics between all those present, including ourselves. If, individually, we're *part of* the method for dialogue, collectively we *are* the method. Together, we *are* the conversation. If the conversation explodes, implodes or otherwise goes awry, the cause is those present, and each individual will have played a part. And, of course, when a conversation evolves, matures and transcends expectations, this too is caused by those present, individually and collectively. When we're able to think together, to be alongside one another in the struggle for shared understanding, we can all take credit.

In later chapters, we'll attend to the process of collectively creating a holding space, or container (Tenet 2). In this chapter, our emphasis is on our personal container, and holding ourselves in a way that supports us to engage mindfully with our thoughts, feelings, sensations and memories. When we engage with our inner experiences in a spacious way, we create room to select which of them might be of service to the conversation we're in.

## Repeating patterns

To engage with our inner experiences in a spacious way, we take on the task of understanding how the two inconvenient human realities outlined above show up in us. We learn to recognise and accept our:

- habits of body – how we're hard-wired to react viscerally to difference, an embodied survival mechanism that evolved in earlier times; and

- habits of mind – how our life experiences and patterns of thinking mean that our perspective is both incomplete and subject to our preferences.

This matters because, when we're caught up in habitual tendencies of body and mind, we're likely to do the same things over and over. The same is true for whoever we're talking to. Our recurring tendencies can be efficient – and even sufficient. However, they also represent a kind of path of least resistance – and conversations with familiar people in familiar settings tend to fall into familiar grooves, behavioural routines that repeat, regardless of subject matter. When we add in an element of wanting to fit in or belong, it's clear that we're in the territory of Field I (Routines) of the fields of conversation (Chapter 14). In this field, there's a collective tendency to keep things as they are, and not rock the boat. When we try to have a different kind of conversation, this stabilising energy draws us back into the established pattern, or familiar groove. A first step towards making a change in practice is to recognise our own part in this process.

As a general example, let's imagine a situation where someone always leaves a conversation with their boss having lost an argument for more resources or having somehow taken on an additional task they were determined to avoid. The next time a similar situation arises they plan what they're going to say more carefully … yet end up with the same outcome. Why does this happen? Inadvertently, and out of conscious awareness, our someone and their boss have jointly set up a customary 'form' for their exchanges – and each faithfully participates in this routine. Unless our someone engages with the boss in a way that disrupts the pattern, it's highly likely that the conversation will run along established lines.

So, to add context to this illustration, perhaps the conversational pattern between our someone and their boss has its roots in quick dissemination of information and allocation of actions. A review of sales targets or an update on project milestones is handled efficiently, with a focus on agreeing any further actions. When something more complex is raised, such as a delicate staffing issue or a request for resources to support a new activity, it will be dealt with in a similar way. Without some discernible signals that a different kind of conversation is required, supported by mindful efforts to follow through on this, a conversation will probably succumb its usual form.

When we find ourselves in a conversation that seems to repeat over and over, it's useful to ask: how am I contributing to holding this pattern in place? In conversations, routines are often established for efficiency – everyone knows what's expected and/or acceptable and can quickly get down to the 'business at hand'. This works, up to a point. However, if the nature of the 'business at hand' changes, the nature of the conversation probably also needs to change. This is often overlooked.

To create the potential for a different conversation means changing some combination of the setting, how we begin and the energy we bring to the exchange. We can experiment with this as an individual. When we can see how our own behaviour supports the status quo, we create the potential for change: if we participate in a different way, we prompt others to adapt in response. The conversation then becomes less predictable for each person, and is less likely to proceed along established lines. It therefore has greater possibility.

## Over to you …

Take some time to identify some of the 'conversational routines' you're in with those around you. The easiest place to begin is people you talk to regularly – perhaps a partner, a child, a friend, a colleague or a boss. Pick one or two that seem to follow a pattern and reflect on the nature of it: who tends to initiate; how does it tend to begin; who usually talks the most; what's off-limits; and what's the 'feel' of the conversation?

Now reflect on your part in the routine – how do you participate in each pattern and, perhaps, even reinforce it? What one thing might you change? Can you try this out and see what happens?

The thinking you've just done is important for what follows. In the next chapter, I'll outline a case study from my coaching work, in which a repetitive pattern was quickly established. As we review it together, it might be helpful to find a similar example from your own experience, so that you can make personal sense of what holds a repeating pattern in place. When we see our part in a pattern, we create an opportunity to engage in it differently.

# Chapter 17 We are the method: a case study

It can feel frustrating when a conversation seems to be going round in circles – and it's easy to assume that the cause of the repetition lies with someone who's saying the same thing over and over. While it may be obvious that they're stuck in a loop, it's often much less apparent that we're equally responsible. In the case study that follows, we'll explore what happened in a coaching conversation that became repetitive. In keeping with our developmental path, we'll look at it from the perspective of *my* part in what was unfolding, which may offer guidance as to how you might approach this kind of pattern in a conversation of your own.

The case study has two layers: what was happening between my client (a CEO) and his team; and the pattern of exchange in the coaching conversation. In the session, a repeating pattern was established within about half an hour. I felt deskilled and was uneasy about the interaction. The conversation could easily have ended inconclusively, or even badly. However, in this case, I noticed what was going on and changed my approach. I'll do my best to explain how and why.

I'll set out a summary of the key part of the conversation using a method called 'the left-hand column'. I outlined this approach in *Pause for Breath*.[1] It was developed by Chris Argyris and Donald Schön as a research method, and is described by Rick Ross and Art Kleiner in *The Fifth Discipline Fieldbook*,[8] which is my source. The power of the approach is that it brings our attention more fully to our own contribution so that we can reflect on how we're shaping what unfolds.

The approach involves making two columns on a page and, in the right-hand column, recording what was said, as if it's a scene in a play. In the left-hand column, we record what we were thinking and feeling, but not saying, during the spoken conversation. This allows us to look at an account of the exchange that's richer than the oral version alone. We can then reflect on what took place by using some of the frameworks we've explored in these pages.

## Overview of the case

First, let's consider a way of getting the most from the left-hand column format used for the case. To begin, it can be helpful to cover the left-hand column and read the right-hand column only. This allows us to read what we'd have heard if we'd been a fly on the wall. You might try this out with the case below and make some notes about your take on the exchange, how you're interpreting the conversation and any assumptions you're making. Then read the case again, looking at both columns.

# Case Study 2

Context: in a coaching session, my client (a CEO) outlined the challenges he was experiencing with his team of directors. One of them was making important errors/omissions, another was fire-fighting and not making time to attend to significant issues, and so on. We join the conversation as I ask a question.

| What I was thinking and feeling but not saying (left-hand column) | What was said (right-hand column) |
|---|---|
| *I wonder what your part in this is …* | **1. Me**<br>What might you do differently to support your directors to contribute more effectively? |
| *Oh! Not what I expected … you're avoiding the question, making it all about the shortcomings of others …* | **2. Client**<br>Well, what Director A needs to do is … and in the case of Director B, she should … |

| What I was thinking and feeling but not saying (left-hand column) | What was said (right-hand column) |
|---|---|
| *I'll try again …* | **3. Me**<br>So … how might you change what you do to support your directors to do more? |
| *You're still missing the point … banging on about the problems with the team … you're part of the problem and this is getting boring … I'll try again* | **4. Client**<br>Well, Director Y is out of his depth and probably needs to move on … then, with Director X, there are long-running issues which need to be prioritised … |
| *I feel quite uncomfortable asking this again … am I doing the right thing in persisting with this?* | **5. Me**<br>So … what is needed in terms of your leadership? |
| *You're side-stepping again … what on earth can I do now? What's my intent here? Is this important enough to pursue, or am I simply banging my drum in the way he's banging his …?*<br>*[pausing … centring …]* | **6. Client**<br>Well, Director B just focuses on the details and really important things get missed and … well, staff are up in arms about Director Y and he needs to get a grip on his team … |
| *Who or what am I in service to? I want to see if I can unlock a pattern that might be limiting this whole team. I'll regroup … and try one more time …*<br>*I'll reflect back the pattern to him before I ask the question again …* | **7. Me**<br>*[pausing, centring, embodying presence]*<br>Let me give you a perspective on what's happening here. I've asked three times 'what might you change?' and each time you've answered in terms of changes that others need to make.<br>*[pausing, exhaling]*<br>And so, I ask again – how might you change your approach to better support your directors to contribute more effectively? |
| *[Holding my breath …]*<br>*This could go either way …* | **8. Client**<br>*[Silence … pausing …]*<br>Oh! I suppose I might try to better understand why … |

If you tried the approach of first reading only the right-hand column, what changes when you read both columns? Note any observations and any ways in which this case feels familiar: have you witnessed this kind of conversation between others or taken part in something similar yourself, in either role? See if you can find a personal example to work with as we explore the case.

Before we look at the detail, there are two reasons why I chose this case. First, it has obvious repeating patterns, both in the CEO's experience with his team – he kept doing the same things with his directors, and getting the same outcomes – and in the coaching conversation itself. Second, because this was a coaching conversation, I was more aware of the emerging pattern than I might ordinarily have been. Please note that context matters: in a coaching conversation, I have permission – and even a duty – to challenge as well as support. Without this kind of permission, the approach I'm about to describe may be less appropriate.

To understand my part in the repeating pattern of this conversation, we'll look at the case in a few different ways. Principally, we'll use an aspect of dialogue practice called bystanding. It comes from David Kantor's Four-Player Model,[17] which describes four distinct types of contribution, or 'speech action', that are present in a healthy conversation. We'll look at all these speech actions in Chapter 31 – and they're explored in depth in *Pause for Breath*.

For the moment, and without much explanation, we'll use the practice of bystanding to shift our attention from the 'what' of a conversation (the CEO and his team) to the 'how' of it (the shape) by outlining what a neutral observer might see. To bystand, we 'zoom out' to see the conversation as a whole and then describe its pattern. Some people call this 'being on the balcony' – a sense that we're looking at a conversation, rather than being immersed in it.

Before we apply bystanding to the whole case, we can see an example of it within my left-hand column: in real time, and not always skilfully, I'm paying attention to the pattern of the conversation, noticing that I'm not getting an answer to my question. However, I'm muddying that observation with judgement – it's not neutral. I'm also bystanding my own experience – taking note of what's happening within me. When I do this, I change my relationship with myself which, in turn, changes the conversation. For example, when I recognise that I'm feeling uncomfortable and beginning to doubt myself (the left-hand column of box 5), I log this data in a neutral way. I'm not caught up in it, and this means I can act on it. This is an illustration of the way we can bystand our internal dialogue as well as our conversations with others.

When we bystand the case, we'll use the framework of advocacy and inquiry (Chapter 7) to discern the shape of the conversation. Things seem fairly straightforward at first. The spoken sequence consists of questions and responses, which can be broadly described as inquiry (seeking to discover something we don't know) and advocacy (setting out where we stand). From the left-hand column, we get a sense of the quality of the exchange – although only from my perspective.

## Over to you …

If you've identified a personal example to explore alongside the case study, take some time to note its context – the setting, the nature of the relationship and/or any special considerations.

In two columns, write out what you can remember of what was said in the right-hand one. In the left-hand one, record what you were thinking and feeling but not saying. Now, reflect on the relationship between what you said and what you were thinking and feeling – were they aligned, or was there a gap? How did this affect the conversation?

With this preparation, it's time to look at Case Study 2 stage by stage.

## A detailed look at the case study

The first time I ask the client what he might change (box 1), my left-hand column indicates inquiry – I'm genuinely wondering how the client is contributing to the situation. A good start. However, as he responds, I make a judgement that he's avoiding the question. Judgement is advocacy – I've formed an opinion about the nature of his answer. I decide to ask again. We don't have any additional information about the tone of this second asking (box 3) – perhaps I was at ease and thinking he'd misinterpreted the question, or perhaps I was a little impatient and so a little more pointed. I can't remember – and in this review, 'not remembering' illustrates the inconvenient human reality that our view (or understanding of a situation) is partial. Since my memory is incomplete, my representation of the conversation is also incomplete. In fact, this will always be the case, which invites us to be circumspect in our reflections.

In response to the second time I ask the question, the client reiterates the ways in which his directors need to change in order to fix things. As he speaks, my left-hand column shows that I'm becoming more judgemental and even dismissive. I'm clearly listening less attentively and am showing signs of exasperation. There's a good chance this energy will flavour whatever I say next. As I ask essentially the same question for the third time (box 5), two things are happening – I'm uncomfortable about repeating myself again and I'm experiencing some self-doubt. This is the crux of what's unfolding. My body is alerting me to the risks of this situation – the client could take umbrage or withdraw – and, in my mind, I'm losing confidence and second-guessing my actions. Basically, I'm tightening both physically and mentally, becoming more fixed in my outlook, which reduces my flexibility. The conversation feels like it could easily implode or explode from here.

As the client retells his story once more (box 6), we've reached an impasse. If I don't handle myself well at this point, one of three things is likely to happen: I'll be more abrupt in my challenge and alienate the client; I'll give up, allowing the client's interaction with his directors to perpetuate; or we'll go around the loop again. I feel slightly exposed and under pressure, indicating that my autonomic nervous system is activated. In this mild version of survival mode, my physiology has the upper hand and I'm likely to go on the attack, turn away or stay stuck. However, if I can re-set my autonomic nervous system and create some space in my mind, I'll have more options.

In essence, the shape of this conversation is two people on parallel tracks that don't meet. I'm immersed in getting an answer to my question and the client is engrossed in the troubles caused by his belief that his directors aren't up to scratch. We're not really communicating and the disconnect gives rise to dissatisfaction – the quality of the exchange deteriorates.

I'll pause here because you've read the case and so you know that it concludes relatively well. I'll share the details of how things changed in Chapter 19. In the meantime, in Chapter 18 we'll linger on the crux of this exchange and use another lens to look at how it came about. First, take some time to draw parallels with your own experience.

## Over to you …

If you're reflecting on a personal example alongside the case study, consider how your autonomic nervous system might be influencing your part in the conversation. Do you have an impulse to push back, defend, turn away or appease? Do you feel paralysed or helpless?

As you recall this experience, use it to map where and how your body tenses or loosens, and to become more familiar with its way of alerting you to potential hazards.

Now that we have a sense of the shape of the coaching conversation in the case, let's revisit the crux of it (boxes 5 and 6) and apply a framework known as intent–impact.

# Chapter 18 We are the method: intent–impact

Our second perspective on Case Study 2 picks up the theme that our view of any situation is partial. We'll explore this reality using the distinction between intent and impact. This lens distinguishes between the motivation for what we say (our intent) and the way our words land with another person (the impact).

In *Pause for Breath*, I used the headline 'we only know half the story' for the intent–impact framework because, between two people, we can only know our own intent and the impact of another person's words on us. Unless we ask, we don't know the other person's intent or the impact of our words on them. Of four possibilities, we only have direct access to two – and even these may be unclear. We may be vague about our intention when we speak, or acting on autopilot with no conscious intention at all. Our sense of the impact of someone's words on us may be intangible – and it may be later, when a conversation is over, that we really know how we've been affected by what someone has said. And so, these days, I say 'we only have *part of* the story', which better reflects the partial nature of our experience.

For many of us, paying close attention to the inner experiences of intent and impact is new. In habitual modes of operation, we tend to either ignore such things or discount them. Yet one provides useful data and the other is significant in how things turn out. Therefore, we gain fresh insight into our conversational experience when we make room for intent and impact as an aspect of 'we are the method'. This is part of changing our relationship with ourselves. Let's explore this through the case study.

# Impact

We'll start with impact, since it was the effect my client's words had on me that signalled that I might need to change tack. Whilst my internal mutterings show that the conversation wasn't going the way I thought it would go, the little 'oh!' of surprise (box 2, left-hand column) represents a small warning that difference was present.

The nature of this difference is subtle. It's a form of disagreement – the client's most accessible narrative is that the issue lies with his directors, not with him, whereas my view is that we're exploring *his* part in the situation. This gives rise to a discrepancy between the type of answer I'm expecting and the one I get. In response, my body begins to prime itself for fight or flight. And, as the difference between what I'm seeking and the reply grows, my autonomic nervous system gradually ramps up in an effort to alert me to potential danger. In this state of readiness, non-essential functions are paused, and my focus narrows to: 'he's missing the point'. I'm not in a resourceful state. For the moment, creativity, reasoning and flexibility are suspended because they're superfluous to survival.

In addition, I only have part of the story: I have access to the impact of my client's words on me, but I don't have direct data about the impact of my words on him. With the benefit of hindsight, I might wonder what he made of my line of questioning. What did it evoke in him? How was he reacting beneath his professional demeanour? What was really going on for him in this process? This is a version of centred inquiry (Appendix D): we're willing to look into, and reflect on, someone else's experience.

The key principle is that the way our words and questions affect others is variable – people have different sensitivities or triggers. A word or phrase that doesn't provoke a sense of criticism, difficulty or censure in most people can have negative associations for others, causing them to react adversely. When we allow for such variations, we can see the value of asking others how our words have landed with them.

The quality of many of our conversations would be enriched if we were more attuned to the 'impact' element of our words – how they affect others – and more attentive to the way we're affected by what's said. These aspects of a conversation naturally draw us towards considering the 'look and feel' of our interactions, their 'how', energy and quality.

# Intention

Let's turn to the second element of intent–impact: our motivation and intention, and what we're hoping to bring about through our words. This can be a tricky domain. I've found that few people habitually clarify their intentions before going into a conversation. It's even more rare for someone to consciously revisit and refine these intentions as a conversation unfolds. As a result, for most people, most of the time, intention is ill-defined and hazy. Personally, I'm a work in progress on this front – although, for important conversations, I make an effort, because the alternative is to be feeling my way in the dark.

So, what can we glean about intention in the case study? There's a hint that my intention is relatively clear when I first raise my question (box 1): my client has a part to play, whether actively or passively, and I'm inviting him to reflect on this. When I don't seem to get an answer to the question I asked, my intention becomes murkier. When we repeat something, we often have a measure of attachment to an imagined response. And so, when I repeat my question for a third time, I may be simply trying to get my client to answer it. I've got a bit lost, in the sense that I'm no longer sure of my motives.

Whenever we notice that our intention is confused or vague, it can be helpful to pause and review what we're trying to accomplish. We can use a framework such as the archetypal centres of energy represented by head, heart and core/gut (Chapter 12) to broaden any immediate focus with our aims for relationships and the wider system. When we enrich our intention in this way, there's a crucial by-product: we reduce our attachment to a particular result. We're then more open to what others say.

In the case study, I don't have direct access to my client's intention – and I didn't ask him why he responded to my questions in the way he did. This means that we're left to guess what his motivation might have been. I suspect that he was simply trying to help me to understand how the unsatisfactory performance of his directors was hindering progress. I don't remember a 'defending' energy that might indicate that he felt criticised. Perhaps it simply hadn't occurred to him that he might need to make changes in his leadership approach – he was on autopilot, telling a familiar story that had always gone unquestioned. He may not even have heard my challenge.

To look even more deeply into this, we could draw on the imagery of wall–window (Appendix D) to wonder about my client's worldview. How is he seeing the world? Where's he standing and where is he directing his gaze? What might be obscuring his line of sight? For example, he is experiencing the conversation from the perspective of being a coaching client. What are his assumptions about coaching and what it will do for him? Perhaps my client believes that a coach's role is to help him solve his problem, not to ask how he's causing it. From this perspective, it's possible that my question might make no sense. What we hear, how we hear it and what we take it to mean depend on the perspective we hold and the assumptions we make. My client and I could be quite literally on different wave-lengths.

To summarise: we can use the lens of intent–impact to be clear about what we have direct access to and what we can only know if we ask. We can enrich our conversational experience by inquiring into the latter, the intentions of others and the impact of our words on them (and what they take them to mean). In addition, if we're attuned to our own intentions and the impact the words of others have on us, our conversations are likely to be more fruitful.

Let's pause to explore how this approach invites us to engage with 'self' (and others) in a new way.

## Over to you …

As you listen to others, how do you tend to engage with the sensations, feelings and thought-reactions that arise in you? Do you dwell on them, discount them or consider them as a useful aspect of the conversation?

How often do you take care to be clear about your intentions? What changes when you do?

How often do you inquire into the intentions of others? How often do you check how your words have landed? What changes when you do?

How might you pay more attention to intent and impact in your conversations?

We'll now return to the crux of Case Study 2 and look more closely at the moments in which I interrupted the repeating pattern in order to put the conversation on a different footing.

## Chapter 19

We are the method:
crux of the case study

You may recall that the case study is based on a coaching conversation with a CEO who was experiencing challenges with his team of directors. When I asked him what he might change in his leadership approach, his responses focused on what the directors might do differently. I was becoming frustrated. Let's pick up the story from box 5, when I asked my question for a third time.

## Extract from Case Study 2

| What I was thinking and feeling but not saying (left-hand column) | What was said (right-hand column) |
|---|---|
| *I feel quite uncomfortable asking this again ... am I doing the right thing in persisting with this?* | **5. Me**<br>So ... what is needed in terms of your leadership? |
| *You're side-stepping again ... what on earth can I do now? What's my intent here? Is this important enough to pursue, or am I simply banging my drum in the way he's banging his ...?*<br>*[pausing ... centring ...]* | **6. Client**<br>Well, Director B just focuses on the details and really important things get missed and ... well, staff are up in arms about Director Y and he needs to get a grip on his team ... |

This is the crux of the conversation – I ask broadly the same question for a third time (box 5) and get the same kind of response to it (box 6). At this point, I've become attached to getting my client to acknowledge his part in the situation.

However, if I try to force the issue by asking the question again, I'll almost certainly express my exasperation. And so, as it says in the left-hand column of box 6, 'what on earth can I do now?'

To explore what happened next, I'll share a fuller version of my experience in the few moments in which I listened to my client's story again. The layers of realisation that I'm about to describe unfolded in a very short time – it'll take much longer for you to read them, but I hope this 'slow motion' replay will be helpful.

My experience starts with the impulse to 'press on' that's present in my body – a slight movement forward, a girding of my loins – and a recognition that acting on this might prompt the client to push back or close down. It's likely that he too is feeling frustrated at this point. The obvious alternative is to drop the issue. While this might feel more comfortable in the moment, it leaves the underlying pattern in place and the client will continue to be dissatisfied with his directors. This doesn't sit well with the coaching context of this conversation.

The raw impulse to act and 'get an answer' tells me that my physiology is taking charge and limiting the information available to me. Unless I'm inclined to allow my autonomic nervous system to dictate what I do, I must regroup, and work with my body to support my mind to regain access to all its faculties.

## Centring and bystanding

I use the four-part centring practice (Appendix B) to come into alignment and ease, which creates space in my mind. Essentially, I take my attention off the problem and regain access to the bigger picture and to my creativity and ethical compass. From a more centred state, I realise that the conversation is stuck, and can accept my own part in bringing this about. I wonder what I'm really trying to do. My favourite inquiry for this is: who or what am I in service to? This question helps me to clarify the context and to consider what I might do next. Let's revisit boxes 7 and 8 to explore this further.

# Extract from Case Study 2

| What I was thinking and feeling but not saying (left-hand column) | What was said (right-hand column) |
|---|---|
| *Who or what am I in service to? I want to see if I can unlock a pattern that might be limiting this whole team. I'll regroup … and try one more time …*<br>*I'll reflect back the pattern to him before I ask the question again …* | **7. Me**<br>*[pausing, centring, embodying presence]*<br>Let me give you a perspective on what's happening here. I've asked three times 'what might you change?' and each time you've answered in terms of changes that others need to make.<br>*[pausing, exhaling]*<br>And so, I ask again – how might you change your approach to better support your directors to contribute more effectively? |
| *[Holding my breath …]*<br>*This could go either way …* | **8. Client**<br>*[Silence … pausing …]*<br>Oh! I suppose I might try to better understand why … |

My role as a coach is to support and challenge the CEO client in service to his leadership. This means that I'm also in service to his colleagues and the wider system, and that these constituencies have a place in my deliberations.

As I pause, I notice that frustration is a theme of the conversation – the CEO's frustration with his directors, my frustration with the CEO, the possibility that the CEO is frustrated with me – and it seems reasonable to hypothesise that the directors are frustrated by the CEO and his leadership. I'm now part of the problem and, as I consider my options, I touch into a desire to release this sense of frustration in all of us. This reflection helps me focus on what matters rather than on my reluctance to ask the question again. I wonder: how do I give this my best shot?

In this situation, centring helped me to zoom out and see the interaction with a neutral clarity – for whatever reason, my client and I had become enmeshed in our own world and had fallen into simply repeating ourselves. This observation represents an inner 'bystand' of the conversation, and I can use the same practice to offer the client a glimpse of the pattern we've established.

The intention of a spoken bystand is to shift attention from the 'what' of a conversation (the CEO and his team) to the 'how' (the shape of our exchange). To make this shift skilfully, a bystand is offered neutrally: we stick to observable details, and frame them as perception rather than fact. We can use the centring practice to support us to offer a bystand in this way. If we also expand our sense of space to include the recipient of our words, they're more likely to land well. We'll look at this in more detail in Chapter 21.

Taking all this into account, in box 7 of the case study, I centre again, and say:

> Let me give you a perspective on what's happening here. I've asked three times 'what might you change?' and each time you've answered in terms of changes that others need to make.
>
> [pausing, exhaling]
>
> And so, I ask again – how might you change your approach to better support your directors to contribute more effectively?

This time the question evoked a silence. When the CEO eventually spoke, he began to reflect on ways he could behave differently to enable his team members to deliver more for the organisation. This moment in the conversation illustrates something I've found to be a useful principle: the quality of a question is revealed by the length of the silence that follows it.

## The quality of a question

Let's leave the case for a moment to explore the implications of this assertion, which I often use as a way to reframe silence. Many people are a bit spooked by silence and, when a question evokes it, they easily fall into self-doubt, judgement, assumptions, humour or supplying an 'answer'. A silence creates a space in our own head as well as in the room, and if we're not accustomed to this internal 'pause', all sorts of habitual thoughts can rush in, fill the space and compel us to speak. If, instead, we regard silence as an indicator that our question has prompted some reflection and fresh thinking, we may wonder what will happen next. This takes attention away from ourselves and the rush of thoughts.

If there's no silence after a question, it's likely that what's said is a recycled standard response. When we're operating on autopilot, we tend to offer previously used explanations or remarks in answer to questions. I sometimes describe such 'auto-responses' as the 'ready meals' of conversation – previously prepared and packaged for quick reheating and consumption (and a bit short on nutrition). Many conversations take the form of rapid exchanges of these ready-meal equivalents. And when these are fit for purpose (effective), they *are* efficient, especially for the day-to-day task of getting stuff done. However, when we apply a ready-meal habit to a matter that calls for more thorough consideration, we can end up with a superficial decision, agreement or course of action that doesn't deliver and/or doesn't stand the test of time.

To continue the nutrition analogy, when we want to access new thinking, individually and together, we create space for those present to gather the raw ingredients for a conversation. We then spend time preparing, combining and cooking them, and savouring the results as they're shared. This takes a lot more time, but yields more nourishment and satisfaction. This kind of conversation tends to bring longer-term benefits, including enriched relationships and insight into the interdependencies of the wider system.

What I'm suggesting is that, when a question is asked, we refrain from unthinkingly recycling pre-prepared opinions or statements. Instead, we pause and search for the raw ingredients of what we really think and feel, in this moment. This is where the silence arises: we're thinking, considering and reflecting before we respond. In silence, we can engage with ourselves in a new way – as my client did when he began to wonder about *his* part in the way his directors were operating.

## Over to you …

Can you recall a time when you've been 'lost for words' and didn't have a ready reply to a question you'd just been asked? What happened in that moment? How did you find the words to respond?

And can you recall a time when a question you asked was followed by a noticeable silence? What happened in that moment? How did the conversation continue?

What insights arise from these reflections?

The essence of this exploration is that, if we answer a question on autopilot, it usually gives rise to a fairly transactional exchange and is useful only in a limited context. Whereas, if we pause, search and compose a response from scratch, we'll enrich a conversation and change the tenor of it. Who knows what may then emerge?

## Re-setting body and mind

Let's return to the case study and reflect more generally. The origins of the pattern that arose between my client and me are archetypal: a person (let's call them Fred, but in the case study, it could be me or the CEO) thinks they're saying something clearly, but they're not getting the response that they expect or want. Typically, Fred then simply reiterates his request, instruction or question in similar terms. When he gets a similar response, a conversational pattern begins to form.

The pattern might be 'tennis match' style, such as point and counterpoint; back and forth; request and inaction; proposal and resistance. This is a 'narrowing' conversation, becoming tighter and tighter around ground that's only somewhat shared and which hasn't been clearly delineated. There's a risk that this kind of pattern becomes conflict – either overtly (things kick off or someone pulls rank) or covertly (someone becomes compliant or gives in).

Alternatively, the pattern might be more circular in nature, in which responses divert the conversation so that the repeating request, instruction or question is avoided or sidelined. The pattern becomes a polite and unspoken agreement 'not to go there'. This kind of conversation becomes looser and more ambiguous: it has no centre or it misses the point.

In each of these patterns, the conversation becomes stuck and so tends to either erupt through frustration or dissolve through lack of interest. There are two aspects to intervening in such a pattern of unproductive repetition: doing something different and doing it in a skilful, embodied way.

My conversation with the CEO was in 'narrowing' territory and, in box 6, we were on the brink of an explosion or implosion. Looking closely, we can see that I reframed my question slightly each time. On the face of it, this is doing something different – trying slight variations on my theme to see if this prompted a change in response. However, I was making this change in quite a transactional way – applying a technique, rather than paying attention to what was below the surface.

In addition, the energy I was bringing to my question was becoming more pointed. Underneath a carefully presented professionalism, I was getting more insistent. The associated energy was frustration – and, to be effective, I had to adjust both my mind-set and my body-set.

Although this sounds simple, each re-set offers a challenge:

* with mind-set, we're likely to be attached to something – a particular course of action, view or outcome – and it may not be easy to unhook ourselves from this preoccupation, especially if we think we're right; and

* with body-set, we may not notice the sensations of our body chemistry kicking in, tightening their grip and limiting our options.

However, if we realise that we need to re-set and use the four-part centring practice to do this, we're in a buy-one-get-one-free situation: as we adjust our body-set, we also affect our mind-set. It only takes a few seconds. We turn our mind to our posture, alignment, breath and the space around us. This takes our attention off the presenting issue, which loosens our attachment to it. As our body-set becomes more easeful, the process of shutting down non-essential functions is halted and our mind recovers its perspective. We regain access to creativity, ethics, compassion and generosity. We have more information and more options.

In the case, this embodied process supported me to change my stance and offer something different: my sense of the pattern itself. My client might have challenged

190

this, but I kept it factual, with no inference or judgement. I was simply 'commentating', like someone describing a sporting event, and offering my words as a perspective. The four-part centring practice helped me to access this neutrality, changing my relationship with myself and with my client: I was no longer trying to force the issue. Instead, I was inviting him to consider how he was responding to my question. My focus shifted from his interactions with others to the exchange between us. I let my description of the pattern land (pausing) and saw a change in his demeanour. I asked my question again with a sense that it would now be received differently.

Neutrality is an essential attribute of a bystand. On an occasion when I wasn't neutral, I added some interpretation to my description of the pattern that I observed, commenting that one of the people present 'seemed to be upset'. The person concerned didn't recognise this description of herself and turned her anger and frustration onto me. Rightly so. I had an agenda and was subtly trying to point out the error of her ways. I now take greater care with my bystands.

## Over to you …

Take a moment to find your own example of a situation in which you repeated yourself several times. What was the response to each reiteration? Is there a pattern in the exchange?

If so, try different ways of describing it, as neutrally as you can. With this insight into the nature of the exchange, what might you do differently the next time you notice that you're repeating yourself?

## Self as instrument

We've been exploring the relationship between dialogue and the way we engage with ourselves. I'd now like to make this connection more general by suggesting

191

that the way we relate to 'self' (and to others) largely determines the shape and quality of all our conversations. Let's consider this.

When our relationship with self reflects qualities like honesty, integrity and openness, we're likely to be able to make ourselves available to others. We bring our whole self to a conversation with a sense of ease. This invites others to do the same, and the door to dialogue opens.

If, in contrast, our relationship with self is murkier and is protected or airbrushed, we present a less coherent self to others. It's likely that they'll pick up on this and, even if this happens outside conscious awareness, it may influence the look and feel of a conversation. I'm suggesting that, if I'm guarded about who I am and what I'm about, my conversations will be guarded. If my interest in an issue or other people is insincere, my conversations will reflect this. If I set myself apart, believing I'm more gifted, important or indispensable than others, I'll flavour my conversations with this energy and others will respond accordingly.

To accept that our conversations and our relationships with others mirror the way we relate to ourselves is a compelling reason to steward ourselves well in our important interactions. The field of Gestalt psychology[18] offers support for this in a principle that's enshrined in the phrase 'self as instrument'. We are (literally) instrumental in everything we do. This principle invites us to guide our 'self' with the same care a specialist would apply to using any precision tool, such as an artist and their brushes or a surgeon and their scalpels. An artisan or craftsperson is never casual in the way they deploy the tools of their trade – in the same way, we might aspire to handle the instrument of self with awareness and skill.

The way we treat the 'tools' of dialogue also matters. If we pay lip service to them and apply them transactionally as techniques, we'll get limited benefit from them. We'll have scraped the surface of their potential. However, if we embody a practice and make it part of who we are, we'll influence others and the conversational field, creating the possibility of change.

In the next chapter, we'll explore our stewardship of self through the lens of embodying the four dialogue practices of respecting, listening, suspending judgement and authentic voicing.

# Chapter 20   We are the method: embodying the four dialogue practices

Engaging in dialogue is a way of being, a quality of energy and presence that arises in and through our conversations – it's hard to describe, but we know when we experience it. In this chapter, we'll explore this quality of energy and presence through the lens of the four dialogue practices formulated by William Isaacs, Peter Garrett[3] and others. The practices are described in Isaacs' book and are: respecting, listening, suspending judgement and authentic voicing. Inhabiting the four dialogue practices is a gateway to being in dialogue, and looking at them separately is like the mirror-signal-manoeuvre stage of learning to drive: we get to grips with the elements through repetition and they blend into a single experience.

In dialogue, since we are the method, we *make* a conversation (individually and collectively) in the way that an artist makes their work. Yes, there are frameworks we can use to guide us, but if we apply them in a perfunctory way, like a practical tool that we pick up and put down, nothing will change. If we inhabit them and make them integral to who we are and how we relate to others, our conversations are transformed.

To expand on this: when we pick up a physical tool, it can be an awkward and unfamiliar movement or a deft one. A tool is a dead weight or a living thing, depending on the skill with which it's handled. What do I mean by this? If I pick up a stick, it's just a stick. If I hold it and move with it in a way that reflects my martial arts practice, it becomes something I can wield to protect myself or to hurt someone. In addition, because I have many years of practice with sticks and swords, my personal space expands to include the stick – it becomes part of me.

You can see this principle at work with someone who uses a 'tool' daily: a plumber, an artist, a joiner, a musician, a cyclist. Their personal space expands to include their tool, it becomes integral to them. When they pick up their tool you don't see person and tool separately, you see person+tool as a natural system, joined in a way that makes them one. The tool moves as an extension of the body it's attached to. This is quite different to the way the same tool moves in hands that don't know it so well.

Something similar applies to using the frameworks of dialogue: we can't simply pick them up and use them well. This is especially true of the four dialogue practices. For example, we don't embody respecting by simply saying we're going to respect others. Even if we're truly committed to doing this, we're unlikely to be able to sustain an orientation of respecting (all) others for any length of time. Our natural predispositions and go-to thoughts will kick in: we'll discount the views of some people, defer to those of others, withhold our voice, or become overbearing. To embody respecting, so that it becomes the ground from which our conversations grow, involves systematically reconditioning our mind-set and body-set until respecting becomes our default setting, whatever the circumstances. Similar considerations apply to all four practices.

There's good news. The embodied practices outlined in these pages – which are all drawn from the Leadership Embodiment approach developed by Wendy Palmer – provide us with a one-stop shop for reconditioning our mind-set and body-set. When we access a centred state, we naturally inhabit all four dialogue practices. We adopt one practice (centring) and get four free. However, since it takes time to build our capacity for centring, it's worth following a dual track and working with the individual dialogue practices as well.

We can appreciate this from a story often told by a former colleague and client, Lorna Jackson, who's now a good friend and fellow traveller. Lorna loved the principles of dialogue as soon as she was introduced to them. She could see their potential. However, she had mixed results when she tried to use them. This changed when she began to use LE practices to support her efforts. The practices enabled her to work skilfully with her tendencies to impatience and frustration, which were often apparent when she challenged a course of action. When she centred, the energy of her challenge changed, allowing her words to be more readily received by others.

I share this story to encourage you to adopt an embodied 'short cut' to approaching difference differently by using the LE practices regularly and often, especially the foundation centring practice (Appendix B). Inhabiting the practice is likely to be a long haul – and, while this may seem to contradict the notion of a short cut, it doesn't. There are immediate and discernible benefits to centring, even when we're inexperienced. However, to be able to access centre when tension creeps (or explodes) into a conversation, the practice must become a 'muscle memory'.

As with any physical art, we embed a practice by taking small steps and repeating often. As we use the centring practice, we'll have setbacks and may need to regroup and try again. We'll also have triumphs, which spur us on – sometimes too much, so that we overreach ourselves and have another setback. Continuing to practise through these lumps and bumps in the road calls for fortitude and a clear sense of *why* we're putting ourselves through this discomfort: we wish to improve the quality of our interactions with others.

In summary, the LE centring practice supports the 'how' element of the four dialogue practices, working with them as energetic qualities. As we inhabit these qualities, they permeate our conversations. This takes us beyond any mundane application of a tool or technique: it changes the way we carry ourselves, which changes everything.

## Over to you …

We all use tools and devices every day – identify one that you use in a way that feels part of you – whether it's a keyboard, car, piece of sports equipment, musical instrument … or something else.

How did using this implement become so natural to you? When did you first pick it up? How did you learn what to do with it? What's the difference between how you handle it now and the early days?

How might these reflections inform the way you develop a centring 'muscle'?

We'll now look at each dialogue practice in more depth, starting with respecting.

# Respecting

If you ask a group about the ground rules they'd like to put in place for a workshop or an important conversation, it's likely that 'respect' will make an appearance. In these settings, the call to include respect is often about being shown or given respect, and may indicate that this quality is generally lacking. However, as a practice, respecting is complex – when we extend too much respect to others, we're in the realm of deference, and when we extend too little, we discount and/or disparage others. What constitutes 'just right' in terms of respecting?

And what about respect for self? If we have too much self-respect, we tend to arrogance, and may be likely to impose our views on others. And if we have too little self-respect, we may think that our view is unimportant and not speak up.

More generally we might wonder: how does respect show up? Do people have to earn respect? What influences whether we extend or withhold respect? Do we expect to receive respect? Do we respect ourselves?

In the context of dialogue and how we handle difference, we can ask: to whom do we extend respect? Many of us have opinions about who 'deserves' our respect – I certainly do. We make judgements according to our preconceptions, forgetting our view is partial – we don't know the circumstances of those we deem to be worthy (or not) of our respect. When we find it hard to respect someone, they may be doing their best in poor circumstances, whilst someone we find easier to respect may be squandering their privileges.

In dialogue, the heart of the practice of respecting is to offer it to all – to be mindful that each person has a place and each voice is of value. This calls for humility – and we can only give it our best effort. In addition, respecting everyone means including ourselves, and balancing regard for others with self-respect.

Personally, being aware of the demanding standard of offering respect to all helps me to catch the symptoms of disrespect – discounting, dismissing, rolling my eyes, being off-hand, denigrating – when they arise in me. Then, sometimes, I'm able to adjust – although there'll always be people who remain 'beyond the pale' in my eyes. When I can't find respect for someone, the best I can do is to be compassionate towards them and myself, and be curious about how they came to be who they are.

Widening our circle of respect is key to discerning inclusion (Chapter 13) and to handling the energy of difference in a way that creates possibility. While we can wrangle with words and reason in defining respect, we can also explore respecting through experience.

When respect is present, we know it in an embodied way. A respectful environment reflects a quality of energy, rather than something that's said or done – we each feel we have a place and that what we say has value. When we embody respect, we receive and appreciate what others have to say, as well as holding our own voice to be of value. A sense of freedom and ease develops, and this supports people to talk openly about what they think and feel.

We also know, in an embodied way, when respect is lacking or leans towards deference. Some things aren't said. Some people don't speak. Some voices are more valued than others. A sense of watchfulness arises, and this inhibits frankness.

The presence or absence of respect isn't about technique, it's about how we carry ourselves and how we receive others. It's an embodied practice and, if we take exception to someone and/or to something that's been said, we fall out of respectful presence. A climate of respect will quickly dissipate if we start trying to persuade others of our view, and so discount theirs, or if we withhold our voice because we don't trust others to receive what we say. Respect is hard-won and easily lost. It always serves us to think about how we foster it.

While there isn't a specific Leadership Embodiment practice for 'centred respecting', the energy of respecting is inherent in the centring practice. In choosing to centre and organise our energy into this resourceful state, we embody self-respect. When we centre, we access the best of ourselves … and in doing so, we convey that those around us are worthy of the best we can offer. In a centred state, we embody respect towards others.

{ } Over to you …

To what extent do you support my musings on the practice of respecting? What do you challenge?

To find your own stance on respect, think of someone you hold in esteem and describe this as an embodied experience. Then think of someone who holds you in esteem and describe how this feels and what it gives rise to. From these examples, what can you infer about respect? What does it feel like? What qualities and attributes does it give rise to?

As you identify an embodied sense of respect, can you imagine what it would be like to extend respect to people that you have less regard for? What might help you to make this shift, at least some of the time?

We've explored respecting through thinking about it and inquiring into it. We've also considered how we know whether it's present or absent through our embodied experience. Now, let's explore listening in a similar way.

## Listening

Listening is another quality that's frequently mentioned when a group is exploring ground rules for a workshop or an important conversation. In such settings, a call for listening often refers to a desire to be heard and taken notice of. This may reflect a feeling that 'no one' listens, with 'no one' often meaning 'those in power'. When there's little or no acknowledgement in a conversation, we can address this by signalling our appreciation when people speak up, whether we agree with them or not.

The act of listening is multifaceted. For instance, we can be curious about what we listen *to* – do we pay more attention to some topics than others? What influences what we screen out and what we get immersed in? Do we listen more to others than to ourselves?

We can also pay attention to what we listen *for* – do we tend to listen for facts or metaphor, for narrative or patterns, for the familiar or unfamiliar? Whatever our preferences, they'll alert us to what we might miss or discount.

And what about our motivation? Are we listening for information that we can make use of? Are we listening to understand, to connect, to participate? Are we listening to challenge or find fault or advantage? How does our motivation influence *how* we listen?

Another facet of listening is attending to our internal dialogue – the plethora of thoughts, sensations, feelings, memories and connections that arise as we listen. How do we take account of this inner experience and balance it with listening to others?

As with respect, we can listen too attentively or not attentively enough. When we listen too closely to a particular person or opinion, it can feel stifling to the speaker, and may also discount other people and points of view. When we're distracted in our listening, we may miss key information and those around us may think it's not worth speaking, which further reduces the information available. So, what constitutes 'just right' in terms of listening?

The dialogue practice invites us to simply listen, to *receive* what others are saying, including their view and allowing for the possibility that it may influence our thinking. It's about receiving what's being said (or not said) without interpretation or inference – witnessing another's narrative without adding our own. This is easy to write or say – and is hard to do. However, the embodied practice of centred listening (Appendix E) can support us to let words land in a neutral way, so that we can consider whether or not to pick them up.

In dialogue, the heart of the practice of listening is to be open to receiving and hearing all voices. However, in reality, most of us are selective in our listening: we favour some voices and discount or ignore others. We might ask: how can we create space to include the voices we find harder to listen to, whether they express difference, articulate difficult truths, are less fluent in their delivery or belong to people we don't like or rate? The centred listening practice can also support us with this.

Including all voices calls for generosity – and we can only give it our best effort. A first step is to acknowledge our tendencies, filters, biases and motives – with greater awareness of them, we're less likely to misconstrue what other people say and do. We can consciously pay attention to the people we tend to tune out, the opinions we tend to give no credence to … and work hard to stay present to them. We may discover something we don't yet know – and, in this way, listening is at the heart of inquiring.

As with respecting, while we can wrangle with words and reason to describe how we listen, the energetic climate of a conversation changes when listening is present. Attentive listening brings with it a settled quality of energy, and we may experience this as being able to 'hear a pin drop'. The very air seems receptive, open, curious – and we each know we have a place and that what we say will be heard. We know when listening is embodied, individually and collectively: it permeates the conversational field.

To practise listening in the spirit of dialogue, we can use the Leadership Embodiment centred listening practice. The more often we repeat the practice, the more available it becomes, building our capacity to receive whatever's being said with acceptance and curiosity.

Over to you …

To what extent do you support my musings on listening? What do you challenge?

To find your own stance on listening, reflect on which of your friends, family members or colleagues listens well – what characterises their listening? For those you didn't include, what is it about the way they listen that prompted you to leave them out?

Now reflect on how you listen to others, and explore when and how you listen well and when and how you're less attentive. Perhaps you listen more carefully to some people than others? Perhaps you favour some topics and discount others? More generally, what influences how well you listen?

Then consider what you tend to listen for and what you tend to ignore.

What insights arise about your listening practice? What would help you to listen well to a greater range of people and views, at least some of the time?

Let's turn our attention to the practice of suspending judgement.

## Suspending judgement

The phrase 'suspending judgement' may be less familiar than respecting and listening and so calls for some explanation. We've already met the essence of it in the wall–window activity (Chapter 10). At the beginning of the activity, we set ourselves up to feel the energy of difference in the form of opposition or resistance. Then, when we notice ourselves tightening around our point of view, we centre and step aside for a moment. This represents 'parking' our opinion to create space to enter into someone else's world. This is the basis of suspending judgement.

'Parking' our view for a moment creates space to think and to inquire. In the wall–window activity, we step into this space by moving to stand behind our practice partner so that we can literally see what they're seeing. We tune in to their view, accepting their reality, even though we disagree. This creates the conditions for inquiry, which might take the form of asking for more detail or context.

How might the movements of the centred inquiry activity be translated into something we can do in a conversation, in real time?

My personal experience of this is that, when I find myself reacting adversely to something that's been said, it's usually evidence that I'm attached to a different view or position. My pattern is to believe I'm right (corollary: they're wrong) and my auto-response is to correct them (nicely, of course – at least initially). This corrective energy, however polite, can quickly lead to a point-and-counterpoint situation with little room for manoeuvre.

There are two opportunities to intervene in this potential tussle – the first, and best, being that I refrain from my tendency to put people right. If I'm on autopilot, I might miss this opportunity. However, as the energy of disagreement rises, I'm likely to recognise it as an experience of the first stage of the wall–window activity. This offers the second opportunity to intervene – I can park my opinion, or suspend my judgement, and enter into more exploratory territory and energy.

To suspend judgement, it helps to remember that, even if I believe my view to be a checkable fact, it may not apply in the current context. In my left-hand column, what I'm thinking and feeling but not saying (Chapter 17), I ask myself 'what if … [the thing I'm so certain about] … doesn't hold water in this situation?'. What I'm really parking is my *attachment* to my view. This creates the space to receive other perspectives and consider them. With this more spacious mind-set, I'm more likely to seek more information and broaden the terrain of a conversation.

When we suspend our position, judgement or belief, we're not agreeing with the alternative(s). We're simply acknowledging that our view is partial, which opens our mind to include other perspectives.

As with the practices of respecting and listening, the essence of 'suspending judgement' often appears when a group considers possible ground rules for a workshop or an important conversation. It tends to show up in the form of a request to be non-judgemental, a shorthand for 'don't judge me or what I say'.

This is territory where I hold a strong view (or judgement): I don't believe it's possible for most human beings to be non-judgemental. I believe we're hard-wired to judge, habitually assessing the situations we find ourselves in and appraising the character of the people we come into contact with. We make judgements as part of deciding whether or not we're at risk. We appraise things, people and ideas, to assess what we value or like (or not). As leaders, we weigh up who to delegate work to and who we trust to handle delicate situations well, and we're paid to make these judgements. How might we recognise, and work skilfully with, the reality of our tendency to judge?

One approach is to notice how and when our convictions constrain our thinking. It's our certainty about, and attachment to, our view/judgement that limits what's possible rather than the view/judgement itself. If we're aware of our judgements, we can hold them lightly or loosely, and even set them aside for a while. This creates the potential for change – in our mind and in the minds of others. This is the art (and heart) of suspending judgement. And, when we truly embrace this practice, it becomes simply 'suspending' everything and being present to what is.

As with the other practices, we can overuse or underuse the practice of suspending judgement. When we suspend judgement too often and too broadly, we accept things that it might be better to question and explore. When we rarely suspend judgement, we tend towards being certain of our stance, discounting what others have to say and polarising everything into right and wrong.

We can also apply suspending judgement internally, to the way we regard ourselves. If our self-regard is low, and we believe ourselves to be less well-informed or less experienced than someone we're talking to, we might stay silent for fear of looking stupid. This can happen in everyday situations, such as when we don't seek clarification of a medical diagnosis or a recommendation made by a mechanic or an electrician. If we're able to 'park' our judgement about ourselves for a moment – what if it's *not* a daft question? – we're more likely to speak up.

The practice of 'parking' our judgement about ourselves may be even more powerful when our self-regard is high and we believe ourselves to be better informed and/or more experienced than others. When we're convinced that we're right, it can be helpful to wonder what we don't yet know. In almost every situation, there are uncertainties, ambiguities and interdependencies that we don't have sight of, and they're often outside our influence and control. Remembering this can help us suspend our resolute confidence in our view, and create room to ask for, and take account of, a variety of perspectives.

In dialogue, the heart of the practice of suspending judgement is holding all views lightly and with a sense of appreciation and curiosity. We change our orientation and, instead of asking 'is this view of value?', we lean into asking 'what's of value in this view?'. Rather than quickly dismissing or concurring with what's said, we start looking for hidden gems that will enrich our thinking.

To do this requires awareness – and we can only give it our best effort. A smattering of humour also helps – as we catch ourselves in our judgements, in our predictable opinions and certainties, it helps to smile wryly and recognise them. This lightens both our mood and our hold on such convictions.

As ever, words and reason only go so far in describing the experience of suspending judgement. When we're in the presence of someone who's suspending judgement we know, in a visceral way, that both we and our view will be valued. It's a quality of energy, a sense of spaciousness, acceptance, curiosity and generosity of spirit. Our legacy fight/flight system rests – there's no present danger.

When we're able to embody the practice of suspending judgement, others are more likely to share their inner dialogue – what they're thinking and feeling and wouldn't usually say. It also becomes possible to say the impossible. We're privileged when others trust us with things that they find difficult to express. When judgement is suspended collectively, the climate becomes one of wonder, a palpable feeling that our differences will give rise to new insights.

Suspending judgement is essentially about our orientation towards what we think and what we hear. It's an embodied recognition of the human reality that our view is always partial. The bottom line is that, when someone feels they may be judged, they'll edit what they're prepared to say or withhold their voice completely. The practice of suspending judgement is key to bringing each person's authentic voice into a conversation.

## Over to you …

To what extent do you support my musings on suspending judgement? What do you challenge?

To find your own stance on the implications of being judgemental, being non-judgemental and suspending judgement for a moment, call to mind an occasion when you made a judgement about someone which later proved to be unfounded. What might have changed if you'd been able to suspend your initial assessment and/or ask for more information?

Now call to mind an occasion when you felt judged – how did this impact what you said and did? What might have changed if you'd felt able to speak and act freely?

From these reflections on suspending judgement, what insights arise?

When sharing the four dialogue practices with others, I usually draw attention to the fact that three of them focus mainly on how we receive what's said: only one is about how we speak. Before we look at the speaking practice, let's briefly revisit the wall–window activity (Chapter 10), which offers an opportunity to experience the three receiving practices in an embodied way. If you tried the activity, you may have found that it encapsulates the energy of respecting, suspending judgement and listening. In essence, the three practices combine to become centred inquiry – we notice we're in opposition, or disagreement, and we centre so that we're in respectful opposition. We suspend judgement, stepping aside for a moment. And we're willing to look at what someone else sees and to listen to what they say. I encourage you to explore the activity again and to reflect on how you might apply it in a real situation.

Having got a feel for the three 'receiving' dialogue practices, let's consider 'transmitting', and bringing the practice of authentic voicing to what we say.

## Authentic voicing

Whether we're inquiring or advocating, the dialogue practice of 'authentic voicing' supports our spoken contribution. To speak with authentic voice, we express what's true for us, whether that's an opinion or something we're curious about. In addition, we try to offer our words in a way that allows them to land with others, always recognising that they may see the world differently. We pay attention to both what we're saying and how we say it, to our intent and the potential impact.

As with the three 'receiving' dialogue practices, we can overuse or underuse our authentic voice. When advocating, we may take airspace from others if we put too much of our 'self' into a conversation. We can also over-explain, give too much detail and/or be too insistent. Too little authentic voice in our advocacy shows up when we don't contribute, speak formally as if we're in a role, recycle pre-prepared statements or speak in generalities.

When inquiring, too much authentic voice may show up as persistent questions on one theme, requesting detail that isn't useful for the wider conversation and/or seeking information for our own ends. Too little authentic voice might show up as a lack of interest in, or an unquestioning acceptance of, what's being said.

There's something reciprocal about the practice of authentic voicing. When I find the courage to be open and genuine, and to mindfully make more of myself available to others, it seems to free them to acknowledge their concerns. As I find the words to articulate what matters to me, I don't second-guess what others might think or feel, as this might tempt me to adapt, edit or embellish my words in the hope of a soft landing. I don't try to protect myself from imagined judgements or adverse reactions. Instead, I try to speak with honesty and without attachment – trusting myself with what I want to say and trusting others to receive and accept my words. In contrast, if I withhold my voice, I'm signalling that I don't trust myself to express what's true for me and/or don't trust others to bear the weight of it.

In essence, when we practise authentic voicing, we deepen our contact with both self and others through our shared humanness. In an uncertain and complex world, we need this quality in our leadership conversations. If we're disloyal to ourselves, what is our loyalty to others worth?

To gain insight into this practice, we might ask: when I speak with authentic voice, how do I feel? What influences the level of frankness I'm prepared to bring to what I say? When we listen to others, we might consider what distinguishes authentic voicing from other contributions. How do we know when someone brings more of themselves into an exchange and shares things they don't often reveal?

### *What we say: intent*

An inherent challenge of speaking with authentic voice is that we're not always clear about what's true for us. Many of our easily accessible thoughts are intertwined with past experiences and with our emotions, biases and preferences. When we examine our view closely, we often find contradictions and/or complexity in what we think/feel/sense. This is normal, a part of being human.

When we want to advocate and express our view, we can untangle the threads of ambiguity in our thinking, feeling and sensing by using approaches such as de Bono's Six Thinking Hats[12] (Chapter 10) or the head-heart-core approach (Chapter 12), which we'll revisit in Chapter 31. When we unravel the complexities of our stance, we practise inclusion within ourselves: we accept the differences of our inner voices, regarding each as a facet of what's true for us. This supports us to distil the spirit and intent of what we truly wish to say. And, before we speak, we can check our motivation: how will our advocacy contribute to the conversation? To what extent will it be relevant or useful? How can we offer our words respectfully and without attachment?

When we want to inquire and better understand what we're hearing, it can be helpful to clarify what we're asking and why. Sometimes, we ask questions to satisfy our personal curiosity, to build an opposing argument or to expose a flaw in someone's reasoning. There are scenarios in which such motivations have a place. However, in dialogue, we inquire to discover what we don't yet know or what isn't yet available to those present. We're seeking information and insight that might add to shared understanding. With this motivation, we can use the head-heart-core practice to clarify what we're looking for and to invite others to discover *their* authentic voice.

In dialogue, the heart of the practice of authentic voicing is to put more of our 'self' into what we say. Authentic voice calls us to speak to our immediate experience and reality rather than offer a prepared script, a rehearsed argument or a rehash of what others think. It reveals what we often keep to ourselves: emotions, uncertainty, values, aspirations and human frailty. It requires courage to speak with authentic voice. When we offer more of ourselves to a conversation, we also draw on the qualities that support the 'receiving' practices: humility, generosity and awareness.

If we're unused to expressing our *real* thinking, our feelings or our deeper sense of a situation, our authentic voice can be a little rusty. When used, it can feel raw, intense, naked. We may speak more slowly, more tentatively than usual. We may be searching for words. If we're used to speaking quickly, articulately and confidently, we may become self-conscious when we reach within ourselves to express what we truly believe.

We may also find that the truth is an acquired taste. When we hear others express what's deeply true for them, we may experience the kind of discomfort we'd feel if a colleague undressed in front of us. We can use the centred listening practice (Appendix E) to support us to receive intensely personal words.

We can also use Leadership Embodiment practices to support us to align our energy with our words so that we have a positive impact. Let's look at how we say what we want to say.

### How we say it: impact

As with the other dialogue practices, authentic voicing is a quality of energy, rather than the words being said. We know in an embodied way when it's present in others. And others will know in an embodied way when it's present in us. Let's explore how our energy affects the way our words are received and perceived by others.

We'll start with a relatively checkable fact: a very large part of communication is non-verbal. The statistics to quantify 'a very large part' vary, but usually reference something between 70% and 93%. We communicate eloquently through our body and our energetic presence and, even if those around us aren't consciously aware of this, they pick up energetic cues and are influenced by them.

We can see this most clearly in animals and young children. Have you seen a child shrink into themselves in an appeasing stance before you open your mouth to scold them? When you've caught a cat doing something off-limits, have you watched it dive behind the sofa before you yell at it? Or a dog dipping its head and tail before you tell it off? The child or pet knows that you're cross before you're aware of it yourself.

Such experiences indicate that the energy of an emotion runs through our body before we know it's there and before we express it. Irritation, frustration, unease and dislike (and positive experiences such as kindness) show up first in the body, and the message takes a few seconds to reach the brain, and a few more seconds to be voiced. Animals and young children pick up the message from our body and energetic presence and react to it. In humans, some of this acuity is lost with age and, in many cultures, we learn to override such sensory data with habits of thought and behaviour. However, we still pick up the cues, often unconsciously. And, when we work with embodied practices, we become more aware of them.

Another way of recognising the effect of our energy on what we say is to experiment with saying the same words in different ways. For example, we can ask 'why?' in many ways. 'Why?' can sound and feel incredulous; it can seem to be criticism or an accusation; it can invite us into revealing more about our motivation; and/or it can prompt us to think or explain. You can test this with a colleague or friend – brief them to ask 'why?' in a variety of ways and notice the impact it has. You may find that you respond to the tone of the word and/or to the demeanour of your practice partner. It's often the energetic message that 'lands' first and prompts a response or reaction.

In summary, we can say the same words with different energy, and it's the quality of energy that largely determines how they land. For example, if we begrudgingly agree to do something for someone, we communicate reluctance. If we agree cheerfully, we communicate willingness. In each case, we take on the task – but the relationship is likely to be affected by the reluctant or willing energy with which we agree to it. In addition, when we give out mixed messages, such as agreeing reluctantly, our energy and words are out of sync. This may be confusing for others. In contrast, when our energy and words are synchronised, we communicate clearly and well.

We'll explore a practice for centred speaking in the next chapter, looking separately at advocating and inquiring and the nature of their respective energies. For the moment, let's pause and reflect.

{ Over to you ...

To what extent do you support my musings on authentic voicing? What do you challenge?

To find your own stance on the practice of authentic voicing, and speaking candidly about what matters to you, think of an occasion when you were able to do this – what did it make possible? What flowed from what you said? How might you more often reach within yourself and truly express your immediate reality?

Now think of a time when you heard someone speak in a way that was compelling, even if you didn't agree with what they were saying. What drew you in? What do you recall about their energy and presence? How did their words land with others?

From these reflections on authentic voicing, what insights arise?

In this chapter, we've explored how we might embody the four dialogue practices in our conversations. To reflect on this, and to prepare ourselves for the next chapter, let's link the practices to advocacy and inquiry.

When advocating and expressing our view, the practices of authentic voicing and respecting both self and others are key to *what* we might say. We reach within ourselves to draw out what really matters to us, whilst considering its place in the wider conversation. In terms of *how* we say it, we embrace the practices of suspending judgement of self and others and listening to self and others to support us to speak in a way that makes it possible for others to receive our words.

When we're inquiring, the practices of listening (to our own concerns as well as to what others say) and suspending judgement (of self and others) can act as a reminder that each view is a partial view – both incomplete and influenced by our preferences. This orientation creates space within us and we begin to wonder what we might discover. This internal shift means that, when we ask someone to say more, we're expressing authentic voice: we genuinely want to better understand their perspective. In showing sincere interest, we naturally embody the practice of respecting.

Although we've explored these four practices individually, they work together. In fact, when we look closely, they overlap and almost become a single practice, but one that's difficult to name or describe. For example, when we listen well, we both suspend judgement and embody respect – towards self and others. When we do this, all those present, including ourselves, are more likely to speak with candour. To experience the single practice that's difficult to name or describe, we can access centre. When we do this, we effortlessly embody all four dialogue practices.

Let's turn our attention to the practice of centred speaking.

# Chapter 21  We are the method: centred speaking

When we make a spoken contribution to a conversation, we can bring conscious awareness to our energetic presence (or the vibe we give out) and to shaping our personal space to synchronise our intent and energy. The way we do this depends on whether we're advocating or inquiring.

Each of these speaking contributions has an inherent shape, which brings a characteristic energy to our words. The shape and quality of this energy combine with our intention (or motivation), and this affects the impact we have on others. When these elements align, we communicate clearly and the impact of our words reflects our intent. When any element is out of alignment, those listening may find what we say confusing in some way. We'll look at this in depth in Chapter 31. Here, we'll focus on the practice of aligning our energy and intent, starting with inquiry.

When we inquire and seek to discover what we don't yet know, we naturally inhabit the circular energy described in Chapter 7. This energy can be visibly expressed when someone spreads their arms in a sweeping gesture with open palms, indicating greater inclusion.

To practise centred inquiry, we consciously bring to mind a circular or spherical personal space, reaching about an arm's length in every direction. We uplift, align our posture and exhale, and then imagine this energetic space expanding evenly in all directions, so that we include those present. We do this whilst staying connected to our own centre and alignment. Bringing this circular energy to mind is a personal form of consciously holding a container, giving our words an invitational and receptive tone. When we expand this container to include others, we convey openness and curiosity towards them and their views. In essence, we're setting aside our own view for a moment, and creating room to explore the views of others. This is similar to the approach described in the wall–window activity

(Chapter 10). We can see a 'bird's-eye' representation of centred inquiring energy in the diagram below.

## Bird's-eye view of energy
### Centred inquiry

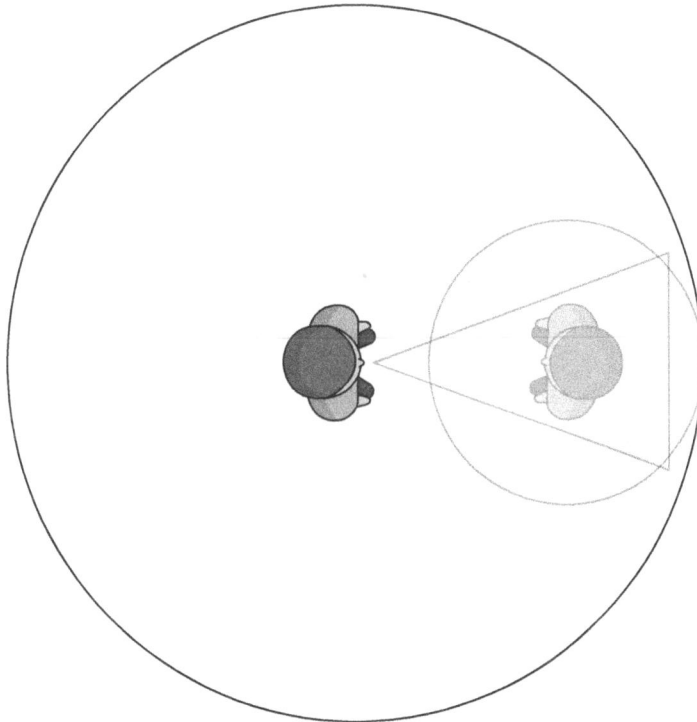

**Key:**

 Centred inquiry, energetic space is expanded evenly to include others

 Included energetically, whether listening, inquiring or advocating

In contrast, when we advocate and speak for or against something, we naturally inhabit a personal space that's pointed and is essentially triangular or wedge-shaped, as described in Chapter 7. This energy is visibly expressed when someone emphasises what they're saying with a pointing gesture. The extended arm and hand represent one side of the triangular energy of their advocacy. The pointed nature of this shape indicates clarity. We can see a 'bird's-eye' representation of centred advocating energy in the diagram below.

## Bird's-eye view of energy
### Centred advocacy

Key:

Centred advocacy, energetic space is expanded
evenly to include others and hold them in parity

Included energetically, whether
listening, inquiring or advocating

To practise centred advocacy, we consciously bring to mind a triangular or wedge-shaped personal space, imagining strong supporting sides and a clear, incisive point or leading edge that extends about an arm's length in front of us. We uplift, align our posture and exhale, and then envisage this energetic space expanding, front and back, left and right, above and below, so that the point or leading edge reaches into the distance. We imagine the sides and the space behind us widening proportionately. The enlarged triangle of our personal energy includes others, whilst we remain connected to our own centre and alignment. Bringing this triangular energy to mind reflects a clear intention to set things in motion and, when we expand this energy to include others, we communicate that we're focused on a bigger picture and invite them to consider it.

When we speak from a centred state, our contribution tends to be motivated by the collective good. We may advocate for what matters to us, but we do it in the context of recognising that our view is simply one perspective. We may inquire into something that interests us, but we do it in the context of its value to the wider conversation.

If we don't centre, the energy of what we say will tend to reflect our tendency towards fight or flight and may not align with our intentions. In these cases, it's the energetic message that lands. Our advocating may lean towards convincing, persuading and/or insisting, or we stay silent or speak vaguely and/or without conviction. Uncentred, an inquiry may feel stifling, persistent and/or prurient, or may be superficial, half-hearted and/or feigned. We'll explore these off-centre experiences in Chapter 31.

For now, we'll clarify the steps of an embodied practice for centred speaking, which is also shown at Appendix G.

## Embodied Practice 6

**Centred speaking[†]**

1. Do a four-part centring practice (Appendix B)

> Become uplifted and aligned in your posture and exhale slowly, imagining the breath spiralling down through your body and into the ground, forming a root.

> Become aware of the space you occupy – pay attention back and front, left and right, below your feet and above your head. Allow the space to hold you.

> Whilst maintaining an uplifted posture, soften your forehead, jaw and shoulders – imagine that they're melting, like butter, and succumbing to gravity …

> Invite a little more ease (or your chosen quality) into your being …

2. If advocating …

> Consciously tune in to the energy of purpose and intention and a sense of triangular or wedge-shaped space that has strong sides and a clear point or leading edge …

> … and then extend this energetic space so that the point or leading edge reaches into the distance, beyond all those present, allowing the sides and back of the triangle/wedge widen proportionately to include them …

3. If inquiring …

> Consciously tune in to the energy of invitation and curiosity and a sense of circular or spherical space …

> … and then extend this energetic space evenly in all directions, back and front, left and right, above your head and below your feet, allowing it to include all those present …

## 4. Speaking

Maintaining your alignment within your extended energetic space, connect to what matters, and say your words into the shared space, rather than delivering them to (or at) a person …

*Advocacy:* offer your point of view, position or opinion, with clarity and without attachment; or

*Inquiry:* seek to discover what you don't yet know or understand, with curiosity and without attachment.

## 5. Preparing to listen

After you've spoken, do the centred listening practice (Appendix E), bringing to mind a circular space in preparation for receiving what others say and letting their words land in the shared space.

*† Based on the work of Wendy Palmer.*

If you want to try out this practice in a real situation, a conversation that seems to be 'on repeat' might offer a baseline from which to assess the impact of it. A familiar, recurring conversation also offers the possibility of doing some preparation ahead of time, and clarifying the point you want to make or the question you want to pose. You can use the archetypal centres of energy outlined in the head-heart-core practice (Chapters 12 and 20) to do this, asking:

- head – what's the point I want to make, or the question I want to pose?

- heart – when I speak, how do I want others to feel and how do I want to feel?

- core/gut – what's the bigger picture here?

It's best not to have a 'set' thing that you want to say – just a sense of what matters. The head-heart-core practice can help you prepare for this. Then, you can use the centred speaking practice to become a little taller and a little more present, fully inhabiting your personal space and connecting to your leadership spirit. And then ... see what happens.

A second way to explore centred speaking is to work with a trusted friend or colleague as a practice partner. In Chapter 11, we used this approach to explore how we can use the centred listening or 'letting land' practice to *receive* unwelcome news (Appendix F). Now we can look at the inverse: using the centring speaking practice to *give* unwelcome news. This practice is also shown at Appendix H.

## ⬚ Embodied Practice 7

### *Giving unwelcome news to a practice partner*[†]

Ask your practice partner to describe something that would represent unwelcome news for them (invite them to choose a 2/10 difficulty, such as a disappointing response to a presentation or request for resources, not a personal criticism or a major life event). Ask them to observe how your words feel when you offer them from an uncentred state and from a centred state.

> 1. First, notice that the news you're about to give is unwelcome to your partner – how does this affect you? Perhaps you're aware of some physical tightening or shrinking or a sense of wariness, discomfort or dread ...

> 2. Then, give the unwelcome news to your partner without making any effort to centre or to collect yourself.

> 3. Pause ... and do the four-part centring practice (Appendix B), aligning and uplifting, exhaling and consciously shaping your personal space and energy for advocacy: triangular or wedge-shaped.

4. Expand this triangular/wedge-shaped personal space so that the point or leading edge extends beyond your partner, widening the sides and back proportionately. Your partner is now included in the 'big triangle' of your personal space, and within your advocating energy.

5. Focusing on the point or leading edge of your big triangle and the shared energetic space the triangle defines, say the same unwelcome words again.

6. Debrief with your partner – compare how the unwelcome news landed in steps 2 and 5. What insights arise?

7. Now change roles and repeat …

† *Based on the work of Wendy Palmer.*

To bring both this chapter and 'we are the method' (Tenet 1) to a close, let's step back for a wider perspective. The principle of stewarding ourselves is a high ideal – and I often fall short of it in my own conversations. Thankfully, we don't need to embrace this ideal all the time (even if that were possible). Initially, we simply aim to become more aware of the way we carry ourselves, our internal dialogue and our conversational habits.

As we've explored this first tenet, we've encountered frameworks such as the left-hand column (Chapter 17), intent–impact (Chapter 18) and the four dialogue practices (Chapter 20). We can use these approaches to begin to gather data on our experience in our conversations. With some awareness and honesty, we'll be able to assess our practice and notice the impact we have. This offers a baseline from which to begin to change our practice: we can try a new approach in a range of routine situations and see what happens. And then, with practise, we may be able to use it when it matters.

The alternative to changing our practice is that our current habits persist and, in doing the same thing, we get the same outcome. As we understand our part in what's playing out in our conversations, we always have at least one good option in problematic situations: don't make it worse. One of my clients, known for his razor-sharp critiquing of any proposal, summarised this: 'I don't know how to apply the practices, but I do know that it's wise not to persist and risk making things worse.'

As my client examined the impact of his quick-witted assessment of what others said, he understood that pointing out potential pitfalls didn't achieve his aim of improving the quality of decisions. With this insight, he realised that it was sometimes better to stay quiet. In essence, 'doing nothing' is a version of doing something different and, if we change how we engage with others, they usually change in response. When my client's colleagues could no longer rely on him to shoot things down in flames, they had to think a little harder and put forward their own objections, if they had them.

As we pay more attention to intent and impact, we become more aware of the part we play when things don't go well. Another client noticed that, whenever she lost her rag and berated her team members, she then spent a couple of days beating herself up. She didn't want to be this 'shouty' person and was also keen to sidestep the ensuing period of self-reproach. With this motivation, we worked on building a centring practice and developing alternative strategies for expressing herself. Alongside this, she found an effective way to remind herself of her intention to change. She came up with a short phrase, or mantra, to repeat as she felt the red mist approaching: 'regret follows a blow-up'. To avoid the former, she needed to avoid the latter ... and, when she succeeded, she felt better about herself. Over time, this small change in practice became a virtuous circle, to her benefit and that of her team.

## Over to you ...

As you reflect on the relationship between the way you carry yourself and how your conversations unfold, can you identify a recurring habit that limits or derails your exchanges? Describe this pattern and give it a name. When it occurs, how do you feel afterwards?

Going forward, how might you 'pause' when you next notice the habitual pattern arising? How might this change what happens next?

It's time to shift our attention from individual to collective energy and to explore the second tenet: consciously holding a container.

## Chapter 22

Consciously holding a
container: introduction

**Three tenets**
Consciously holding a container

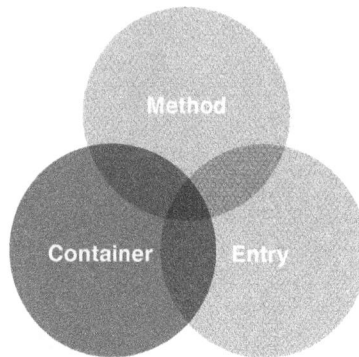

*The premise I work with is 'no container, no dialogue'. More precisely,
no consciously held container, no dialogue.*

– William Isaacs, *Dialogue and the Art of Thinking Together*,[2] page 244

One of the most common approaches to a conversation is just to turn up and see
how it goes. We might spend a little time thinking about what we want from a
conversation but often don't give as much thought to the setting and conditions that
might bring about this result. We might think that we don't have time to consider
such things. However, in the chapters that follow, I hope to inspire you to invest time
in fostering a fruitful environment for your important conversations. My premise is
that doing this up front will save time and energy later. If we don't set things up well,
we're likely to be fielding unintended consequences for some time to come.

In this chapter, we'll explore the relationship between the holding space for a conversation and what's possible within it. The conditions within which a conversation takes place are now commonly referred to as a container. For dialogue, Isaacs describes a 'container' as a setting in which deep and transformative listening becomes possible. It's a holding space capable of accommodating disparate views and energies in a way that supports shared understanding – and it's consciously formed and held. Simply, to create conditions in which the energies of difference can be transformed, we attend to the 'how' of our conversation alongside the 'what'.

## The nature of containers

My starting point for exploring the nature of containers is a belief that every conversation has one, whether or not we pay attention to it. When ignored, a container still shapes the way a conversation unfolds, just as the layout of a room may go unremarked and yet subtly enable or limit collaboration. To 'consciously hold' a container that supports dialogue, we actively seek to influence the quality of our conversational environment. We attend to tangible aspects of this, such as venue, how and when people arrive, and thoughtful set-up and beginning. We invite participation in ways that encourage listening, respecting, openness and curiosity. We use physical and relational factors to shape the quality of conversational energy, creating a space that holds us so that we're able to talk freely and to truly listen to others and to our inner experience.

We can think of this holding space, this container, as being similar to the useful 'emptiness' that's characteristic of a bowl. A bowl is often defined by a tangible substance such as clay, glass, willow or wood – but its value as a utensil lies in the space in the middle. This analogy illuminates a paradox – with a bowl, we can see and touch the material from which it's made, but it's the 'non-material' within that we actually use to hold liquid, food or other items. If we relate this to the container for a conversation, what are the parallels? What tangible elements might constitute 'material' that we can shape into a suitable 'empty space' within which to talk and listen?

Another attribute of a physical container is that the material from which it's made determines what it can hold: a flimsy plastic tray distorts when filled with hot contents; a bowl woven from willow won't hold liquid; a glass dish may shatter when filled with boiling water or ice. In a similar fashion, the nature of a container for a conversation determines the intensity, turbulence and discomfort that can be (safely) handled by those present. A routine conversation may be satisfactorily held by social customs, a formal agenda and a chairperson, whilst a 'higher, deeper, wider' conversation (as one client describes dialogue) calls for something more complex.

In essence, there's a connection between the *outcome* of a conversation and the *climate* within which it's held. By 'outcome' I mean not just the immediate 'upshot', but the impact on relationships and the wider system. Climate is harder to articulate. It's a mash-up of energetic feel, quality of engagement, levels of safety, rhythm and tone of voice, perceptions of power, freedom to speak … very little of it is concrete, and yet it's palpable. It's the energetic quality of the space – an embodied experience that unfolds in us and through us. We are the method.

In *Pause for Breath*, I expressed a slight reservation about the term 'container', which seems to imply a solid object, something that's created and is then relatively unchanging. This reflects the everyday use of the word for items such as a box, basket or cup – once made, this kind of container is (usually) fixed in size and shape, at least for a period of time.

In contrast, a container for conversation is made and re-made many times, and changes in feel, shape, texture and size as people talk together. A container forms, often out of awareness, from an elusive alchemy of people, the relationships between them, their interactions and the context within which they're meeting. These elements are enmeshed and, when any single aspect changes, the whole flexes and adapts. In response to what's unfolding within it, a container expands or contracts, or becomes stronger or weaker, and to hold it consciously means paying attention to these changes. My work in the field of dialogue has been shaped by a belief that the essence of consciously holding a container is to be aware, collectively, of the making and re-making of it.

Ultimately, I think of a container for conversation as a living thing: it evolves as we talk together. It's dynamic, being continually formed and re-formed by, and through, the conversation that it holds. It's as if we grow a collective 'skin' that's sufficiently safe and permeable to hold us, our differences and our talk, and evolves as our conversation evolves.

A container often forms naturally and out of awareness, as people connect and build relationships. And, sometimes, the process needs a little more attention, a little more conscious nurturing. This may be especially true in organisational settings, where the majority of conversations are pragmatic and purposeful. Then, when a complex scenario requires exploratory and nuanced consideration, it can be difficult to set aside habitual ways of engaging. This is why 'consciously holding' a container is so important: if we don't actively attend to our container, familiar patterns of engagement quickly re-emerge. In Chapter 12, we called such established patterns a conversational operating system.

Overall, we begin to recognise that shaping the setting for an important conversation is a creative undertaking, an art. Rather than regarding the setting as something that pre-exists, something that we simply walk into and make use of – or don't take into account at all – we actively think about it and seek to influence it.

In the remainder of this chapter, I'll briefly outline my personal journey with containers. It took me some time – and two major setbacks – to grasp the importance of them. In sharing my experiences with you, I hope that you'll realise their significance more quickly than I did. First, let's pause and reflect.

## Over to you …

Think of a conversation that reached beyond what you imagined was possible – perhaps everyone left inspired to take action; or some anticipated resistance either didn't materialise or melted away.

Reflect on what might have made this outcome possible. How were practical details handled, such as setting, timing and so on? What was the make-up of the group? How did the conversation start and how did people engage? How did the energy of the conversation evolve? What most surprised you?

How might these reflections inspire you to approach your next important conversation differently?

## My journey with containers

In my case, the importance of the quality of the 'holding space' for a conversation dawned slowly. In my earliest dialogue-related work, I worked alongside another independent practitioner with a very different style. We sought to use our differences in a way that *modelled* how they might be creative, although we weren't always successful in this.

In this partnership, I tended to outline dialogue frameworks such as Kantor's Four Players, Scharmer's Four Fields of Conversation and intent–impact while my colleague introduced practices such as check-in and paying attention to the conditions for conversation (the container). We used interventions such as a 'fishbowl' to support conversations between different constituencies within an organisation, as described in Chapter 11.

In one assignment, we shared some of the principles of dialogue with a senior team and then joined them in their regular meetings to support them to use the approaches in real time. This work helped the team recognise that their meetings tended to take the form of a 'serial monologue' in which each manager spoke only to their own agenda. There was a sense that they weren't really listening to each other or engaging with the collective potential. Some team members admitted that their approach to the meeting was to 'get out without an action against my name'. When the team reached 'agreement' on an issue, there was often no follow-through. And, whenever there was a sense that a deeper conversation might occur, there'd be a 'stutter' and those present would 'back off'. Moving beyond these habitual 'routines' proved challenging.

Working with this team opened my eyes to the influence of established patterns in regular meetings. Whilst the team's conversational operating system was deeply embedded, reflecting the patterns of the wider organisation, my colleague and I did have some small successes. We observed that team conversations often stalled and were inconclusive, and we likened this circling of different views to planes in the 'stack' above an airport – with no one being willing to actually 'land' an opinion with candour. This shorthand description offered team members a way to bystand (or neutrally name) this pattern when it occurred. The team then had a choice – do we address this, or let it stall the conversation? Once a pattern is brought into awareness, it's harder to let it run – and yet, the team often allowed this to happen. The alternative proved to be even more challenging for them.

As my awareness of containers developed, there were some hiccups along the way. In a particularly clunky incident, I was introducing embodied practices to a group and was too prescriptive, caught up in a 'right way' of doing things. I was also under time pressure. In my hurry and inflexibility, I didn't listen carefully enough to someone who was uncomfortable with what I was asking participants to do. In not respecting her concerns, I inadvertently put her on the 'naughty step'. As I did so, I viscerally felt the collective container shrink, which limited what was possible for the group.

There were also 'light bulb' moments. In the check-in for one workshop, I saw how a single contribution could change the climate. Initially, the check-in followed rather familiar lines: individual updates and quite general ideas about what each person might want from the session. Then, about halfway through, someone spoke personally and authentically. I can't remember what she said – only that her heartfelt honesty made me sit up and pay attention. Suddenly, the possibility of a different kind of conversation became tangible, and others followed this spirit. Witnessing this, I began to think more carefully about the relationship between check-in and the container.

As I learned from my experiences, I was gaining confidence as a practitioner. Then I had two major setbacks that stopped me in my tracks. In each, I misjudged the balance between stretching my practice and being clear about my limitations. These episodes prompted me to regroup and to become more conscious of the nature of a container for a workshop or conversation.

In the first situation, my colleague and I were hosting a three-day residential workshop in which we were aiming to create something deeply experiential and provocative. We got into difficulties – one participant left abruptly and another was quite disturbed by one of the sessions. Afterwards, with the help of another seasoned practitioner, we debriefed our experience as hosts. While I used different language at the time, my sense of the root cause of what happened was a flaw in our hosting container. Our working alliance wasn't resilient enough to hold our own 'stuff' … and so the wider container couldn't possibly hold what was present in the group. It was a painful and illuminating experience.

227

In the second situation, I was working solo with a small executive team. I can't be sure of the details now, but it's likely that I'd been engaged to deliver a few workshops to support the team to use the practices of dialogue to enrich their leadership conversations. In the first workshop, and very suddenly (or so it felt to me), an exchange between two of the directors became heated and rancorous. It quickly became obvious that their mutual animosity went back years, but had been unexpressed – until now. While we'd paid some attention to creating a container, it wasn't able to hold the energy that erupted. And, as a practitioner, I wasn't experienced enough to support the team to navigate the flare-up in a productive way. Unsurprisingly, the team decided to cancel the remaining workshops.

Chastened by these incidents, particularly the second one, I took a break from working in the complex currents and tides that are often present within teams and organisations. I did a lot of reflection on what had happened, both independently and in coaching supervision. I did more reading and began writing *Pause for Breath*, which helped me to articulate my ideas and my practice more clearly. Through these processes, I realised that I hadn't properly grasped the principle of 'no consciously held container, no dialogue'.

## Over to you …

Take a moment to reflect on my experiences with the strength of existing patterns of conversation and the challenge of creating a container in which to change them. Do any of my examples resonate with you and, perhaps, offer insight into something you've experienced?

What might you learn from my mishaps, and how might this help you in your own development?

Following the two major setbacks that I've described, I decided to focus on working with small groups of unrelated leaders, supporting them to change their practice in their leadership conversations. In these programmes, I brought together dialogue practices and key elements of the Leadership Embodiment approach. In addition, I attended carefully to creating the conditions for both learning and being in dialogue.

My aspiration for each group was that, as the programme progressed, our conversation would evolve and we'd find ourselves in dialogue. This meant putting the conscious establishment and evolution of our container at the centre of the programme. To support this, I aimed to transition from bearing the majority of the responsibility for the container in the early sessions to being a part of collectively holding the container in the later ones.

Over the years, I hosted many of these programmes. While each was different, reflecting the composition of the participant group, they gradually came to have a similar overall structure of six one-day workshops spread over six to nine months. The first three workshops focused on setting things up, outlining key dialogue frameworks and introducing LE practices. They followed a broad structure of handling self in conversations, navigating exchanges with others, and raising awareness of the influence of collective energy in a conversation.

The second three workshops focused on case-work, with each participant contributing one case in the form of a left-hand column (Chapter 17). This allowed us to apply the frameworks and embodied practices to real situations. The cases tended to focus on occasions where something had gone awry, and we explored the case-bringer's role in this. By this stage, our container had to be able to hold the self-consciousness of a senior leader disclosing their fallibility. When we were collectively able to create the conditions for this, it was immensely valuable: each case was 'personal', and yet often archetypal, so we were exploring themes and patterns that everyone could learn from.

Within this overall approach, each programme was shaped by those who participated – their tendencies, style and predispositions – and the container we co-created. We attended to our container from the start. In the first workshop, we shared our thoughts about the conditions that enable a conversation to go well. We captured these qualities on Post-it notes arranged around the four dialogue practices (Chapter 20). In this way, we captured the 'idea' of the container we aspired to.

Then, in each subsequent workshop, we invested precious time in considering how we'd bring our container to life: how would we *inhabit* the conditions we'd identified? By paying deliberate attention to this early in each session, we brought the quality of the space we intended to hold into our awareness. This made it more likely that we'd heed our aspirations and realise them.

Initially, participants often found this 'repetition' frustrating. However, when their good intentions went by the wayside during a session, they began to appreciate the aspirational nature of the container that we'd described. Until we put them into practice, the words on the Post-it notes were just words. In revisiting them each time we met, and developing our understanding of what it might mean to embody them, our container grew in substance, becoming more tangible. We gradually grew into our words and inhabited them. Our conversations changed – together, we became the method.

Through repeatedly bringing our container into consciousness, I believe we were more quickly able to cultivate the honesty, openness and curiosity that underpin meaningful case-work. Our conversations naturally expanded to be frank, reflective, supportive and illuminating. We also laughed together, bringing a lightness to our explorations. We began to put into practice what we were learning and the groups became laboratories for dialogue. And, as a practitioner, my understanding of the nature of containers grew. Consciously holding the container, collectively, had become central to my work.

In outlining some of the experiences that led me to understand that every conversation has a container, whether acknowledged or not, I hope I've inspired you to pay attention to this facet of conversational practice. In the next chapter, we'll develop this theme by revisiting the four fields of conversation (Chapter 14) and using it as a starting point for describing different containers.

# Chapter 23 Consciously holding a container: the four fields revisited

As a starting point for consciously holding a container, we can consider whether an existing container is able to hold all the ideas, interests, differences and preferences that we want to air and explore. If it isn't, there's work to be done. Scharmer's Four Fields of Conversation framework offers a template that can help us describe and understand the shape and quality of different conversational spaces.

We met the fields of conversation in Chapter 14, when we explored the axes of the framework and the nature of each field 'at its best'. In this chapter, we'll look at the quality of energy in each field. To prepare the ground, let's briefly recap the framework, so that you don't need to leaf back through the pages. The diagram showing the fields at their best is reproduced overleaf.

The four fields are delineated by two axes, one that distinguishes between mindful and habitual engagement, and one that differentiates between speaking in a way that fits in with group expectations and expressing our individuality. Each field naturally supports a particular kind of conversation, with associated customs and practices that are often unspoken and unquestioned. When the conditions for a conversation are implicit rather than explicit, they're not 'consciously held'. This means that we're leaving the climate for a conversation somewhat to chance. Sometimes this doesn't matter. But when we find out that it *does* matter, it's usually too late. We can use the fields to explore the potentials and limitations of four different kinds of conversation. This can support us to create appropriate conditions for the conversation we want to have.

# Fields of conversation

Spaces

**Engaging mindfully**

**IV Dialogue**

At its best:
participative,
connective,
systemic

**Engaging**

**III Exploration**

At its best:
curious,
reflective,
reciprocal

**Collective voice (belonging) is primary**

◀ Voice

Voice ▶

**Individual voice (differentiating) is primary**

**I Routines**

At its best:
contained, courteous,
collective
endeavour

**Engaging**

**II Breaking open**

At its best:
respectfully
robust,
candid, creative

**Engaging habitually**

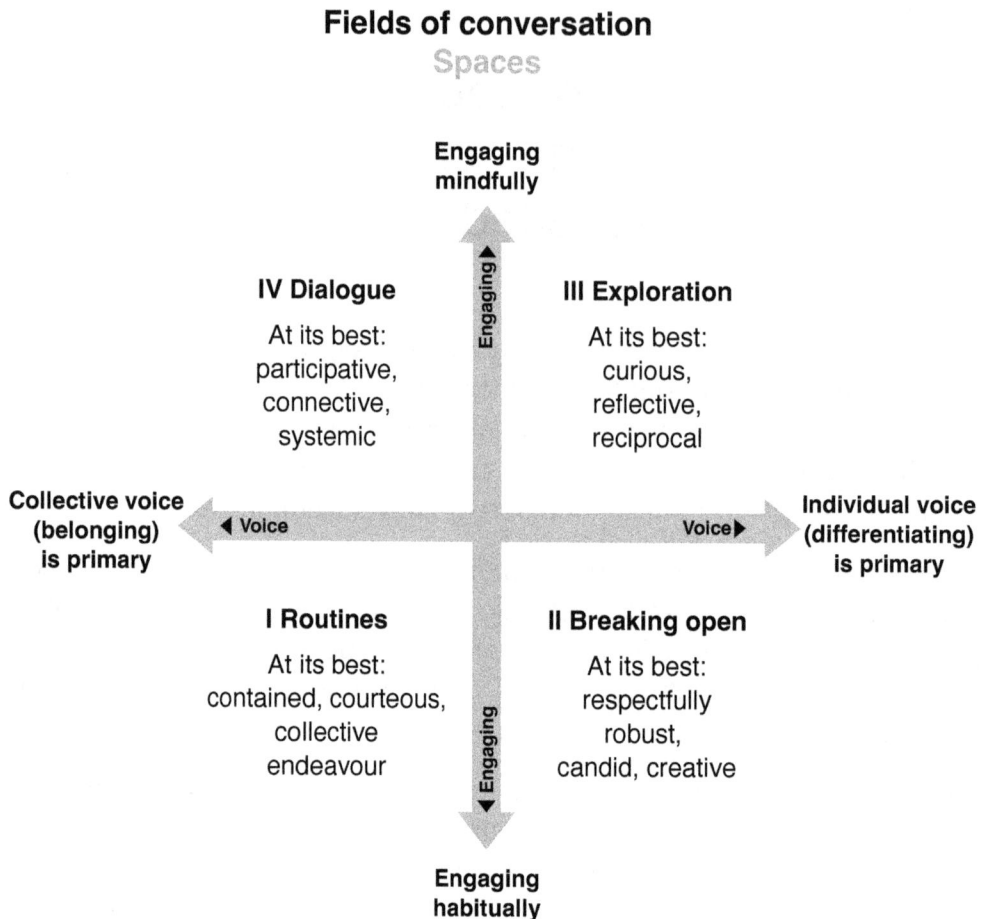

Drawing on the work of Otto Scharmer

The essence of Field I is that, at its best, it's a fruitful space for everyday business, offering a familiar space that supports efficiency and cordiality, and can be supported by conventions such as a chairperson and an agenda. If we loosen these conventions, we allow greater freedom in the conversation, which encourages diversity of view and increased frankness. Differences may then become apparent.

When they do, we're in the realm of Field II which, at its best, is a robust yet respectful exchange of views (debate) that can help us thoroughly consider the benefits and drawbacks of different options. However, the presence of difference puts people 'on alert' – their survival pattern is activated. This state of alert may be exacerbated by the uncertainty inherent in a shift away from known routines: people are more watchful, cautious and reactive. If we don't attend to this mood, a conversation may contract into the safety of familiar routines, or flare up into conflict.

If the differences expressed in Field II can be acknowledged and held in parity, those present may become interested in them and be willing to explore how they've come about. With this orientation, there's less insistence on our own view and more curiosity about the views of others. This is the terrain of Field III. At its best, this field is a holding space in which differences can be mulled over and probed in a constructive way, creating the possibility of fresh insights and changes of heart. However, without care, a conversation in Field III can drift into a new form of Field I, shaped by tacit assumptions of what's appropriate to the setting and situation. Alternatively, the habitual behaviours of Field II can be reactivated, dissolving curiosity and prompting a return to debate. Field III can also give rise to generative dialogue (Field IV) – of which more later.

For now, let's turn our attention to the energetic feel of each field and then, in Chapter 24, we'll explore what this means for the energies of difference.

## The four fields – energies

When we understand the nature of the energies at play in each field, we gain insight into the way individual and collective actions either hold them in place or reduce their influence. The diagram overleaf indicates whether the energy of a field tends to be settled or unsettled, allowing us to explore how this might affect our efforts to establish and hold a container in which the energy of our differences can be creatively channelled.

## Fields of conversation
### Energies

**Engaging
mindfully**

**IV Dialogue**     **III Exploration**

Energy is ...

Energy
settles

**Collective voice
(belonging)
is primary**  ◄ Voice    Voice ►  **Individual voice
(differentiating)
is primary**

**I Routines**     **II Breaking open**

Energy is
settled

Energy is
unsettled

Engaging

**Engaging
habitually**

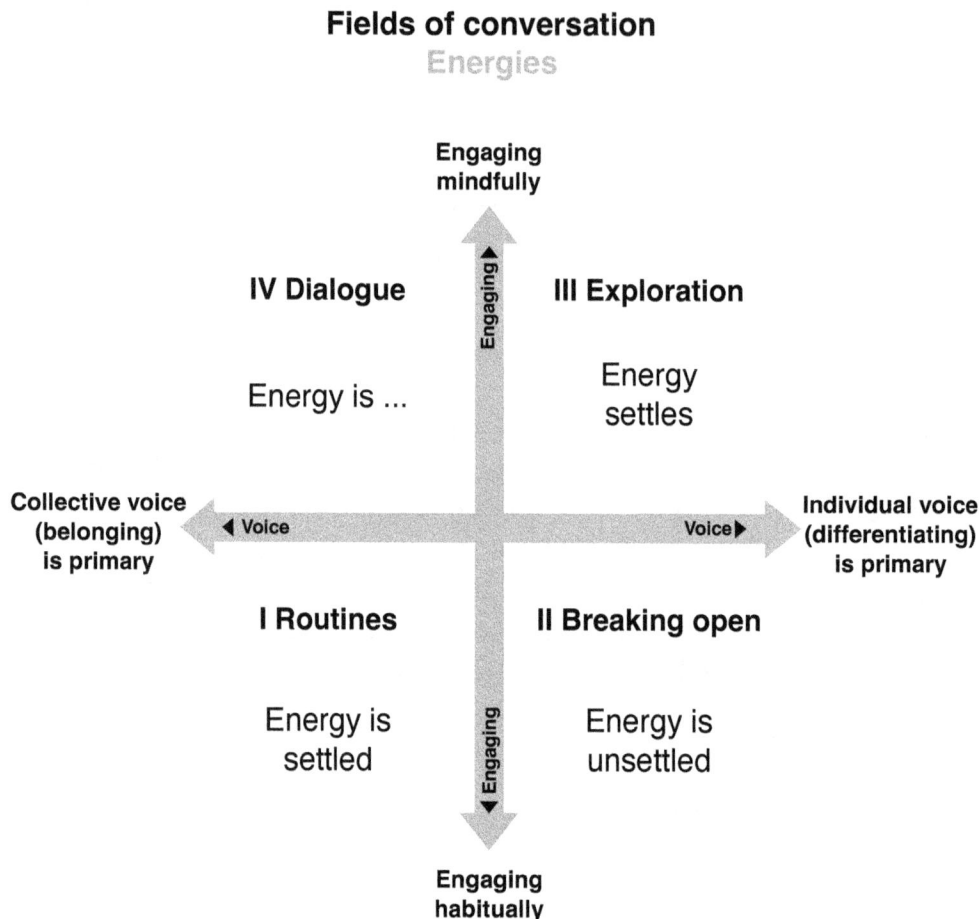

Drawing on the work of Otto Scharmer

## *The energy of Field I*

In Field I, Routines, energy is quite settled because it's bounded by the adhesive quality and tone of collective voice (a tacit agreement about what it's OK to say) and habitual ways of engaging with each other. In fact, it has a kind of homeostatic inertia – if the group (or any individual within it) tries to stimulate a different kind of conversation, the shared patterning that's been established and sustained over time stealthily reasserts itself. The container for Field I isn't usually consciously established or held, and it only becomes evident when proceedings feel constrained rather than contained.

You may have had this experience. It can show up when a group that meets regularly for a particular purpose (such as governance or project management) decides to have a session to think creatively and strategically about the future. Despite genuine commitment amongst those present to talk candidly and imaginatively about possibilities, there's a greater force at play: the Field I conversational operating system of their regular meetings. This collective patterning, which quite literally has a life of its own, draws the group back into their usual routine. The conversational OS doesn't allow the new 'app' to run – it supports the group's original purpose but limits their efforts to engage with a different purpose in a different way.

The settled energy of Field I is valuable for everyday business and interactions – provided there's reasonable coherence in the thinking of those present. However, unspoken assumptions about being 'on the same page' can cause frustration in those who wish to express a different view. Left unattended, this frustration can grow – and may eventually be expressed as non-compliance or subversive disruption 'outside the room', or as an outburst within the room.

## Over to you …

What does this description of Field I energy bring to mind?

Can you find an example of a regular meeting that has a familiar, settled energy? How might you describe this energy? What does it support and what does it constrain?

What tends to happen when those involved in this regular meeting try to have a different kind of conversation?

The threshold between Field I and Field II is often marked by a swift change in energy, such as a flare-up kindled by overt disagreement or a withdrawal, as if the air has been sucked from the room. Whether expressed or suppressed, the underlying cause is frustration.

### The energy of Field II

In Field II, Breaking open, we remain in the terrain of habitual engagement but now individual voices have greater weight. The presence of differentiated voices unsettles the settled energy of an established routine. This generates discomfort – especially if what's being expressed challenges the norms of Field I. In this disturbance, individuals may feel exposed, at risk and/or mildly threatened. In unfamiliar territory, those present succumb to survival behaviours that have served them in the past – their autonomic nervous system is activated and physiology is in charge. This reactivity shows up in the form of raised voices, pointed comments, implacable resistance, tense silences, flippancy and/or taking cover until the storm has passed. No one quite knows what to do and so, according to their habitual tendencies, they fall into joining the fray, trying to smooth things over or riding out the turbulence. None of these actions support the inclusion of diverse views.

The collective energy of Field II arises from the energy of individual survival patterns, which are likely to include fervour, disengagement, apology, hesitancy, insistence, frustration and/or defensiveness. An absence of listening and/or acknowledgement means that these energies, whether they're expressed or suppressed, tend to intensify. We can appreciate how this comes about if we wonder why someone vehemently repeats their view (whether for or against a proposal): it may be that they feel unheard and unrecognised. Similarly, when someone remains silent, it may be because they notice that others are being discounted or ignored, and feel it's not worth speaking out. Listening to, and acknowledging, different perspectives is key to navigating the energies of Field II.

It's the nature of the energy in Field II that invites us to make a deliberate effort to create and hold an appropriate space for our differences. If we don't consciously do this, the container for Field I will be in place if/when things kick off. This container has to expand and/or strengthen if it's to hold the unsettled energies of Field II. If it doesn't, the conversation tends to contract to fit the container, or to explode, often with collateral damage.

I can offer two examples of the way that Field II energy can shape an experience. In the first, I was a participant on a development programme and, on the first day, we agreed a form of container for the work we'd be doing together. In a later module, one of the course leaders intentionally wrong-footed the group and, as participants, we challenged this. We requested time to debrief what had happened, in accordance with the agreed container. The request wasn't supported – it seemed that the container was simply a form of words, not an embodied reality. On a personal level, I was angry and I repeated the request for a debrief. When this was denied, I lost confidence in the container and expressed my individual voice by leaving the programme.

In the second example, one member of a senior team was known for pointing out the potential problems in any proposed change. Let's call him Joe. In the collective routine, the response to Joe's input was that everyone rolled their eyes and discounted what he said. The pattern became so ingrained that Joe often didn't raise his concerns – and so the conversation contracted to fit the container. However, when Joe did speak up, it was because something really mattered, usually the wellbeing of staff. To function well, the team had to recognise this pattern and find ways to hear the point being made. They had to change the collective routine – and they did.

The way we navigate the turbulence of Field II is key to creating conditions in which differences can be heard, acknowledged and held. On an individual basis, this means being able to handle ourselves with grace when the chips are down, which is where embodied practices come in. When we access a centred state, we change our relationship to our experience. If we have an emotional reaction to someone's view, centring creates spaciousness around this experience, giving us some detachment from it. This allows us to bystand our feelings so that we can describe them without being immersed in them. For example, I can say that I feel quite angry about something, without enacting the anger and being limited by it. In doing this, I also refrain from inflicting the anger on those who don't deserve it.

In addition, when we embody a composed and open presence, we're more able to discern the essence of what's being said, even if it's being expressed unskilfully. We embody the practices of listening, respecting and suspending judgement. In these conditions, those speaking are more likely to feel heard and understood. Generally, when we experience acceptance, we stop repeating our preoccupations. Such conditions also support us to risk speaking up or speaking out about something that we find difficult to say, or that others might find difficult to hear. In this way, and through using embodied practices to settle our own energy, it becomes more possible to hear diverse, and potentially provocative, views and to hold them in parity. If one person does this it can make a difference. If several people do it, it changes the field.

There's more! Our centred energy affects those around us, as a positive or moderating influence – and may even support them to pause and think more deeply about what they're hearing. The way we carry ourselves individually affects collective energy and so is central to shaping the container and building capacity to handle differences skilfully.

So ... Field II is the field in which the time spent consciously establishing and holding a container reaps rewards. It's the field where the energy can be transformed by listening to what each person has to say and recognising that they're expressing something that matters to them, even if it isn't universally welcomed. When people are gathered in a room, we can often feel collective energy beginning to settle. In virtual settings, this shift in energy may be more difficult to discern, but I believe the principle still applies. We'll explore some aspects of virtual containers in Chapter 25.

Over to you ...

What does this description of Field II energy bring to mind?

Can you find an example of a conversation that erupted into unsettled energy, disturbing those present? What prompted this change? What was the impact?

What happened next? Did the conversation blaze into a stand-off? Was it shepherded back into safer terrain? To what extent were those present able to remain constructively engaged with, and hold, what was unfolding?

What was your part in what played out?

As with the threshold between Fields I and II, the threshold between Field II and Field III is often marked by a palpable change in energy. In this case, it's a settling, similar to the way a river quietens and slows when it widens after some rapids – it's still flowing and vibrant but in a less lively way. I attribute this change in energy to what I call an 'amnesty of opinions' – a sense of relief and ease that arises when those present let go of the views they're attached to and insistent about. Collectively, those present now embody the quality of 'suspending judgement' and the air is alive with possibility. As we discovered in the embodied activity wall–window (Chapter 10), judgements don't dissolve, but we're aware of them and park them for a while. This frees up space to consider other options.

### The energy of Field III

In Field III, Exploration, individual voices remain to the fore, but with greater awareness, individually and collectively. We're in the first of two spaces characterised by mindful engagement. The energy settles as those present become more attentive, more considered, more curious, more reflective. It feels like there's room for manoeuvre and capacity to take in new information. There's even the possibility that a mind might change. The settled energy isn't always comfortable. It can be intense and/or vibrant, a sense of being in a struggle with ourselves and with others. We're in relationship with each other and with creative potential. For me, this brings a flutter of anticipation and barely suppressed excitement, which is a different 'vibe' to the sense of earnest seriousness that might be evoked by the phrase 'mindful engagement'. Perhaps Field III blends gravitas and animation, a paradoxical quickening and slowing that's both fertile and fruitful.

Whilst Field III sometimes occurs spontaneously as the relationships within a group evolve, its collective energy is strengthened by conscious attention. However, even when we've articulated an intention to create and hold a container for dialogue, we're unlikely to travel directly from the settled energy of the routines of Field I to the (different) settled energy of Field III.

To access Field III, we can expect to navigate the minefields of Field II. If we try to avoid this gritty energy, our container is likely to be flimsy: even if we've consciously expressed the conditions we wish to foster, they're unlikely to become an embodied reality. Old habits die hard, and it takes time to grow into a shared intention to hold and inhabit a Field III container. On the upside, collectively weathering the tricky ground of Field II is likely to generate respect, connection and confidence. This represents a change in the way the container is being held and, if we make this change conscious, a Field III conversation becomes more possible.

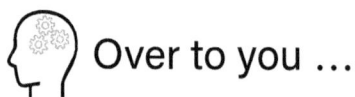

## Over to you …

What does this description of Field III energy bring to mind?

Can you find an example of a conversation that, after a gritty phase, seemed to settle into an engaged, productive exploration? What prompted the settling? How might you describe the settled energy? What did it make possible?

As you reflect on this, and on your experiences of Field I and Field II energy, what changes might you make in your practice?

As Field III strengthens, deepens and/or expands, a sense of coherence may arise, signalling the threshold between Fields III and IV. In the associated shift in energy, self-interest – and perhaps even any sense of self – dissolves. In Field IV, we become the container and the conversation truly becomes an entity in its own right: when someone speaks, they give expression to its voice. This is different to the 'collective voice' which constrained Field I – it's liberating, unconventional, authentic, naked. It's an expression of something universal, articulated by a human voice.

### The energy of Field IV

To describe the energy of Field IV almost defies words. The energy simply is as it is, defined by those present and their conversation. We *are* the energy of this space, just as we *are* the voice of the conversation. I got a glimpse of this experience whilst on an ALIA programme. ALIA stands for Authentic Leadership in Action, and it was on their European 'Leadership Intensive' in 2010 that I first met Wendy Palmer. I returned the following year, when my chosen module was based on Otto Scharmer's *Theory U*.[16] It was during this module that the experience I'm about to describe occurred - it happened during a group activity in which we were asked to solve a tangible problem.

In groups of about six people, we were given a small wooden board with a large nail tapped into the centre of it. I'm guessing now, but the board was perhaps five to six inches square and the nail was perhaps three to four inches high. We were also given ten slightly smaller nails. The task was to find a way to place *all* the smaller nails on the head of the bigger one.

As the group that I was in of sought a solution, the process that unfolded was fascinating. It was a study of the primacy of collective voice, then frustration leading to fragmentation and individual effort, and then a coming-together that gave rise to a conceptual articulation of how we could achieve our task. During the process, some people engaged verbally, some scribbled on bits of paper and some handled the materials and experimented physically. Once the outcome could be described and the smaller nails had been arranged accordingly, there was a final step: to place the collection of smaller nails on to the head of the upright larger nail. For reasons I don't remember, this delicate task fell to me. It required a steady hand ... and a steady mind. I remember doing a centring practice: uplifting, exhaling, expanding my sense of space to include my colleagues, the table, the nails ... I remember watching my hand ... and seeing the ten nails balance on the single nail.

Then the activity was over, and we were the only group who'd completed the task. In the debrief, I remember saying, 'It was as if it wasn't my hand, it was the group's hand'. I experienced the whole group as having a steady hand and a steady mind. We were as one. It simply fell to my body, my hand, to do what was required. This was a Field IV experience.

In Field IV, the energy of difference is transformed into fuel for insight, innovation and inspiration. Any personal 'edges' between different perspectives dissolve so that they all become facets of something bigger. Each facet is important, even essential. In such a conversation, genuinely fresh thinking can occur.

### Over to you …

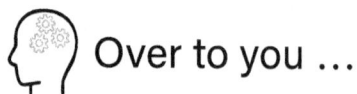

As you reflect on my description of a Field IV experience, try to connect with it viscerally – can you find a similar experience of your own? It can occur in any setting, and you may recognise it through both heightened senses and an experience that nothing is happening, that time, feeling and thinking have stopped.

Take time to capture the nature of this experience in your own words – it's your personal articulation of Field IV energy.

In this chapter, we've been exploring the nature of the energy in the four fields of conversation, gaining insight into what holds each field in place or prompts it to change. It's important to note that no field is inherently better than the others – they each serve different purposes. As we become more aware of the relationship between the conditions in which a conversation takes place and what then unfolds, we gain a sense of what we need to attend to in a particular situation.

For example, if we need to have a robust conversation about the pros and cons of alternative courses of action, a Field II conversation with some appropriate 'ground rules' may be ideal. In contrast, if we try to create the conditions for a Field III conversation when we're meeting to review the governance of a project, we won't add any value – our efforts may even cause difficulties. The key is to consciously hold a container that's fit for our purpose.

Now that we have some familiarity with the energetic containers of the fields of conversation, let's explore how difference might be handled in each of them. I'm articulating this territory for the first time – and, in this way, and even though it isn't in real time, I have a sense that we're thinking together. I hope you feel this too. Thank you for your readership, and your part in co-creating the next chapter.

# Chapter 24  Consciously holding a container: the four fields and difference

Recently, I was hosting an introductory day on the topic of 'embodying dialogue practices'. I'd designed a day in which to share some essential principles of this work, including the four-part centring practice (Appendix B) and how we can use it when things get heated. I was writing this book and my creative juices were flowing: I suddenly 'saw' a way of describing how difference is often treated in each of the four fields of conversation.

To get us started, the diagram overleaf shows the familiar outline of the fields – but with new text summarising how difference is typically handled in each field. I'm drawing primarily on personal experience to formulate this. Therefore, please treat what follows as a hypothesis – untried and untested – and put it to your own test.

My experience of Field I, Routines, is that difference is typically discouraged because it sits uneasily with the received narrative(s) present in a group. This field is delineated by collective voice and habitual engagement and, in order to fit in, we may moderate or withhold some of our more challenging thoughts and opinions. If we do express an alternative view, we'll probably do it from a place of reactivity – off-centre, we'll either over-cook it or discount it in some way. This can make what we say harder to hear, and increases the likelihood that others will react rather than respond. Even if we're able to centre and express difference in a skilful way, others may experience it as a mild threat to the settled, established way of operating, the usual routine.

This means that, collectively, a group will tend to find a way to return to a stable and familiar state of affairs, by minimising or smoothing over any differences or by simply ignoring them. The mantra of Field I might be 'don't rock the boat!'. In our context, this means 'don't rock the container' – let's keep things as they are. In this kind of environment, differences between individuals or constituencies within a group will occasionally become set-piece battles that remain unresolved. Such exchanges get assimilated into 'the way we do things', becoming part of the Field I routine.

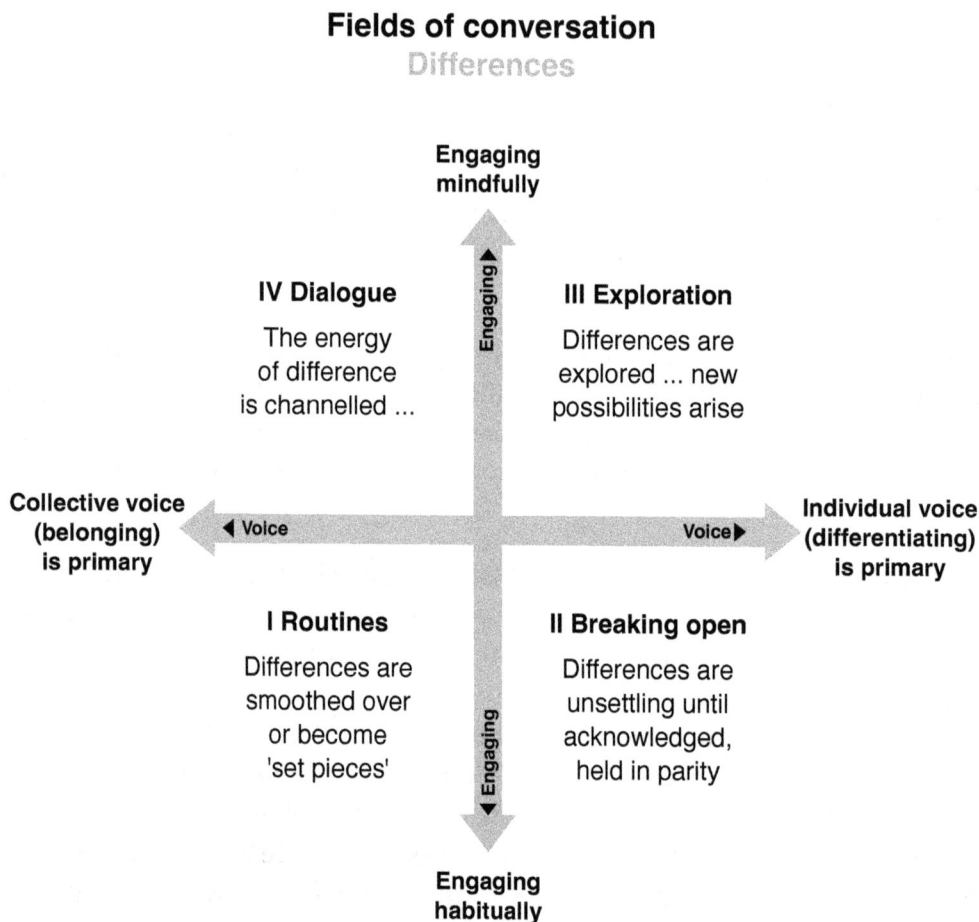

## Fields of conversation
### Differences

**Engaging
mindfully**

Engaging ▲

**IV Dialogue**

The energy
of difference
is channelled ...

**III Exploration**

Differences are
explored ... new
possibilities arise

**Collective voice
(belonging)
is primary**

◀ Voice

Voice ▶

**Individual voice
(differentiating)
is primary**

**I Routines**

Differences are
smoothed over
or become
'set pieces'

**II Breaking open**

Differences are
unsettling until
acknowledged,
held in parity

Engaging ▼

**Engaging
habitually**

Drawing on the work of Otto Scharmer

When tensions cause a conversation to erupt into Field II, Breaking open, differences become more apparent and those present may begin to take sides (either openly or covertly). This is the field bounded by individual expression and engaging habitually (and, often, reactively). On autopilot, the opinions that are expressed are often forcefully advocated, provoking divisions. Energy becomes raised and unsettled, or brooding in a way that feels ominous, like a volcano about to blow. In addition, there may be a simmering tension from opinions that are withheld. Either way, there's a sense of fragmentation, of disconnection.

The conversational boat (or container) is well and truly rocked and rocking …

When a boat is rocked, what usually happens is that some people react by moving suddenly to somewhere that seems safer. In doing so, they increase the instability of the boat. Others react by shouting instructions about how to steady the boat. Both these actions heighten the energy of the situation, which adds to the rocking motion. In conversations, these tactics show up as wading in (on one side or another) and/or attempting to smooth things over and guide everyone back to comfortable ground. In both boats and conversations, some people simply keep their head down and wait for the storm to pass.

These are crucial moments. In a boat, if someone is able to bring a calm and composed presence to proceedings, the amplitude of the rocking reduces. In a conversation, someone with a centred presence and some awareness and skill can steady the container by acknowledging different positions (or sides) and holding them in parity and balance. It can also be useful to gently remind everyone of the shared reasons for talking together. These actions begin to realise the potential of Field II.

In the context of dialogue, we want to find ways to really listen to one another, even when we're in the unsettled energy of Field II. To continue the 'rocking boat' analogy, one wise voice can softly call others to their senses, encouraging them to pause and gain perspective. This usually dissipates some of the energy of strongly held opinions and, although the 'rocking' continues, it becomes less pronounced.

Differences now become a little easier to hear. And, if they're acknowledged, individuals may feel less need to 'beat the drum' of their point of view. This is the 'amnesty of opinions' that was briefly described in Chapter 23. As we let go of our fiercely held positions, we free up internal space in which we can hear and consider the views of others.

The amnesty heralds the emergence of Field III, Exploration, which is shaped by individual voices and mindful engagement. This is the space in which consciously holding the container comes into its own as those present begin to take an interest in differences and how they arise. Although differences still have the potential to rock the conversational boat, those who've steadied themselves no longer add to the 'rocking'. The boat is balanced enough that differences can be considered and explored – they've become thought-provoking, rather than alarming. This offers the real possibility that the energies of difference can be harnessed creatively.

Personally, I believe that supporting and inhabiting a Field III conversation will be 'enough' in most circumstances. Something else may or may not unfold from it, but a conversation in this container will be markedly different from the more familiar exchanges of Field I or Field II.

Sometimes Field IV, Dialogue, will emerge from the collective energy of curiosity and possibility present in Field III. When it does, it offers fertile conditions for fresh thinking. This is generative dialogue, in which the boundaries between people and views dissolve. The space is delineated by collective voice and mindful engagement. Do you recall the Field IV experience described in Chapter 23? In it, those present accessed a state of collective grace or presence. When this occurs, the words spoken express the voice of the conversation itself. The energy of difference becomes a kind of creative tension amongst partial aspects of a bigger whole. From this, new insights can arise.

In the boat analogy, those in a Field IV experience become the boat itself, they become the container. However, the energy of this field is a temporary state. Eventually, individual and collective capacity for remaining mindful will falter. Then the boat can once again be rocked, and the conversation may return to Field I or II. However, with awareness it's also possible to regroup when the Field IV container is rocked, and to move through the fields of conversation once more.

## Over to you …

As you read these descriptions of the energies of difference in the four fields, what comes to mind? What resonates? What is it more difficult to give credence to? Can you find personal examples that reflect the experiences outlined?

Reflecting on this chapter and the preceding one, how might you approach the next conversation in which significant differences are likely to be present?

Often, we have no role in shaping a container for a conversation and so we have to find ways to act skilfully in conditions established by others (whether consciously or not). We can use the embodied practices set out in these pages to support this. In addition, by drawing on what we observe and experience in the realms of public discourse, we can better understand how we're affected by difference when we have little or no scope to influence the shape and quality of a conversation.

It can also be helpful to understand the look and feel of societal conversations because no container, even one that's consciously established and held, stands alone. Every container sits within another container, and each has its own conversational patterns or operating system, most of which are beyond our influence. Let's explore public discourse using the fields of conversation.

## Into the ether

Any conversation will ultimately be located in a wider societal container and, without care and conscious holding, will be influenced by it. The currents and tides of this broader context can show up starkly in public discourse, especially in exchanges on social media. We can use the fields to describe some of these patterns and gain insight into how they play out. We touched on this theme in Chapter 14

– let's develop it further by focusing on the relationship between individual and collective voices in the context of difference.

We start with Field I, bounded by habitual engagement and an emphasis on collective voice. To explore what this field might reveal in the context of societal conversations, we can think about 'constituencies' that link people. Most of us have connections with, and/or belong to, different groups, interests and causes. Each constituency is likely to have its own conversational patterns and routines, its own Field I container. We might identify as part of a family, friendship group, political party, profession, sports team or cohort of enthusiasts of a particular activity or pursuit. We might also feel connected to a group based on factors like ethnicity, gender, sexual orientation, eating preferences or fields of activism. Part of the power of any collective is a sense of bonding, of belonging – which sometimes brings with it a call to fit in.

For most of us, identity is multifaceted. We're part of a variety of different circles, some of which feel more central and more defining than others. As a result, distinguishing between collective voice and individual voice isn't straightforward or linear. When we're in a group, particularly if we've joined it for a sense of community, it's natural to unconsciously emphasise the parts of our identity that relate to it. In doing so, we may downplay, discount, or even forget, aspects of our wider humanness.

In some settings, such as social media platforms, we can be actively selective about which parts of ourselves we make known. There are many reasons why we might embrace this opportunity – and, when we do, what matters is whether we're acting with awareness or on autopilot. If we're on autopilot, we may be drawn more deeply into highlighting particular aspects of our identity. If we make our choices more consciously, we're more able to remain connected to a broader sense of self.

When we join a group, particularly in social media settings, we may also join a Field I conversation focused on one or more shared interests. This provides a valuable sense of connection and cohesion. We can talk freely amongst like minds and there's a sense of community. However, if a group supports *only* those with similar values and stances, this can be taken too far and become an 'echo chamber'.

As we've discovered, an allegiance to collective voice means that, when different views are expressed (the boat is rocked), they tend to be ignored, smoothed over or shouted down. This may discourage healthy questioning, and allow group members to develop a sense of certainty about their view of the world and become intolerant of those who don't share it. In the unregulated environment of social media, where the summary dismissal of an alternative narrative can happen without consequence, exchanges can quickly escalate into the terrain of Field II. This is the container in which things can become heated – the boat is rocking, and this is likely to continue until different perspectives are acknowledged, included and held in parity.

In the arena of social media, acknowledgement comes from 'likes' or a menu of brief pre-scripted endorsements. Exchanges are linear and often in short forms that have little nuance and are open to a range of interpretations. We can see a similar pattern in the repetitive soundbites favoured by politicians – their statements are 'liked' or not by commentators and through polls. In both cases, it's hard to engage in meaningful exploration of differences, and they can quickly and easily become divisive. These are unskilful versions of Field II engagement – they're all about individual voice and reactivity.

This presents a huge societal challenge: how do we, individually and together, find ways to work skilfully with our differences in important public discourses? Changing the shape of a Field II conversation involves finding ways to hear and acknowledge the opinions of others, even if we vehemently disagree with them. Essentially, we respect the right of another human being to hold their view, however wrong-headed and wrong-hearted we think they are. It's only when someone feels that their agenda will be taken into account that they can find capacity to listen to others.

Hearing and acknowledging strongly held views may prove impossible in public settings. However, we can build our capacity to handle ourselves well if we engage in this kind of conversation. Each time we're able to respond skilfully to difference, we contribute to germinating systemic change, one conversation at a time.

{ } Over to you ...

To explore these ideas further, select a societal issue that stimulates strongly held opposing views. Be clear which 'side' you lean towards and, using some of the ideas set out here, reflect on how your chosen issue plays out 'in the ether' and amongst commentators in the media.

Then think about what happens when someone in your circle – whether at home or at work – mentions the issue in passing, to you personally or in a group. What kind of engagement follows? What do you think underpins the interactions taking place? To what extent does your example reflect the public pattern?

With the help of the four fields, we've considered how the context and climate of a conversation shape what unfolds when the energies of difference are present. In Chapter 26, we'll develop this theme and look at some of the practicalities of creating good conditions for dialogue so that we can harness these energies to generate new thinking.

Before that, let's consider the ways in which a conversation held in a virtual medium is different to one held in a physical space. What does a virtual setting call for in terms of establishing and consciously holding a container?

# Chapter 25  Consciously holding a container: virtual matters

Before 2020, I always focused on in-person settings for my leadership development work. I sometimes did executive coaching and coaching supervision sessions on the phone, but all my workshops involved human bodies gathered in a room. In fact, before 2020, the phrase 'in person' didn't really figure – there was an assumption that learning events (and many other forms of gathering) largely involved being physically present. However, the arrival of the Covid-19 pandemic changed this for us all: much interpersonal activity, whether conversations, meetings or development workshops, shifted online, mainly to visual platforms such as Zoom.

This was a huge challenge for me. On a personal level, I find visual-virtual very difficult – there's something about the medium that shuts down an important part of my brain. Having recognised this, a few years before the pandemic I spent eighteen months actively using video interfaces and trying to find a way to work skilfully with them. In the end, I concluded that I'm less able to do good work in such settings. Since then, whenever I've been asked to use Zoom, MS Teams and similar platforms, I've declined and asked if it's possible to work in person or by phone. If it isn't, I don't take on the work.

For a long time, I framed my inability to function well in screen-based environments as a personal limitation. I felt awkward each time I requested an audio-only conversation – and thought that I was, perhaps, passing my 'use-by' date. However, the rapidly escalating use of visual-virtual platforms during the pandemic focused attention on the effects of using them, such as the feelings of exhaustion that often accompanied or followed immersion in online meetings. This experience was common enough to acquire a name: Zoom fatigue. Further, when I explained my preference for audio-only settings to others, I found that I wasn't alone.

It turned out that I was well-placed (and motivated) to explore the roots of my personal concerns and the experiences being described by others. I read many articles and revisited trusted references to gain a broad understanding of the place of virtual channels in conversations, meetings and developmental work. In this chapter, I'll share some of what I discovered with you, and offer a response to a question that I'm often asked: how do the principles and practices of dialogue work on platforms such as Zoom and MS Teams?

Essentially, this is a question about virtual containers. In what follows, I'll distinguish between in-person containers and two types of virtual container: audio-only and audio-visual. The sensory data that's available in each holding space is different and it's helpful to be aware of this when selecting a container for an important conversation.

Whilst we'll be focusing on synchronous virtual containers, in which people meet to talk and listen in real time, there are also asynchronous virtual containers, such as voice notes, emails, texts and posts. In these interactions, there's a gap between one person writing or speaking and another receiving their words. Our book-based conversation is an extreme version of this. In such settings, there *is* a container: a sense of what it's OK to say; an energy created by the tenor of an exchange; and a tendency to engage habitually, which creates a pattern. However, the container is often not consciously held.

On the upside, the asynchronous nature of these settings offers an opportunity to pause, and to consider what we'll write (or say), examine how we're interpreting what someone has written (or said) and be thoughtful about how we'll respond. We can actively use the time lag, and even extend it, to create space to think about our intent and the impact we might have.

When asynchronous exchanges are in written form, there's an additional challenge: they're stripped of the visual and tonal cues of spoken words and nuance is often lost. A recipient will read and interpret what's written from their own perspective, concerns and assumptions, which invites us to be mindful of what we write and how we write it. If we're short of time, this can be difficult. However, when we react quickly to what's written, any time 'saved' now can easily be lost in managing the consequences of ill-judged words.

I'll leave this as a brief and tantalising line of thought for you to explore further. In these pages, our context is creating the conditions for dialogue, and this is more likely to be based on synchronous interactions.

Before we get started, I'll set out some personal context. As ever, what I write is informed by my experience and preferences and, if you understand this background, it may help you to assess whether what you read applies to your circumstances. First, whilst I have direct experience of creating powerful audio-only containers, the choices I've made mean that don't have it for audio-visual containers. Therefore, I usually answer questions about Zoom/MS Teams with some combination of 'I don't know' and 'I don't have much experience of this, but similar principles apply'. In truth, creating a virtual container is a subject in its own right and is beyond the scope of my body-based approach. However, it's an important question and so I'll outline what I've discovered (so far) and invite you to explore what works for you.

In general terms, I have a bias towards in-person containers and the richness of the energetic data that's available in them and I suspect this will flavour what follows, however hard I try to be neutral. Beyond this preference, I don't believe either an audio-visual or an audio-only environment to be intrinsically 'better' than the alternative. Each virtual medium offers different conditions for conversation, and the choice about which to adopt is part of paying attention to the container.

A second bias is a desire to rehabilitate the value of audio-only environments, as I believe their benefits are often overlooked. The default option for a virtual conversation seems to be to use an audio-visual platform – perhaps on the assumption that this is superior to an audio-only setting. I gently challenge this, partly because we increase the options for a container if we include audio-only channels. This can only be helpful.

Over to you …

Take a moment to reflect on your natural preferences (and biases) when you choose a medium for your conversations – given a free hand, do you tend to select an in-person, audio-visual or audio-only setting? Which options do you tend to avoid? What motivates your choices?

As you reflect on your tendencies, what unexamined assumptions underpin them?

As we explore virtual settings, our context is consciously holding a container that will support us to handle our differences skilfully and generatively. For any conversation, our conscious choice of setting will depend on many things, such as the number of people involved, their location (and perhaps time zones), the reason for gathering to talk and/or the quality of the technology available. There's no 'one size fits all' approach – in-person, audio-only and audio-visual settings each have different characteristics. For dialogue, it's important to consider our options, especially if it's impractical to meet in person.

## Sensory data in virtual settings

In choosing between audio-only and audio-visual containers, a key consideration is the availability of sensory data and the quality of it. When we meet face to face, we're able to see and hear others without external filters. The available audio and visual data are synchronised. We also have access to sensory data that requires proximity – the most obvious example is touch, but taste and smell also fall into this category. This proximity data is automatically absent when we meet virtually.

In addition, when we meet in person, we tune in to the quality of presence of others, their energy and the way they're carrying themselves. These inputs are types of vibration, discerned across spaces, and such energetic data is more elusive across technological interfaces. Even in proximity, we have to pay attention to pick up nuanced vibes and non-verbal cues.

In our virtual exchanges, we can't replace the missing sensory data. However, we can think clearly about the impact of their absence. In using a video interface, some visual data is available and, on the face of it, this may seem like a better option than an audio-only environment. Sometimes it is. However, audio-only environments do have compensations, and we'll consider these later in the chapter.

Essentially, there are trade-offs to be made between the two virtual settings. For example, in virtual spaces, what happens to the 'peripheral awareness' that we use when we're in a room with people? When we're focused on a screen, our field of vision narrows and, as a consequence, our attention tends to become more concentrated. In the act of focusing, we become less aware of our peripheral vision. We can, quite literally, lose sight of the bigger picture.

This matters because, as human beings, we tend to prioritise what's in our visual field, and our attention becomes correspondingly narrow or broad. When our peripheral vision (and sensing) is activated, our awareness is spatially open and we think more freely. In contrast, when our gaze is directed towards one thing, we tend to think practically and efficiently. This means that, when we're thinking with others, screens support us to be focused, efficient and effective. If we want to be creative, they may not offer the best environment.

Personally, when my gaze is focused, the problem-solving, task-oriented functions of my brain predominate. I have less access to the creative patterning and insight-related areas that I regard as my particular strengths. My 'peripheral' mind seems to activate only when my gaze is resting on the horizon or middle distance, which is easy to do when I'm on the phone – I look out of the window. I have to work harder to 'lift my gaze' – and my mind – from the lure of a screen.

To conclude this brief exploration of sensory data, please note that a specific feature of the Leadership Embodiment four-part centring practice (Appendix B) is that we access our peripheral awareness. We can use this practice to connect to the bigger picture in any medium or setting, including those that are screen-based.

{ﾂ} Over to you ...

Take a moment to notice how you've responded to what I've set out about the data available in different containers – what do you readily agree with? What do you dispute? What's made you think?

What might you do differently next time you're selecting a setting for an important conversation?

Let's consider the two virtual containers in more detail, noticing how they differ from in-person settings and from each other.

## Audio-visual settings

We'll start with audio-visual, which has the attraction of retaining visual data. However, this data is arranged in an unfamiliar way, as multiple 'headshots' on a screen. This contrasts with the organic nature of visual data in physical settings. When we're in a room with a group of people, we see a few faces 'straight on' and some in profile, whilst others are out of our line of sight. We also have some awareness of the bodies around us, and may pick up movements and non-verbal interactions in our peripheral vision. This kind of data gets lost in visual-virtual settings – and there are two aspects to this.

First, with a group of people in a room, we indicate that we're speaking to someone in particular by a turn of our head or body and/or by making eye contact. This isn't possible when interacting with an array of faces. Second, it won't always be clear what any gesture, movement or change in expression relates to. We might see someone roll their eyes, for example, and it won't be clear whether this is a response to something in the online conversation or something that's happening in an individual's immediate vicinity. There's a lot of scope for misunderstanding.

In addition, two features of the visual display can make screen-based conversations more challenging than in-person exchanges. One is that the human brain isn't wired to take in, and make sense of, a number of faces arranged in a grid. Our natural sense of what's going on in a group comes from millennia of evolution based on small numbers of people gathering in proximity. Even those who are adept at reading and navigating interpersonal dynamics have to pay more attention in this unfamiliar setting. There's no natural 'order' to the flow of changes in expression, and dynamics between and amongst people become harder to observe. In evolutionary terms, we're unaccustomed to taking in and processing this form and volume of visual data – which means it can feel overwhelming. When handling an information overload, we tend to exert more effort, disengage and/or close down.

When looking at a headshot amongst headshots, it's also much harder to perceive energy, nuance and even authenticity. In a room, we're tuning in, getting a visceral sense of collective and individual 'vibes' – and we intuitively assimilate this. While we can attribute a vibe to what we're seeing on a screen, it's an indirect experience of the energy – we're reading a situation and interpreting it. The quality of energetic data is diminished, and this can make it more challenging for those present to feel heard.

A second feature of screen-based engagement is that being face to face with someone is a more intense experience than sitting side by side, or being slightly 'off-set' in a seating arrangement. Early in my career, I was given some related advice: don't sit directly opposite the person you find most challenging or difficult. This was a particularly helpful steer for someone inclined to be combative. Basically, tension is more likely to escalate if we're in direct eye contact with someone, because our limbic brain registers this as a potential threat and puts us on alert. Our fight/flight system is activated and we become watchful, or even vigilant. Whilst this will influence different people in different ways, it might be useful to consider the effect of being face to face with many individuals on a screen.

The impact of each of these screen-based 'visual effects' can be mitigated with some careful thought and by taking a conversation more slowly, allowing time to process the complexity of the environment. This is particularly important when difference is present. Even when an established group has built trust and respect through working together over time, it's immensely difficult to handle diverse perspectives through a screen. With more room to misinterpret what we hear and/ or see, there's increased potential for differences to become inflamed. This invites us to pay greater attention to a virtual container than to an in-person one.

There's another facet of screen-based interactions that can affect the quality of communication. Whilst both visual and audio data are available, we don't receive them in real time. The data is delayed in the transmission process, with a different delay for visual data and audio data, creating a lag. Essentially, light and sound travel at different speeds – and even with super-fast broadband, good bandwidth and uninterrupted service, they're slightly asynchronous. So even when things are going well, this distorts what we hear and see over the wires (or airwaves).

This means we have to work harder to process what's taking place. When there are disruptions to internet services, visuals 'hang' or become pixelated, and voices echo, stutter or cut out. As speech is an embodied activity, all this adds to the load of making sense of our experience. We can, of course, choose to live with the resulting disturbances to the human communication 'feed'. However, for me, vital data is lost.

Whatever the nature of an audio-visual conversation, these factors are in play, complicating even harmonious, benign and/or routine exchanges. For dialogue, when we're likely to be navigating complexity and difference, we may want a container with less potential for misinterpretation. In addition, dialogue calls us to attend profoundly to both what's said and how it's said, which may mean that in-person or audio-only settings are more appropriate.

{💭} Over to you ...

Take a few moments to reflect on your experience of screen-based conversations, choosing a couple of examples that went well and a couple that were unsatisfactory. What might have influenced the outcome? What supported success in the good conversations? What limited what was possible in the other conversations?

When you set up your next screen-based conversation, how might these reflections inform you?

## Audio-only settings

In an audio-only environment, our experience of others is voice only. With no visual data to process, we free up bandwidth which we can use in different ways. In *Dialogue and the Art of Thinking Together*, there's a chapter on the practice of listening in which Isaacs explores the sense of hearing and contrasts it with the sense of seeing. He examines the nature of these two sensory inputs to offer insight into the potentials and limitations of our experiences in conversation.

Isaacs observes that modern Western culture is dominated by sight, and that we've become habituated to the rapid pace of intake associated with visual phenomena, placing less emphasis on other modalities and rhythms. Hearing is a slower process than seeing – to properly accommodate it, we need to work at the speed of sound rather than the speed of light (which is hundreds of thousands of times faster). However, hearing also gives us a 'feel for' the vibrational energy of what someone says and is more nuanced and precise than sight. Our voice carries an energetic message and, as we discovered in Chapter 20, this is what 'lands' with others. We get other data through our eyes, such as expression and gesture, and this may augment our sense of what we're hearing. However, visual data can also distract us from the more subtle energetic elements of what's being said.

Without visual cues, we tune in to others in a different way – with, perhaps, more scope to listen to ourselves and pick up internal data such as sensations and feelings. There is (quite literally) less going on, and we have more bandwidth to make sense of what we're hearing. We have more space and time to perceive factors such as tone, pitch and timbre alongside attributes such as confidence, diffidence, mood and intensity. Variations in these energetic qualities can be nuanced and layered. When there's a lot going on, whether in a room or on a call, this richness is easy to miss. Personally, I find that the advantages of an audio-only space can sometimes outweigh those of being in a room with others.

To summarise, it's clear that audio data is central to conversations and that kinaesthetic data is automatically excluded when we're physically distanced from others. Therefore, a key question for selecting the medium for a virtual container is: will visual data enhance or limit the quality of our exchange?

The answer will, of course, depend. Sometimes the benefits of seeing will outweigh the potential drawbacks of audio-visual channels, and sometimes the visual dimension will detract from the quality of the listening environment. The essential theme is 'no consciously held container, no dialogue'. We must choose well.

## Consciously holding a virtual container

Let's return to the theme of *actively* establishing and sustaining conditions that will support the conversation we intend to have. In dialogue, we consciously create a container, an agreement about the climate that we'll foster. If we don't attend to this, a container will form, unnoticed, and will reflect factors such as the setting we choose, any preconceptions of those present, and the habits of behaviours they carry with them. These considerations apply equally to physical and virtual containers.

Virtual settings have some attributes that enable good conversations and others that hinder them. They differ from physical spaces, and the art of creating a container in a virtual setting is fairly new territory which, by itself, might suggest that we give it more attention. Ghislaine Caulat,[19] a thought-leader and researcher in the field of virtual leadership, invites us to take these factors into account when we establish a virtual container, saying:

> Virtual working requires leaders to learn to radically rethink the fundamentals of communication and cooperation and to be prepared to question several taken-for-granted principles.[20]

To navigate virtual settings skilfully, Caulat's research calls for new forms of leadership and new ways of engaging with each other. However, she reports that leaders and team members often simply transfer the customs and practices of physical spaces into virtual settings (whether audio-only or audio-visual).

One of Caulat's findings is that it's helpful to have a level playing field in terms of the way participants access a conversation. The aim is to ensure that the same sensory data is available to everyone, as far as is humanly possible. In each setting – in-person, audio-only and audio-visual – different sensory data is present and, when people participate in a conversation using a variety of modalities, it can affect both its quality and its outcome. What Caulat suggests is that, when a conversation is held in person, *everyone* is present in the room. There's no 'dial in' or 'log on' option. In fact, to uphold the principle of equity of access and experience, she goes so far as to propose that, when two (or more) people dial in or log on from the same location, they should do so from separate rooms. This applies to both audio-only and audio-visual settings. She reasons that, when others aren't able to witness it, silent visual communication between people in the same room causes an imbalance in a conversation.

For dialogue, these principles seem important. In Chapter 13, we explored inclusion and holding people and views in parity, and I understand this aspect of Caulat's work to be a call for parity of experience for participants. This seems radical – and is an invitation to reflect on the quality of the container that's created when some people gather in a room and some log on or dial in. This isn't to say that we should avoid such arrangements, only that we should understand what they constrain as well as what they enable.

I can offer an example that supports the principle of parity of access. Some years ago, I was asked to do a series of introductory in-person Leadership Embodiment workshops for the National Health Service in Scotland. It was proposed that one of the workshops would be video-conferenced to participants in remote locations. I turned this option down as I felt that my attention would be on participants in the room, and that I might overlook the remote participants. Instead, I suggested that we do a workshop solely for these participants and that I'd adapt the material for this virtual setting. Although this was a development activity rather than a more conventional conversation, it still seemed important to aim for a level playing field for all who took part. The virtual workshop was a great success and the participants were fulsome in expressing their appreciation that, for once, they were the centre of the workshop 'action'.

Whatever the context, if people are meeting virtually, Caulat suggests specific measures that help to establish a good container. Here are some of her proposals, which I've linked to the four dialogue practices to highlight their relevance to our exploration.

First, Caulat invites us to signal that a virtual conversation has the same status and attention as an in-person one by not squeezing it into diaries or compromising on location or time. This embodies the quality of respect. In addition, if people are joining a conversation from different time zones over several meetings, we can vary the timing to share the inconvenience involved. This, too, is respectful to all.

Second, we can ask people to dial in or log on from an appropriate space, with minimum background noise and distractions, so that they can give their full attention to the conversation. This supports good listening.

Finally, we can embrace the principle of creating a level playing field, where everyone has access to the same sensory data. This offers parity of experience and signals inclusion: we're in this together. It also encourages participants to listen more attentively and makes it easier to be curious – and to suspend judgement.

When we foster an emphasis on the 'receiving' practices of listening, respecting and suspending judgement, I believe that we naturally adopt and embody the speaking practice of authentic voicing: we become more discerning about what we say and how we say it. We start to experience a virtuous circle, whether in a virtual or physical setting, and our conversation slows down and becomes more spacious.

## Over to you …

Take a moment to revisit your natural preferences and biases when selecting a setting for a virtual encounter – have these been influenced by what you've read in the last few pages? What's your response to Caulat's work and her more radical proposals? What do you find thought-provoking, and what simply provokes you?

What, if anything, might you change when you're next arranging an important conversation where it's not possible to meet in person?

In this chapter, we've looked at factors that might affect our choice of container when we can't meet in person. Let's now turn our attention to more general practicalities for consciously establishing and holding a container for dialogue.

# Chapter 26 Consciously holding a container: practicalities

While the idea of container is relatively easy to understand, the realities of consciously creating one to foster dialogue can be challenging. To consider how to go about this, we'll start with things we can attend to before we meet. Then, we'll touch on how we can begin to collectively hold a container, once we're gathered. We'll revisit the metaphor of a conversational operating system and its role in determining what's possible in a conversation. Then we'll use it to support the practice of regularly revisiting a container to keep it in conscious holding. All this will, I hope, make the case for paying active and sustained attention to a container – especially if the stakes are high.

There are two key aspects to the art of establishing a container for engaging with our differences and exploring them. One is to carefully select the setting for the conversation, whether this is a physical or a virtual space. The other is to take account of human factors, such as the readiness of the people involved, how they come together and how the conversation begins. While there's practical support for navigating these factors throughout these pages – especially in Chapters 13, 25 and 33 – it's an art rather than a science. We can draw on frameworks and guidance but, in the end, we'll be sensing our way into what works for our particular circumstances.

In this chapter, we'll focus on two things:

- when and how a container begins to establish itself, which informs when it's useful to start the process of consciously holding it; and

- how we cultivate and sustain collective capacity to 'consciously hold' a container once our conversation is underway.

Whether we're gathering in bricks and mortar or in a virtual setting, a container begins to form at the moment we decide to meet. We tend to think that a conversation starts once everyone's sitting down together, or has logged on/dialled in. In fact, in energetic terms, it starts much earlier, as soon as we form an intention to talk together. This nascent energetic field evolves as we make choices about timing and setting, which establish boundaries within which people will show up and get started. The container further develops as arrangements are put in place and we invite people to join the conversation. Essentially, the way we set things in motion affects how people arrive and engage, and the container is then influenced by the interests, histories and habits they bring with them. This leads us towards the territory of our third tenet, 'entry is everything'.

Initially, and whether explicitly or not, the person or people convening dialogue are 'consciously holding' the container on behalf of everyone else. In every aspect of setting a conversation in motion, the convener (or convening group) can adopt the spirit of 'entry is everything' by consciously choosing words and actions that ensure that their means reflect their ends. As we saw from our exploration of Caulat's work in Chapter 25, when arranging a virtual gathering we can take care to signal its importance and create a level playing field of access for participants. We can take similar care with an in-person encounter, indicating why it matters and finding a suitable venue with reasonable travel logistics for all involved.

Once timings and physical or virtual 'venue' space are determined, we continue to foster good energetic conditions by giving thought to why we're convening the conversation. We consider who to invite (Chapter 13) and what we're calling for from them. When we extend the invitations, it may be worthwhile doing so in more than one way – perhaps by talking to each invitee in a phone call or Zoom chat and following up in writing.

As I set this out, I can almost hear the cries of, 'Seriously? We don't have time to do that!' Please remember that I'm not suggesting you take this care for every conversation, just for the important ones in which difference will be present. For these conversations, the choices are stark: invest time and energy in this kind of preparation, or spend (more) time and energy handling fallout, during and/or after the meeting.

In my view, when the stakes are high, we don't have time to *not* do this kind of preparatory work. Time spent supporting invitees to understand the purpose(s) of a conversation, and what's expected of them, individually and collectively, is never wasted – it starts to sow seeds for what's to come. It signals that this conversation will be different, and this begins to shape the container for it.

If we don't pay deliberate attention to these initial conditions, we leave them to chance. And, as Caulat discovered in her research, this means leaders and team members often simply transfer their familiar customs and practices into the conversation. This applies for both virtual and physical spaces. In addition, when we leave things to chance for an in-person meeting, hotels and other venues compete to sell us *their* version of a good environment. It's easy to fall in line with what's on offer. However, whenever we walk into a space set up by someone else, we inherit a system of assumptions that may or may not support our purposes. We inherit the layout of their physical container, and what follows is affected by the way people move into it and claim it.

## Over to you …

How might you test my proposition that the energetic field for a conversation begins to take shape as soon as we form an intention to meet? One approach might be to compare and contrast two hastily convened meetings – one that went well and one that didn't. How was each conversation set in motion? What was attended to and what was left to chance?

In the meeting that went well, what was already in place to support it, despite the fact that it was hastily convened? In the other, what led to the difficulties that arose?

What conclusions might you draw about the influence of initial conditions on how a conversation plays out?

Once gathered, how do we begin the process of building collective capacity to consciously hold the container for our conversation? The key is to take time at the beginning of a conversation to consider how we want to talk and listen together. We began to look at this in Chapters 13 and 24, and will revisit it in Chapter 29. There are many ways of approaching it, and the one we choose will depend on our context. What different approaches tend to share is that they ask an 'opening question' that invites participants to engage with the 'look and feel' of the conversation ahead. This may be slightly unfamiliar territory for those present, and so it can also be valuable (and save time in the long run) to invite them to explore the opening question in pairs before speaking in plenary.

When we don't take time to talk about the environment we want to co-create, habit will probably draw everyone straight to the subject matter they want to focus on. I know I'm not alone in finding the pull of tasks, decisions and problem-solving irresistible. The short-term attraction of content and the possibility of achieving something easily seduce me into skipping over the non-urgent business of creating a container. When things are going well, this doesn't matter. If things get messy, it's too late – it's likely that emotions are already running high, ambiguity and uncertainty abound, and self-interest predominates. This makes it much harder to 'hold' the conversation: if we haven't explored how we'll engage with each other, we're ill-equipped to handle such situations.

When a group has articulated the conditions they wish to create, it pays to point out the obvious – only those present can bring them to life. We are the method. When we make this explicit, we call on everyone to do their best to embody the desired conditions. However, in their own way, it's likely that each person will fall short at some stage. This is a natural part of the process. We're setting a course towards new habits, behaviours and ways of being. It will take time, commitment, forgiveness and perseverance to inhabit them. Which brings us to the matter of revisiting the desired conditions each time a group meets, so that we bring them back into consciousness.

## Conversational operating system – rebooting

In my dialogue programmes, when I impose the discipline of attending to the container at the beginning of *each* workshop, group members go along with me at first. They raise their eyebrows but, on the whole, they try to engage. As the process repeats, session after session, compliance gets more cursory and it's accompanied by a sense of humouring me until we get to the 'real stuff'. Despite intellectual understanding of the relationship between container and outcome, each cohort of participants seemed reluctant to build collective capacity to embody the aspirations we'd set out as we began the programme.

You may conclude that I found this frustrating – and you'd be right. However, I was most frustrated by my inability to explain why revisiting the container matters – I tried many different ways of doing this, without any real impact. And then, Dorothy Atcheson, a fellow coach supervisor, offered a fresh perspective, saying: 'Oh! We need to reboot the conversational operating system each time.' This links the process of refreshing the container to the metaphor of an operating system that represents the underlying coding for a conversation (Chapter 12). When we consciously articulate, and agree to hold, a different set of conditions for our engagement, we're upgrading our conversational OS. And so, just as the OS reboots when we restart a device, we reboot our conversational OS, or container, when we reopen a conversation.

To elaborate on this, once a conversational OS has been established in, for example, a team, all conversations reflect the 'look and feel' of it. The underlying coding runs in the background, but is tangible in the way people talk and listen to each other. This OS determines whether or not a particular conversational form, or app, will run. And so, for example, if a team whose conversational OS supports quick decision-making and action tries to adopt the practices of dialogue without changing the underlying coding of their conversations, they're unlikely to be successful.

Changing the underlying coding of our conversations takes persistence. Even when we understand that dialogue requires different conditions, and we take time to articulate what they might be, there's a long road to travel before we inhabit them. As we try to put our aspirations for our container into practice, they'll founder on the reality of established habits and routines. Old habits do die hard. Collective old habits even more so.

This is where rebooting the conversational OS comes in.

Just as we shut down a computer to allow updates to install, and then reboot it so that the system can reintegrate, we can think of 'closing' a conversation and its container when participants depart. When we reconvene, we then reboot both conversation and container, checking that they remain fit for purpose. In bringing to mind our container and the part we each play in holding it, we make it more likely that we'll hold it consciously. In addition, a reboot might allow for 'automatic updates' as the container evolves under our care and attention.

So, rather than being something 'we don't have time for', revisiting the container is essential maintenance if we want to change our conversations. And, as we grow into our container and become increasingly able to embody our aspirations, we develop as individuals and our relationships deepen. We're naturally changed by our collective experience and by our efforts to support it: we grow as the container grows. We come into new relationship with ourselves (we are the method).

In the next chapters, as we explore the third tenet 'entry is everything', we'll look more deeply into the symbiosis between individual and collective experience. First, let's pause and reflect.

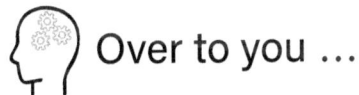

## Over to you …

In the context of dialogue, how does the metaphor of rebooting a conversational operating system land with you? Does it make you more likely or less likely to prompt a group to revisit the container each time they meet?

If the metaphor inspires you to be disciplined in revisiting container conditions, how might you bring this to life? If the metaphor doesn't work for you, what *would* inspire you to bring a container into conscious holding each time a group meets?

This completes our exploration of the second tenet, 'consciously holding a container'. In these chapters, we've revisited Scharmer's Four Fields of Conversation as an aid to understanding some of the qualities of the energetic space in which a conversation is held. We've looked at how difference is typically handled in each of the fields and considered some of the ways in which virtual containers differ from in-person gatherings. We've touched on some practical aspects of consciously establishing and maintaining a container.

We now turn to the third tenet: entry is everything. As we delve into it, we'll discover that there are many points of entry. In fact, perhaps, everything is entry. Let's inquire.

## Chapter 27 Entry is everything: introduction

**Three tenets**

Entry is everything

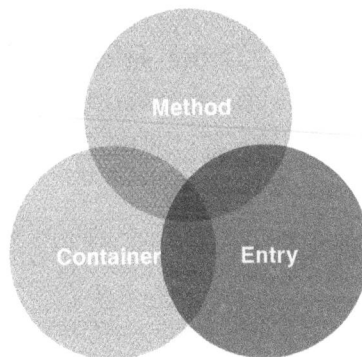

*Entry is everything. The way you approach a situation will determine a great deal about how it will unfold.*

– William Isaacs, *Dialogue and the Art of Thinking Together*,[2] page 293

In Isaacs' book, the phrase 'entry is everything' appears in a chapter on convening dialogue. The supporting paragraph reads:

> I have found that the first few moments of any exchange contain the seeds of the totality of the interaction you shall have. The importance of these initial conditions, of the way you choose to interact with people, sets much in motion. In this sense, any move you make is an intervention into the system you are entering.

271

These words resonate with my Buddhist studies and the principle that each moment conditions the next (Chapter 4). They also reflect the essence of Gestalt psychology and the idea that each moment or event carries within it all that will arise within a system. The Dalai Lama describes this principle as the whole universe being contained in a single atom.[21] In addition, the words reach into my hinterland, speaking to me of fractals and the breathtaking intricacy and beauty of images created from their replication. In these images, each component part, or fractal, is a coherent distillation of the whole system. Every essential element is present in each piece. The principle of 'entry is everything' seems to lie at the intersection of quantum physics, Buddhist thinking, psychology and mathematics. It's a mighty provenance.

The practical implication of this principle is that, if I go into a conversation in a bad mood, I'll imbue what follows with that energy. If I have mixed motives, either knowingly or unknowingly, I'll probably communicate this confusion in some way. If I feel composed, and clear about why I'm participating, this will permeate my contribution.

## Entry and entering

When we embrace the possibility that the way we begin largely determines what's to come, we're more likely to take care with 'entry'. In addition, entry is where we (often) have the greatest agency to shape a conversation: we can prepare a setting and a beginning, but it's more complex to influence things once they're underway.

We can use the framework of advocacy and inquiry (Chapter 7) to get a glimpse of the connection between the way we open a conversation and what follows. If I begin with a statement (advocacy), I tend to set a direction, drawing attention to a focal point. If I begin with an open question (inquiry), I tend to encourage sharing of different perspectives. A skilful entry may well combine both advocacy (direction) and inquiry (exploration) by briefly delineating purpose and scope, and then inviting wide-ranging contributions and deliberation. This has the effect of offering some parameters for the conversation whilst inviting engagement, curiosity and reflection.

More subtly, the tenor and breadth of a conversation will be influenced by the energy we bring to it and how genuinely we're seeking the input of others. For example, paying lip service to consultation or asking questions that 'lead' others to the conclusion that we want them to reach tends to limit what's possible. Such tactics may be skilfully deployed, and those present may go along with them. However, they're unsuited to dialogue.

From the perspective that *each* moment conditions the next, the principle of 'entry' goes beyond Isaacs' emphasis on convening and the 'first few moments of [an] exchange'. This reflects my experience of martial arts, where the action of enter*ing* a situation is at least as important as the initial conditions. The practice of entering offers a way to engage with challenging moments when we don't have the luxury of setting things in motion: it's a resource when we're already in the middle of something.

A key practice in the martial art of Aikido, on which the Leadership Embodiment approach is based, is 'irimi', which means 'entering'. Broadly, irimi involves being present to, and making space for, the incoming energy of an attacker, and stepping into it without losing our centre. We open to, and include, an incoming energy and blend with it in a productive way. As we do this, there's a moment when we see the world from the other person's point of view. When practised with awareness, the practice of irimi offers us a glimpse of an alternative worldview.

The principle of irimi, or entering, is relevant to handling difference in our conversations. Being present to, and holding space for, different perspectives, is a foundation for skilfully channelling the energies associated with them. It's a foundation for dialogue.

We've already met the practice of irimi in the form of the wall–window activity (Chapter 10). The essence of wall–window is that we meet difference by centring and then stepping off our position for a moment and moving to a place where we can see the other person's point of view. In doing this, we're not agreeing with them. Rather, in being willing to look, we create the potential for a new, blended perspective. Energetically, we're communicating that we see and hear our partner. And, energetically, they sense this inclusion and acknowledgement, which settles their system.

Personally, I see 'entering' as stepping into the reality of 'what is' without giving up my own centre. When we open our awareness to include 'what is', we make better decisions about how to engage. Centring creates a moment of choice and the act of entering gives us a sense of agency: we actively engage with a challenge rather than waiting to see what happens.

In LE, the word irimi is used as a shorthand for 'entering into adversity'. When we're faced with someone offering a view that we find difficult to hear, we centre, suspend our judgements and certainties, and step into the situation to explore it from a resourceful place. When we *include* the someone and their view in this way, the boundary between 'self' and 'other' dissolves. We create conditions in which we might find a response that benefits both of us. This reflects a founding principle of Aikido: we try to protect the 'attacker' as well as ourselves.

To embrace the principle that both entry and entering matter, we can amend the end of Isaacs' paragraph to propose that:

> At every point in a conversation, the way we choose to interact with others sets much in motion.

This is the ground that we'll explore in the chapters that follow. First, let's look briefly at preparation and why it matters.

## Preparation matters

You might recall the phrase 'preparation and beginning' from Chapter 1. It comes from T'ai Chi Chuan and describes the moments of settling into a 'ready' stance and then beginning the first movement of a form (a sequence of movements). To engage in dialogue, this spirit of 'getting ready' is important – and we often feel we don't have time for such niceties. Yet, if we recognise that moments of entry and entering matter, then preparing for them also matters.

As we explore the third tenet, 'entry is everything', we'll focus on preparation. Whether we're hosting a conversation or joining it as a participant, we can prepare for both our initial entry into it and for moments of entering once it's underway. When we discover how our personal preparation affects the way we participate, we may be inspired to invite others to undertake some *collective* preparation. This natural movement reflects the interdependence of 'entry is everything' (Tenet 3), 'we are the method' (Tenet 1) and 'consciously holding a container' (Tenet 2).

Preparation is different to planning. When we think clearly, we realise that we can't actually *plan* a conversation, because it involves other people and, although we may think we can predict what they'll say or do, they may not oblige. Also, if we plan around our assumptions about how others will contribute, we'll limit the potential for discovery and creativity. Further, without care, our planning assumptions become expectations, and this sets us up for disappointment when things unfold differently. Over-zealous planning seems to me like digging a channel for a conversation, along which all parties are then supposed to travel. The conversation will be constrained by this – can you imagine what might be missed?

Whilst you may already invest in thorough groundwork for your crucial conversations, what you read here may prompt you to pay attention to different things. For instance, instead of researching a situation or topic and rehearsing a rationale for a preferred stance or outcome, we might wonder how we can draw out different perspectives to gain a shared sense of the complexity of an issue. And, instead of considering the steps or stages that we hope to guide others through, we might wonder how we can foster good relationships so that difficult subject matter can be explored candidly. To prepare for dialogue, we consider how we'll attend to relationships and thinking systemically, alongside immediate concerns. Instead of more conventional planning and rehearsal, we focus on preparation.

## Over to you ...

Take some time to reflect on how you currently prepare for your important conversations. What do you tend to focus on? What do you tend to overlook or leave to chance? How much attention do you give to how you'll begin? And to how you'll engage once things are underway?

How might you expand the scope of your preparation for your next important conversation?

In the next few chapters, we'll look at entry and entering more fully. Before doing so, I'll introduce the words *convening* and *intervening*. The Latin base of both words is *venire*, meaning 'to come', while *con* means 'together, with' and *inter* means 'between, among, during'. And so, to convene is to assemble, to gather, to bring together, and to intervene is to come among or between things or people, usually with an intent to influence what's happening. Convening is connected to entry and initial conditions, whilst intervening relates to entering into something that's already underway. And so, in our exploration of entry and entering, we'll distinguish between:

- *convening* a conversation, in which we set up the initial conditions and choose our entry; and

- *intervening* in a conversation, in which we respond to what's unfolding – entering into what is.

We'll consider these processes from both an individual and a collective perspective. In parallel with the emphasis that dialogue places on convening collectively, we'll work with a proposal that it may be helpful to 'convene' ourselves before an important conversation. Mirroring this, we'll then explore how we can 'intervene' in ourselves in moments when we feel an urgent desire to intervene in a conversation: this will support us to be skilful in what we then say and do.

With all this in mind, let's engage with the process of 'getting ready' for dialogue, starting with how we can 'convene' on a personal basis.

## Chapter 28 Entry is everything: convening self

Individually, the way someone prepares for and approaches a conversation (or any situation) is material to what then ensues – entry is everything. For example, during an intense development experience, a fellow participant – I'll call him Hugh – suggested that we have a 'connecting conversation'. I had no idea what he meant by this but, caught on the hop, I agreed to meet and talk.

I was thoughtful about the conversation and did some preparation, deciding that my entry would be to ask Hugh: what does a 'connecting conversation' mean for you? He didn't answer the question. Instead, he moved swiftly into explaining that our interactions had been 'jarring' on occasion. I nodded in recognition. He added, 'Let's start with the appreciative before we get into what jars.' The energy of the conversation had now been set in motion: his opening words were about dissonance, not appreciation. The conversation didn't go well. It left me feeling that I'd been punched in the stomach, hard and often. The energy of the conversation was corrective, not connective.

This exchange occurred early in my exploration of dialogue practices and, believing that I had to make room for all views, I sat it out. Nowadays, I would try to change the tenor of the exchange as soon as I felt the first blow and, if unsuccessful, I'd leave. In dialogue, tolerance, acceptance and inclusion are reciprocal and, if they're not, we might best serve both ourselves and others by stepping away.

Whilst I'd done some preparation for the conversation with Hugh, I was limited by not knowing what it was about. Since he'd asked for the conversation, I wondered what he might want from it and focused on this. I didn't consider what the conversation might offer me. In essence, I knew what I was curious about, but didn't really think about what mattered to me. The conversation began in a way

277

that took it into unhelpful territory and, lacking clear intention, I was unable to redirect it. In addition, I hadn't yet encountered the Leadership Embodiment practices that, nowadays, would support me to recover presence in this difficult situation.

This experience suggests three ways we can prepare for a conversation. Whilst the idea of calling this kind of preparation 'convening self' has only come to me as I've been writing this book, I've been using what follows for many years. For important conversations, three pieces of groundwork help me convene myself:

- clarifying my intentions and what really matters to me – articulating my 'take' on subjects that might be included and how I wish to participate;

- being curious about what I'm seeking to discover – expecting differences and exploring the questions I might ask to draw these out; and

- embodying good practice – preparing to carry myself well and respond skilfully to whatever unfolds.

I use these three pieces of groundwork for every important conversation, whether with friends, clients, colleagues or family, and whether communicating face to face, virtually or in writing. Taking time to prepare recognises the significance of 'entry is everything' and embodies the principle of it for each interaction. In addition, when I have a complex choice to make or a tricky personal issue to resolve, I even use this approach to untangle my internal dialogue, my conversation with myself.

In what follows, I'm imagining that we're able to prepare for a conversation. Obviously, this isn't always the case – some conversations are sprung on us, or a difficult issue arises unexpectedly in the midst of a more mundane exchange. When we're caught by surprise, the best strategy may be to pause, use a centring practice, and say 'let me think about that'. Then, if possible, to set a time to reconvene, creating space for some reflection and preparation.

If we're able to prepare, the three pieces of groundwork can guide us. Let's look at them in more detail.

## Groundwork: clarifying – my intentions and what really matters to me

There are some obvious reasons to be clear about our intentions – understanding why we're meeting; appreciating potential outcomes; and, perhaps, being explicit about anything that isn't in play. There can also be a less obvious benefit: when we've articulated where we stand and 'heard' our own view, it can be easier to step aside and be receptive to what others have to say.

If I don't clarify my intentions, I may be blinkered or confused, which makes me more susceptible to being sidetracked or derailed. It's as if my unidentified wishes, assumptions and biases lurk just below the surface, ready to knock me off balance and wreck my good intentions. Such undercurrents are present in all of us and, unrecognised, they can disrupt a conversation, even between two people. In a group, the potential for misunderstanding is magnified because each person carries their unexamined hopes and fears into an exchange.

In *Pause for Breath*, and inspired by the Ladder of Inference (which we'll meet later in the chapter), I introduced the notion of 'icebergs of inference'. In conversation, what we say represents the visible tip of these icebergs, whilst 90% of what we think and feel remains 'unseen' and lurks beneath the surface. The unseen elements represent the assumptions, inferences and expectations that we haven't explicitly recognised within ourselves. When our personal 'below the surface' stuff meets and clashes with the unspoken and contradictory 'below the surface' stuff of others, it can be a surprise. This can derail a conversation.

We can use the process of convening self and clarifying our intentions to increase our awareness of the complexity that underpins what we think and say. This begins to uncover the uncertainties, ambiguities and/or inconsistencies within us. With greater awareness of our inner workings, we're less likely to be caught out by something we didn't know about ourselves.

### Many voices

A simple way to access some of our inner complexity is to notice when we use everyday expressions such as:

- part of me thinks … and another part of me thinks …;

- on the one hand … and on the other …; and

- I'm in two minds about …

These phrases indicate that we have many voices – and that, somewhere deep inside ourselves, we *know* this. These inner voices reveal that, despite our certainties and our belief in our own judgement, we may not be coherent in what we think. To navigate this inner complexity, we can draw inspiration from the words of Judy Ringer,[22] a teacher, writer and Aikido practitioner:

> We all have many voices. Instead of deciding which one is right, find out what's right about each of them and practise being more fluid in moving among them.

Judy's words invite us to consider that there's something 'right' about each of our inner voices, rather than judge any single one to be right (or to be 'more right' than the others). In essence, when we convene self, we aim to widen our perception by distilling what matters from each inner voice. For example, if we acknowledge that we have some reservations or doubts about our 'headline' opinion, what changes? Or, if we have to make a tough business decision, but feel uncomfortable because it will adversely affect some people, how do we accommodate both rationale and values? In general, as we recognise that our take on an issue is multifaceted, how do we make room for this complexity? How does this affect how we express our view?

As we gain clarity about our inner contradictory and/or dissenting voices, and become more generous towards them, we're more able to regard the voices of others in the same way. Imagine what might change if we were to look for what's right (or what matters) in what others say, rather than judging it to be right or wrong.

## Over to you …

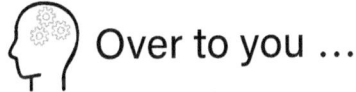

To explore some of your inner voices, recall a situation when you were 'in two minds' about a course of action – what were the competing concerns that made it challenging to come down in favour of one option or another? How might you describe these different influences on your thinking? How did you make a choice?

The principle we're exploring is that, if we assume that our thinking is always more complex than we first appreciate, we may discover unnoticed aspects of our experience such as our values, feelings and sense of what's right. We may also discover paradoxes, doubts or incompatibilities in our stance. Such discoveries can give us greater clarity about what matters and support us to hear the voices of others.

### Head-heart-core

One way to untangle some of the complexity of our inner dialogue is to use the three voices of the archetypal centres of energy and presence that we first met in Chapter 12. At that stage, we used the framing of head-heart-core to explore what a good outcome would look like. This can also be part of clarifying what matters as we convene self:

- purpose/head – what do I want from this conversation?

- relational/heart – how do I want to relate to those present?

- systemic/core – what's my aspiration for the wider system?

When we consider how a conversation might affect relationships and the wider system alongside how it might meet our personal aims, we explicitly recognise the reality that others may want different things. This prepares us to work with difference and (perhaps) to accommodate what others have to say. If we're conscious that our point of view might have an adverse impact on relationships, we'll be careful about how we express it. We may also be less likely to insist on it. Further, we may be more inclined to support a proposal that benefits the whole system even if this means that we won't get what we (originally) thought we wanted.

We can also use the archetypal voices to better understand our perspective on an issue, by asking:

- head – what do I think about this issue? What beliefs and assumptions are shaping my view?

- heart – what feelings and values are in play?

- core/gut – what really matters here?

My earlier book, *Pause for Breath*, contained two practices that explore this ground and they're included as appendices in this book. Practice 20 (Appendix I) invites us to sit quietly with a dilemma and allow different aspects of it to arise. Practice 29 (Appendix J) invites us to use the archetypal voices of head, heart and core/gut to explore something that's important to us. The practices each support us to consider what's right about our many voices and to realise that, in the round, our perspective on a topic is often nuanced and incomplete. With these insights, we may be more open to hearing what others have to say.

This aspect of convening self – clarifying our intentions and what really matters – is a process of becoming aware of our personal container, the holding space for our many voices. We met the concept of a personal container when we explored centred listening (Chapter 11). The context then was expanding our energetic space to include others. Here, we expand our personal container to include our own (many) voices.

One further aspect of clarifying our view is to use de Bono's work on white hat thinking to differentiate between 'checkable facts' and beliefs (Chapter 10). White hat thinking reminds us that most facts are subject to conditions and caveats. The principle, when convening self, is to ask: to what extent is my view relevant in this setting? As we reflect, we may discover some of the assumptions that we're making, which can allow us to be more precise in the way we use language and present our thoughts.

Having clarified what we stand for, we're ready to express our view when called to do so: we're ready to advocate. We've also created space to wonder what others might stand for. What do we not yet know or understand? What might we be seeking to discover? This brings us to the second piece of groundwork.

## Groundwork: being curious – what am I seeking to discover?

In this aspect of preparation, we actively access a sense of curiosity. We wonder what we might ask others so that we draw out *their* motivation, feelings and beliefs, and get a sense of what really matters to them. Further, if we expect difference, opposition and/or resistance, we can prepare to ask how others came to see the world in the way that they do.

To help me foster curiosity, I use the Ladder of Inference, which I first encountered in *The Fifth Discipline Fieldbook*.[8] This framework helps me to remember that each person experiences a situation in a different way. Broadly, it summarises the process of taking in information, making personal sense of it and drawing conclusions.

The first step on the ladder reflects the reality that a human being can't possibly take in all the sensory information available in any moment – a multitude of sights, sounds, smells, tastes and tactile experiences. Therefore, we apply filters, usually unconsciously. The filters might include sensory preferences such as favouring visual data over audio data and/or factors such as our interests, personal biases and professional concerns. The result is a partial impression of what's happening, being (necessarily) incomplete.

Our mind is wired to take this fragmentary impression and search its library of experiences for a memory of similar-enough circumstances to provide a template for an efficient response. The memory will be accompanied by an emotional 'tag' – how we felt in that previous situation. This tag will flavour our assessment of the current moment, predisposing us to react positively or negatively towards it, to see opportunity or threat. The emotional tag brings partiality in the form of preference.

283

In addition, the memory template is unlikely to be an exact fit for the current situation, and this introduces some assumptions into our sense-making. It can be helpful to be curious about our own view and to unpick some of these assumptions as we prepare to be curious about the way others see the world. When we understand that we may not be on entirely solid ground, we open the way to inquire into the views of others.

Personally, I use the Ladder of Inference to help me reflect on the aspects of a situation that might be significant to someone else. This is an example of using the wall–window activity (Chapter 10) to prepare for a conversation. I wonder how someone's profession, experience, interests, concerns and personality might influence both what they take into account and how they make sense of it. This supports me to identify questions that might draw out some of this information, which increases the possibility of finding some common ground.

Over to you …

Recall an example of a conversation where you discounted or dismissed what someone said. If you regard what they said as a 'view', what do you think might have shaped it? Where might they have been standing? What might they have been seeing? What might have been hidden from view?

What questions might you have asked to better understand where they were coming from? If you'd been able to do this in the moment, what difference might it have made?

When we've primed our curiosity, we're ready to inquire – either to set a tone of discovery early in a conversation, or to balance any tendency to trade positions as a conversation gets underway.

The process of clarifying our stance and being curious about the views of others will shape a conversation. However, it's the quality of energy that we bring to our words that determines how they land. I might even go so far as to say that the *energy* of entry (and entering) is everything. The quality of energy we bring to receiving the words of others also matters. With these considerations in mind, how do we support ourselves to positively influence the energy of a conversation? This brings us to the third piece of groundwork.

## Groundwork: embodying good practice – preparing to carry myself well

For the first two pieces of groundwork, preparation is likely to be specific to a conversation and can be undertaken just before it. The third piece of groundwork, which supports us to carry ourselves well whatever the circumstances, requires the long-term preparation of practice and repetition. When we work diligently with a practice that supports us to collect ourselves and come into presence, we build a viable neural pathway for it. The upside of such an investment of time and effort is that the practice can then be applied in *all* conversations. In the absence of this kind of embodied habit, we're more susceptible to being derailed by anger, frustration, self-doubt, expedience and other human limitations. This constrains what's possible in a conversation.

While there are many approaches to collecting ourselves and coming into presence, we've focused on practices from the Leadership Embodiment approach. These practices explicitly incorporate the element of including others. We're not centring for ourselves alone, we're in service to others and the wider conversation. This reflects the founding principle of Aikido (Chapter 27): we try to act for the benefit of all concerned. It also resonates with the spirit of dialogue. Let's look at how LE practices can support the way we speak, listen and include others.

### Three energetic competences

In the LE approach, there are three energetic competences, each of which contributes to building our capacity to be in dialogue. In LE training programmes, these are set out quite concisely. Here, I've adapted each one to include an action, an associated quality of energy and a sense of how we relate to others:

- centred speaking – to speak about what matters with clarity and without attachment;

- centred listening – to listen spaciously and without taking things personally; and

- centred inclusion – to include and accept others whilst maintaining our own centre.

Together, these competences naturally encompass the four dialogue practices of listening, respecting, suspending judgement and authentic voicing (Chapter 20). Let's contrast the centred competences with their uncentred counterparts.

We've already met the practice of centred speaking in the form of both individual and partner activities (Chapter 21). Energetically, speaking about what matters with clarity and without attachment means offering our view in a way that recognises that it's simply one perspective and that others may see the world differently. We want to convey that what we're saying is important to us, *and* that we're not going to impose it on others. With less attachment, we create room for others to receive what we're saying without feeling they have to agree or disagree. We offer our words in a way that invites inquiry, which may encourage others to properly consider them.

If we're not centred when we speak, attachment tends to come 'as standard'. If we're attached to our position, the energy of our words may ring of certainty and/ or of convincing or persuading. To those on the receiving end, this can feel heavy-handed. Alternatively, if we're attached to harmonious relationships, we may speak without conviction, or choose not to speak. In this case, our words may carry little weight for those listening, which reduces their impact. We'll explore this further in Chapter 31.

We've already met the practice of centred listening in the form of both individual and partner activities (Chapter 11). Energetically, listening spaciously and without taking things personally mirrors centred speaking in that it too encompasses non-attachment. We allow the words of others to land in the space, rather than 'latching onto' them and reacting to them. This neutral receiving encourages others to share more of their thinking, feeling and experience. When this kind of listening is present, they may be prepared to risk more of themselves.

If we're not centred when we listen, we tend to be influenced by what we find interesting, what we like and/or don't like, who we like and/or don't like, and our personal agenda. We tend to sift through what's said to see what we can use for our own ends. We're also more inclined to taking things personally, perhaps feeling that we're being undermined, overruled, criticised or discounted. In essence, we react to a point being made, or to the person making it, rather than being curious about the relevance of what's said to the wider conversation.

Inherent in the first two competences is the practice of opening our energetic space to include others and to genuinely accept them in all their humanness. We've lightly touched on inclusion throughout our exploration of centring, drawing attention to the fact that we occupy an energetic space that extends beyond our skin. We've learned that we can become aware of this energetic space and consciously enlarge it to include others, whilst maintaining our own alignment and presence. This communicates acceptance and is key to both centred listening and centred speaking. When we practise centred inclusion, we hold self and other in parity. In addition, the boundaries between self and other dissolve, reducing or removing the 'edges' that can cause friction.

If we're not centred when we seek to include others, we tend to lose contact with our own centre. We lean into them and their world, and exclude ourselves. Alternatively, if we're not centred, we may actively shrink away from including others. We lean into ourselves and our own world, and separate ourselves from others. Either way, we lose parity. We'll explore the impact of this in Chapter 31.

While it can be challenging to practise the three competences consistently and well, we can always bring them to our 'entry'. If we begin a conversation with them in mind and intend to speak, listen and include others in a centred way, it will surely be better than intending otherwise.

This concludes our exploration of the three pieces of groundwork.

To bring to life the principle of 'entry' and what it sets in motion, I'll describe the experience of a coaching client. This client led a part of the National Health Service that dealt with patient data, and he'd done some embodied work with me. He'd been summoned to a meeting with his counterpart in a Government department because he and his team had got something wrong. He 'expected a kicking' – and got one. We reflected on this in a coaching session, and I asked him to show, physically, how he'd carried himself into the meeting. His whole energetic presence and demeanour signalled his expectation of 'a kicking' – he shrank into himself and had a hang-dog air. Silently, he was communicating loud and clear.

Whilst not everyone would have responded to this 'invitation' and supplied the kicking, his counterpart did. We explored how the conversation might have turned out if he had centred, carried himself into the room with calm assurance and made an active verbal 'entry', rather than a passive, silent one. My client recognised that, if he'd begun with an acknowledgement of the mistake and suggested he and his counterpart work together to limit the damage, the conversation would have been quite different. This realisation had a huge impact on him, and he repeats the story often, helping others to see how a conversation can be materially influenced by the energy we bring to 'entry'.

## Over to you …

Can you find a personal example of a situation in which you entered a conversation expecting it to go badly – and it did? What was your demeanour and energy as you approached the conversation? What did you say to begin? How did this sow the seeds for what then transpired?

Now find a counter-example, a conversation that you expected to go well – and it did. What was your demeanour and energy as you approached the conversation? What did you say to begin? How did this sow the seeds for what then transpired?

The theme of this chapter is an invitation to prepare for an important conversation by establishing where we stand and what it might be useful to discover. As we understand our own influences and agenda, and foster curiosity about where others might be coming from, we're preparing to 'enter' a conversation. We're now ready to 'be convened' with others, especially in a conversation where we expect differences to arise. We can also prepare by building our capacity to recover presence and to positively influence the quality of energy in a conversation.

The underlying principle is that, when a conversation matters, we consciously turn away from arriving unprepared and towards being considered and intentional. In addition, we turn our attention away from subject matter and towards the shape and quality of our interactions.

Whilst we can always take time to convene 'self', we may not have a role in convening a group. When we do have this opportunity, we truly have the potential to make a difference. Let's explore this ground.

## Chapter 29　Entry is everything: convening collectively

There's practical guidance on the art of convening dialogue throughout this book. For example, we've already touched on aspects of the early stages of collective entry in Chapters 13 and 26. In this chapter, we'll briefly reprise key themes and then build on them to become even more aware of what we're setting in motion.

Conventionally, a conversation begins once people have gathered. However, as we discovered in Chapter 26, the energy for a conversation starts to come to life earlier. An intention to hold a conversation is the first moment of entry, and many more follow. In each phase of convening, the energy of a conversation evolves. This invites us to pay careful attention to the process.

If the art and practice of convening is new territory, it's sometimes helpful to have a 'convening guide', someone whose principal role is to support a group to consciously attend to their container from the outset. I believe the role of such a guide to be temporary – in order to support a group to grow into holding the space for their conversation, a guide will diminish their involvement over time.

## Invitation matters

Once a convenor or convening group has decided to bring people together to talk, they attend to matters such as who to invite and why; how to invite them; and where and when people will meet. For those taking part in a conversation, the first engagement is the invitation to join it. This is a key moment of entry. The way we frame an invitation and outline the 'what', 'how' and 'why' for coming together will influence how people respond. An invitation may give rise to hopes, fears and/or expectations. It may stir up ambitions, resentments and/or frustrations. It's important to be thoughtful about *what* we communicate and *how* we do it. For example, to convene dialogue, we might be clear about the reason for meeting (advocacy) and what we might seek to discover together (inquiry).

Receiving an invitation to join a conversation stimulates a form of 'entry' in the mind and body of an invitee. It evokes a response (or reaction) in the form of internal dialogue and, perhaps, exchanges with colleagues and/or friends. Even though it may be some time before people meet, the individual energies kindled by the invitation affect the evolving collective energy and container.

In the period between an invitation and gathering in a chosen space, there are practicalities to attend to. The way we handle these also influences the initial conditions. And so, when I'm convening a workshop, I try to attend to 'administration' in a mindful way. I'm not just dealing with practical details – I'm affecting the way the container is taking shape. If my reply to a question is perfunctory or irritated, it will detract from the initial conditions, whereas a warm and generous response will augment them. When I catch myself about to react to a query or request, I use the LE centring practice to regroup and to respond thoughtfully. The situation that I'm describing is one in which people have chosen to take part. When any of those involved feel required to attend or have reservations about participating, the way we handle pre-gathering exchanges matters even more.

To further support the process of convening collectively, especially for dialogue, we can ask participants to prepare, and to engage lightly in the process of convening self (Chapter 28). We might ask them to consider what matters to them and why, and to explore what they might want to discover and/or understand. This can begin the process of setting aside certainties and preoccupations, and stimulate curiosity about what others might contribute.

In general, I'm suggesting that a 'conversation' begins long before people meet and that this influences what then unfolds. In this light, each interaction with invitees is part of a conversation that's already underway, energetically speaking. Whilst the primary focus of this book is dialogue and handling difference creatively, I believe we could usefully pay more attention to the way we convene conventional conversations or meetings. Such encounters are often set up hastily, with scant attention to the process. For example, when an invitation appears in an electronic calendar with little or no explanation, attendees may have wildly differing expectations of what a conversation is about. Small adjustments could make a big difference in such arrangements, such as being clearer about purpose, participants and how each person might contribute.

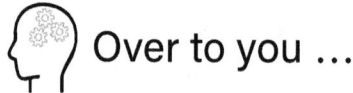

### Over to you ...

How do you typically initiate an important conversation? It may be helpful to reflect on different settings – a key conversation with a loved one, a business-critical conversation with colleagues, a conversation with stakeholders to explore strategic options.

When you decide to arrange a conversation, what happens between this decision and the moment you begin to talk? What do you tend to communicate? How do you tend to do this? What does this set in motion in terms of both possibilities and limitations?

What might you do differently for your next significant conversation?

## Collective groundwork

When people actually gather together, we reach the point of conventional entry. What matters now? In the context of dialogue, we typically consider how we'll check in individually, which prepares us to begin to come together collectively. To support this, we can use the Gibb[6] approach to attend to who 'we' are as human beings before engaging with whatever we intend to do together (Chapters 3 and 4). This process will be enhanced if those present have done some personal preparation before meeting. After we've made contact at a human level, we can ask: if this is who we are, what are we here to talk about? When we've clarified this, we can explore how we'll talk and listen together, asking: what might arise and how will we hold it?

In some ways, convening collectively mirrors the process of convening self – but with many distinct hearts, bodies, minds and voices rather than many internal voices. In Chapter 28, we considered three pieces of groundwork for convening self:

- Groundwork: clarifying – my intentions and what really matters to me;

- Groundwork: being curious – what am I seeking to discover?; and

- Groundwork: embodying good practice – preparing to carry myself well.

In group settings, there are additional considerations because we're convening many voices and, initially, it may not be clear how to include them and gain a shared sense of what matters and what we might explore. When we're convening self, a *personal* container holds our many voices. This natural container is so familiar that we may not be fully aware of it. It's composed of things such as our values, principles, concerns, preferences, personal standards and ways of doing things. It's a repository for our thinking, feeling and expression and, in preparing for a conversation, we work within it to clarify our intentions and what we're seeking to discover.

For a group, there's no obvious equivalent to this repository – so how do we bring the different intentions, uncertainties and questions of many distinct voices into the conversation? To convene collectively, we take time to draw out and acknowledge individual voices. As we do this, we begin to shape a holding space that will allow us to connect with a shared sense of what matters and what we might explore together. Then, as we gain some insight into the range of thoughts, feelings and perspectives of the separate hearts, bodies, minds and voices of those present, we think about how they can be held. And so, to prepare for dialogue, we pay attention to the container. We consider how the values, principles, concerns, preferences and ways of doing things of those present might hold the uncertainties, doubts, deeper feelings, confusion and innermost thoughts that people normally keep to themselves. If we're not explicit about how this humanness will be held – if we're not consciously holding a container – it may be difficult for group members to find the honesty and courage to speak freely.

These considerations call for two pieces of groundwork to be added to those for convening self, giving five in total:

- Groundwork: clarifying – drawing out intentions and what really matters for each person, their 'take' on the proposed territory for the conversation and how they wish to participate;

- Groundwork: distilling – refining collective intentions to gain a sense of what matters to all present;

- Groundwork: being curious – surfacing what each person is seeking to discover – expecting differences, and forming questions that might be explored together;

- Groundwork: container – articulating what will make this conversation possible, considering how those present will consciously hold all that arises; and

- Groundwork: embodying good practice – supporting those present to uphold the container and to carry themselves well in whatever unfolds.

In essence, convening is the collective process of consciously preparing for the conversation ahead. Out of necessity, this 'entry' is done as part of the conversation. This makes it easy to skip over or omit because, once we've gathered, the pull of 'content', purpose and getting things done can capture our attention. Without shared preparation, existing conversational patterns tend to take hold and the opportunity for a different kind of conversation is lost.

### Commonality and difference

Through the process of checking in and collectively engaging with the five pieces of groundwork, we establish some shared ground – this, in itself, is an aspect of containment. In the words of Timothy B. Kelly, Professor Emeritus of Social Work and former editor of the online journal *Groupwork:*

a group needs enough commonality that people can bond and connect and enough difference to give the group energy. In addition, if group purpose is really clear and powerful, a group can tolerate a huge range of difference.[23]

An aspiration to be in dialogue calls for a similar balance between the human connections and relationships amongst participants and a shared focus that's strong enough to hold interest and engagement. The latter gives a centre to the conversation, lessening the attention and energy given to 'sides' (Chapter 14). In this way, having 'a centre' of common ground is an element of the container.

My personal experience of being invited into dialogue that doesn't have 'a centre' is that it's somewhat unsatisfactory. Whether in the easy chairs of a home, a 'circle' in a development programme or sitting around a table, this kind of 'open' dialogue was always hosted sincerely and skilfully. However, without a clear centre, these conversations seemed to be a sequence of separate contributions: I rarely found personal meaning in them, let alone the sense of shared meaning that arises from dialogue. This brings me back to Isaacs, who asserts that we 'can't make dialogue happen'.

In the language of Scharmer's Four Fields of Conversation (Chapter 22), when we try to make dialogue happen, we often encounter a threshold, or crisis, between one field and another (Chapter 23). The threshold between Field I and Field II is a sense of frustration that, despite our efforts and good intentions, we're not getting into dialogue. In my various experiences of 'open' dialogue, I feel we may have faltered at this threshold in the absence of some shared ground.

In the context of 'enough commonality' and 'enough difference', discovering a shared centre supports the container. It also introduces some parameters for shared inquiry, which may assist us to be discerning about the inclusion of diverse views and people. As we articulate and agree the conditions for our conversation, a shared centre can guide us to uphold them.

{ Over to you ...

Take some time to reflect on the balance of 'enough commonality' and 'enough difference' in a group.

Can you find an example of a conversation with a clear shared focus? What unfolded and how did it feel? What might have been missing? What was the balance between commonality and difference?

Can you find an example of a conversation where shared purpose was absent or unclear? What unfolded and how did it feel? What might have been missing? What was the balance between commonality and difference?

What tentative conclusions might you draw?

It's time to turn our attention to entering a conversation once it's underway. Whereas we can prepare somewhat for 'entry' and even arrange for it to be guided or supported in some way, we're now in the territory of discerning whether, when and how to voice what we're thinking and feeling. The word 'discerning' is important: each time we have an impulse to speak or to stay quiet, to make a statement or ask a question, it pays to pause. This pause represents an intervention in our 'auto-response' tendency. Therefore, before looking at entering, or intervening in, a conversation, we'll look at 'intervening' in our inner dialogue and embodied experience so that we contribute in a considered way.

# Chapter 30  Entry is everything: intervening in self

However well we prepare and however good our intentions, when we engage with others and step into communal energy, we'll encounter the unexpected. Other people will arrive with their own level of preparedness and their own take on things.

During a conversation, we may react to something that's said (or not said) and find ourselves ready to fight or defend our view – we have 'a side'. We may get drawn into a particular line of thought and lose sight of (or discount) other possibilities – we've joined 'a side'. We may be surprised, confused, frustrated and/ or otherwise at a loss, and then rely on what's most familiar – caught up in our own uncertainty, we stop listening. We may feel that we're not able to say something that might be difficult for others to hear – we withhold our true voice. We may find ourselves judging others and their contribution – we're neither respecting nor suspending judgement. These are the moments in which it's fruitful to pause and 'intervene' in our auto-response patterns. First though, we need to notice the auto-response tendency, which can be easier said than done.

Everything I've described happens for me, to a greater or lesser extent – and I suspect you have similar experiences. Such 'auto-responses' are part of being human, and each has a mind element and a body element. The mind element arises from the suite of thought patterns and habits that we've developed over the years. These reflect our character, education, professional training and life experience. The body element reflects our personal encoding of the survival instincts activated by the autonomic nervous system. This too has developed over many years.

To 'intervene in self', we become more aware of these patterns and, when they're not helpful, we pause and make different choices. This involves noticing what's happening within us – in both mind and body – as we hear what others say. When we react and feel an impulse to speak, we pause … and look for the cause. Perhaps we want to correct something, solve a problem, promote an opinion, defend and/ or protect someone or something, or register an objection. Whatever the reason, we pause to weigh up how/whether what we want to express might serve collective intentions. This process of pause-examine-consider is a shift towards regarding our embodied experiences and inner dialogue as interesting data, rather than a signal to contribute to the conversation.

For many of us, this is a new way to engage with ourselves, and it supports us to be 'part of the method' for our conversation (Chapter 16). When we bystand our familiar patterns of thought and modes of interacting, it can be exacting, insightful, disconcerting and rewarding in equal measure. It requires a respectful curiosity about our inner experience, and a spirit of candour and acceptance. Coming to know ourselves in this way is lifelong work – and I've found it to be of great value on a personal level. For example, I now (mostly) notice my judgements and, rather than expressing them, I wonder what I don't yet know or understand. I inquire and, on the whole, this enriches my conversations.

As we begin to recognise our habits of mind and body, how can we intervene in them? We've already explored two approaches that can assist us – one for mind, the left-hand column approach (Chapter 17), and one for body, the Leadership Embodiment four-part centring practice (Appendix B). Let's briefly revisit these approaches in the context of intervening in an 'auto-response' pattern.

## Body on alert

We'll start with the body and the 'alert' messages generated by the mild threat or pressure we feel when we're challenged, potentially obstructed, unsure of ourselves, provoked, in a spotlight or in a minority. We already know that this alert invites us to use the LE centring practice, which is the body element of how we can 'intervene in self'. As we access the aligned and open flow state of centre, we counter the effects of the autonomic nervous system. In addition, our relationship with 'self' changes – we touch into an expanded self that has room for other people and possibilities. Our personal preoccupations and concerns diminish.

We began to explore our personal survival pattern in Chapter 8. To refine our sense of how it shows up in our body, we can recall an example of an awkward or challenging moment in a conversation. When we do this, our body usually recreates the sensations of the experience which allows us to become more familiar with them. Perhaps parts of our body tighten or loosen, become hot or cold, or move in some way. Perhaps we experience flutters, heaviness, twitches, shrinking or flinching. Perhaps our breath and/or heartbeat changes. If we draw on different examples, we can build a map of the sensations and micro-movements that arise in these moments of alert.

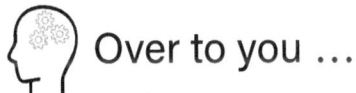

## Over to you …

Take some time with this exploration. Think back to a moment when you felt put on the spot in a conversation. As you relive the moment, notice what happens in different zones of your body. What do you experience in your forehead and jaw, your neck, throat and shoulders? What sensations arise in your chest and belly? What happens to your hands and feet? How does your heartbeat and/or breathing change?

Shake these feelings off and do something different for a while. Then choose another such moment and repeat … then shake it off, pause … and then find a third such moment.

In terms of your embodied experience, what characteristics do the three examples share? Note the overall pattern and be curious about when and how it arises.

Even when we're familiar with the 'alert' signals in our body, it's tempting to ignore them. If we do, they tend to play out in three main ways. One is that we override the alert and press on, probably with a little more determination and (perhaps) force or edge than we might have intended. Another is that we pay too much heed to the alert and back off. A third is that we spar or stall for a while in order to assess the situation or simply for the fun of a scrap. While none of these tendencies is intrinsically problematic, the reactive, off-centre energy that accompanies them affects others. In addition, if a pattern is so strongly embedded that it's effectively our only option, it limits what we're able to do.

In essence, when an auto-response kicks in, we focus on what caused it, becoming vigilant and wary: physiology is 'in charge'. Even if we try to contribute skilfully, our energy communicates that we're 'on alert'. Others pick up on this and react to it. Reactivity is often 'viral': the collective temperature rises and it becomes more difficult for anyone to conduct themselves well. This shift in energy can happen within seconds.

As we become more familiar with our personal survival pattern, we may discover where it starts and/or where it 'shouts' most loudly. Then, when an embodied alert occurs, we can acknowledge it as a signal to do the four-part centring practice (Appendix B), which changes our energetic state. Others pick up this, and respond to it. Their energy settles and they become more able to conduct themselves well. Centring, too, can be viral.

In essence, we have a choice about the quality of energy we bring to an intervention in a conversation. This is important because the *way* we enter influences the effect that we have. We'll look at this in more detail in the next chapter.

Finally, if we're not able to discern how our survival pattern shows up in our body, we can simply assume that, most of the time, we're on autopilot (or off-centre) – and do the centring practice anyway. In fact, there's no downside to centring regularly and frequently. This embodied practice is, in itself, a 'pause': it supports and enhances our ability to see what's going on in our mind and to accept what we find there as interesting data. With this perspective, we can be discerning about what we do with the stories we're telling ourselves. This brings us to the mind element of intervening in self.

# Habits of mind

To prepare to intervene in our 'habits of mind', it's helpful to identify our recurring thought patterns. In my case, these include a tendency to plan, a preference for seeking quick agreement and an inclination to focus on big picture possibilities. Whilst these attributes can be strengths, I can overplay them: too tight a plan squeezes out opportunity; speedy agreement may deter questions and alternative points of view; and I can skip over details when inspired by a vision. Each of these tendencies can cause problems later – and, in becoming familiar with them, I'm more likely to notice when they're not helpful, which creates an opportunity to change tack.

To become more familiar with what's going on in our mind, we can use the left-hand column approach (Chapter 17). We've explored how this framework can support us to reflect on a conversation that's challenged or puzzled us. We can apply the essence of it in real time because, during a conversation, we're usually somewhat aware of 'what I'm thinking and feeling, but not saying'. In the moment, the left-hand column approach invites us to pay attention to the gap between our internal dialogue and what we're saying. To do this, we bystand our thoughts and feelings: we zoom out and notice them. We can also pay attention to our state of mind, the energy of our thoughts – perhaps we're uncomfortable, frustrated, energised, anxious, resentful and/or concerned.

This empirical approach to identifying our habits of mind can be tricky, because we're too close to our thoughts to see them clearly. To use our mind to see our mind involves creating a sense of space – and, preferably, a still quietness. The left-hand column approach allows us to do this. We can also draw on mindfulness practices and apps (which you can find by searching online).

In addition, we can make use of some of the profiling tools used in personal development – such as the drivers and life-scripts of Transactional Analysis; the preferences in inventories such as Insights Discovery or the Myers-Briggs Type Indicator; or approaches that identify unconscious biases or conflict styles. At this stage, it might be useful to collate what you've discovered about your tendencies in any personal development that you've done.

Less obvious habits of mind might be better described as habits of heart – our values, principles and beliefs. These act as lenses through which we see the world, often without noticing they're there. For example, one of my values is authenticity, so I may react negatively to someone who seems to lack sincerity, and then discount what they're saying. Influenced by my sense of what's good or bad, I don't respect their view – or them. The mind element of our auto-response tendencies arises because, however we describe them, we all have prejudices, preoccupations and preconceptions and we filter our experience through them. If we accept this inconvenient reality, we can work constructively with the factors that constrain our capacity to include others and to truly listen to what they say.

Whichever approach we use, when we pause and examine our mind, we create space in which we can consider how and/or whether we share what we find. We may choose to be transparent and reveal some of our 'inner workings' with others. This bridges the gap between what we're saying and what we're thinking and feeling, and allows us to communicate more clearly. We can also use the four-part centring practice to bring body and mind into alignment. This changes the energy that we bring to what we say, which can put a conversation onto a different footing. In a moment, we'll take a look at one approach for doing this and then explore the impact of it in the next chapter. First, let's pause.

## Over to you …

Recall a recent conversation that still puzzles you – perhaps it fizzled out or got derailed in some way. Use the left-hand column approach: in two columns, record what was said (as far as you can remember) in the right-hand one, then, in the left-hand one, record what you were thinking and feeling but not saying. You can look back at Case Study 2 in Chapter 17, if this is helpful.

As you zoom out and observe your inner landscape alongside the outer conversation, what do you notice? How might you have contributed to the way the conversation played out?

We can enrich the data in our left-hand column by drawing on another aspect of the Leadership Embodiment approach. We can use the three archetypal centres of energy and presence – head, heart and core/gut – to gain greater insight into our inner experience.

## Using the three archetypal centres

We met these three centres in Chapter 12, when we looked at intention, and we've revisited them in various ways. Here, we'll explore how we can use them in conjunction with the left-hand column approach. The idea of combining the three energy centres with the left-hand column came from my friend and fellow-practitioner, Lorna Jackson. When she writes up a left-hand column, she uses head, heart and core/gut as subheadings to capture what she was thinking and feeling but not saying. She says that this helps her to recover aspects of her experience that she might otherwise overlook. I now adopt this method myself – it's inspired.

First, let's look at the archetypal centres in a little more detail. Each represents an aspect of our humanness which, when we're off-centre, we tend to overplay or underplay. To start at the top, the head is the home of perception and, on autopilot, it tends to seek to control, organise and fix (over-engagement), or seek to abdicate and be helpless (under-engagement). The heart is the home of connection and, off-centre, it tends to seek approval and acceptance from others (over-engagement), or seek separation and independence (under-engagement). The core or gut is the seat of confidence and, habitually, it tends to seek danger and thrills (over-engagement), or seek certainty and safety (under-engagement). Once we're aware of these off-centre tendencies, and the associated habits of thought, we can intervene with a centring practice.

To use my own patterns as an example: when uncentred, my tendencies are to control, separate and be slightly risk-averse. And, occasionally, I'll over-correct and act with bravado, try too hard to be liked, or shrug and say 'whatever ...' in that bored tone that's recently become common. When I reflect on a conversation using the three archetypal centres of energy in conjunction with the left-hand column approach, these tendencies show up clearly.

303

When we notice the off-centre 'seeking' tendencies, we can come into balance by doing the four-part centring practice. This brings all three centres into equal presence. The centred core or gut, which is confident and powerful, provides a base for the centred heart, which knows it's *already* connected. The centred core and heart support the head to perceive clearly and with perspective.

By combining the left-hand column approach with the three archetypal centres to examine our inner experience, we may realise that one energetic centre is dominant. For instance, we may be headstrong, leading mostly from ideas and reasoning, or heart-led, where we're principally guided by values and relational considerations. Or perhaps we rely on gut-feel to sense what's important. For some people, two of the centres may be prominent, but nearly all of us have one that's less-used. For me, it's the heart centre. For many, it's the core or gut. For some, the head is less active.

The key point is that, when we're on autopilot, it's unlikely that all three archetypal centres are equally engaged when we speak, listen and act. This means we give out a mixed message. We've all been on the receiving end of a mixed message – those experiences where we just *know* that someone is dissembling, or that their heart isn't in what they're saying, or they're being disingenuous. However plausible they seem on the surface, we experience some disquiet, some incoherence. We pick this up from the energy of the speaker, who will know, at some level, that they're being evasive, half-hearted or insincere.

In general, our communication will be clear and congruent if our words and energy are aligned and synchronised. Recording our experience in a left-hand column can help us to see what happens when one or more of the archetypal centres is less active and/or present. When we understand the impact of our misaligned energy, the shortest route to return to alignment is the four-part centring practice. When we centre, our energy and words are naturally synchronised and what we intend to communicate is what lands. It's worth putting in the repetitions that prepare us to access this option in challenging moments.

## Over to you …

Revisit the left-hand column that you were invited to prepare in the previous 'Over to you …' inquiry and use the frame of head, heart and core/gut to take a fresh look at it. What additional information can you retrieve about what you were thinking and feeling but not saying?

Which archetypal centre is most evident? Which is least evident? If you'd been able to give equal weight to head, heart and core/gut in the moment, what might you have said? If you'd been able to centre in the moment, how might you have said it?

Before we turn our attention to intervening in a conversation, I'll share some well-known words from the field of dialogue. In *Theory U*,[16] Otto Scharmer refers to a conversation in which Bill O'Brien (the then-CEO of Hanover Insurance) drew attention to the relationship between our inner landscape and the impact of any intervention we make, saying:

> The success of an intervention depends on the *interior condition* of the intervener.

These words invite us to attend to our 'interior condition' and to relate to ourselves in a profoundly new way. They also invite us to actively and consciously intervene in self as we take part in a conversation. When we do this, our words are more likely to have the impact we intend – this is the theme of the next chapter.

# Chapter 31 Entry is everything: intervening in conversation

Once a conversation is underway, the collective energy created by those present is sustained or unsettled by the way each person carries themselves and contributes. The container is a living thing, fluctuating in response to individual energies. There's a natural pulsing in the feeling tone of the space, a rising and falling, an intensifying and easing. It's almost as if the container breathes with the ebb and flow of our individual and collective capacity to consciously hold it. In this context, everything we do is an intervention, whether we speak or don't speak. Everything is entry.

As we attend to the flow of a conversation alongside our individual experience, we begin to consider how an intervention might contribute to collective concerns. As we do this, we can use the approaches from the previous chapter to support us to intervene in our tendencies to contribute in habitual ways. This creates space to be more mindful of what we might say and whether and how we say it.

In this chapter, we'll look at two things: how an intervention might affect the collective energy of a conversation; and the potential impact of our words on others. The way we intervene is especially important when difference is present because, when we encounter it, our primal patterning puts us 'on alert' and prompts a reaction that's designed to protect us: we attack, defend and/or avoid. When our personal energy is on alert, it can activate a similar state in others. An intervention will therefore be most effective if we attend to the way that the energy we bring to it affects the conversation as a whole.

To consider how an intervention might affect collective energy, we'll briefly revisit the four fields of conversation (Chapters 14, 23 and 24). Then, we'll revisit intent–impact (Chapter 18) and use it to look at how our personal energy influences the way that our words land.

# The four fields – energies and differences revisited

In Chapters 23 and 24, we explored both the energy of each field of conversation and how difference tends to arise and be handled in it. In the diagram below, the essence of those deliberations is combined into one diagram.

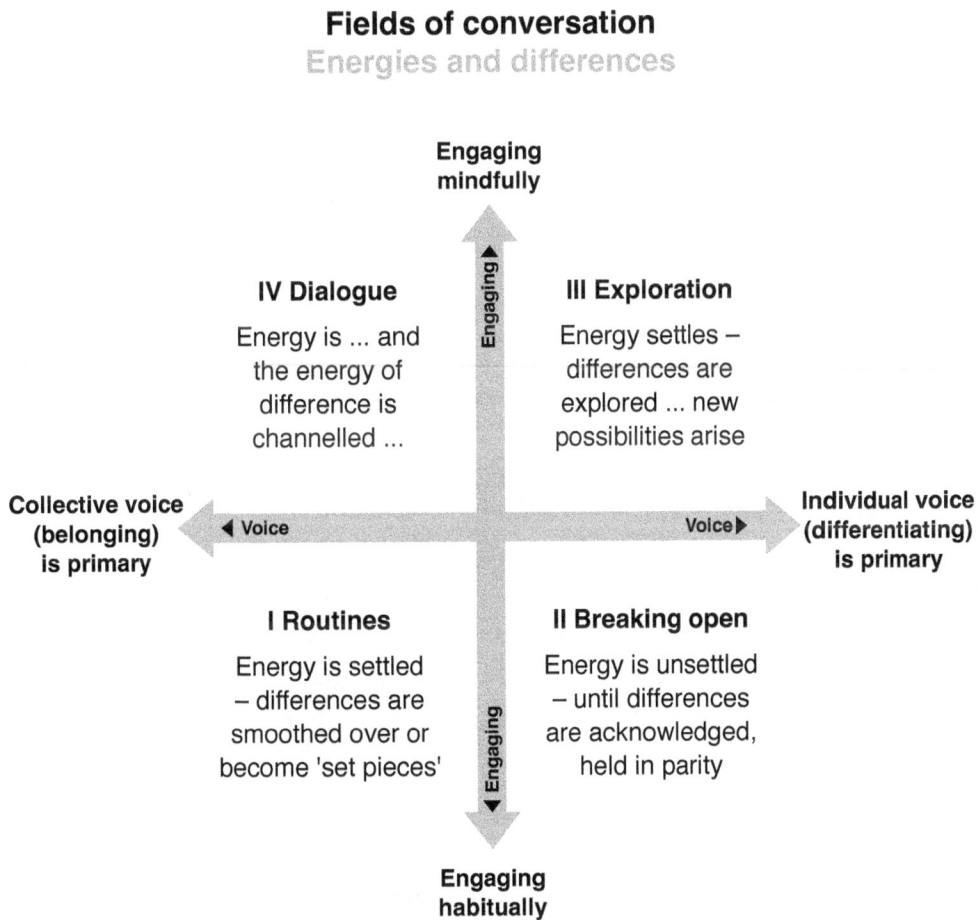

**Fields of conversation**

Energies and differences

**Engaging mindfully**

Engaging ▲

**IV Dialogue**

Energy is ... and the energy of difference is channelled ...

**III Exploration**

Energy settles – differences are explored ... new possibilities arise

**Collective voice (belonging) is primary**

◀ Voice

Voice ▶

**Individual voice (differentiating) is primary**

**I Routines**

Energy is settled – differences are smoothed over or become 'set pieces'

**II Breaking open**

Energy is unsettled – until differences are acknowledged, held in parity

Engaging ▼

**Engaging habitually**

Drawing on the work of Otto Scharmer

In what follows, we'll review key elements of this combined representation and briefly look at what this means for the way we intervene. We'll also pay attention to the thresholds between the fields. The four spaces and three thresholds are:

*Field I:* Routines – energy is settled, tacit agreement not to rock the boat

*[Threshold: the conversational boat is rocked, often out of frustration]*

*Field II:* Breaking open – differences unsettle the energy, the conversational boat is rocking

*[Threshold: the boat is steadied by centring, using the practices of suspending judgement and listening, and acknowledging what's said]*

*Field III:* Exploration – the conversational boat steadies as opinions are less tightly held, energy settles

*[Threshold: individual identities are less tightly held]*

*Field IV:* Dialogue – those present become the boat/container, energy is simply as it is, although it's susceptible to being unsettled

When we view the conversational fields in this way, we can see that each intervention will have an energetic impact. If we're trying to create the conditions for a different kind of conversation, for dialogue, we take account of this. Let's look at how we might intervene in each field and then briefly review the potential of threshold moments.

### Choosing how we intervene

In Field I, bounded by habitual engagement and fitting in, we may decide to nudge those present to acknowledge views that differ from the shared narratives and norms of the collective routine. We can also intervene to invite these differences to be expressed, which may actively unsettle collective energy. This kind of intervention may take us into Field II.

Alternatively, if a conversation is proving to be fit for purpose, we may want to steward our personal energy so that we *don't* unsettle things. When we're aware of

308

the nature of this field, we can consciously choose to reinforce the established pattern and energy or to disturb it: we can choose whether or not to rock the boat.

In Field II, we may want to give careful consideration to the way an intervention will affect the heightened and changeable (even volatile) energy that often arises in the presence of difference. The boat is rocking – and the way we contribute will add to this energy or moderate it. Therefore, it pays to be as mindful as possible about what we say and how we say it. We might also be thoughtful about collective capacity to hold the unsettled energy: in this moment, how much rocking can be contained in a way that supports us to navigate our differences skilfully? If we reach beyond our collective capacity to hold them, differences may become more deeply entrenched, or even irreconcilable.

In this field, the practice of bystanding can be a particularly helpful intervention. For example, we may notice that a pattern of interactions is forming – perhaps, collectively, we're going down a rabbit hole or off at a tangent, or perhaps something is being studiously avoided (an 'elephant in the room'). In being present to the conversation in a different way, then pausing and centring, we can offer this information to others. We aim to reflect observable attributes, in the way a mirror does, and to describe them as neutrally as possible. When we're able to do this, we raise collective awareness of the nature of the conversational entity, and this allows those present to choose whether to continue or change tack.

As the reactive energy of difference enlivens Field II, the antidote is centring, suspending judgement, listening and acknowledging different points of view. Centring directly contributes towards settling the collective energy, and supports us to embody the dialogue practices. When we acknowledge what's being said, we demonstrate that a speaker is being heard. When someone knows that their words are being taken into account, they're more able to loosen their grip on their opinion, even if it's dearly held. All this begins to create space for difference and, when enough people feel recognised, a conversation comes to the gateway of Field III.

As differences become interesting, rather than alarming, energy settles – we're now in Field III. And yet, if collective energy becomes too settled, we might slip into a variation of Field I and, once again, become reluctant to rock the boat. Equally, if the energy is too unsettled, we risk a return to the turbulent waters of Field II.

There's a 'just right' energy for Field III, a kind of creative tension that can support fresh thinking. In choosing how we intervene, we aim to uphold this delicate balance. Sometimes we'll want to enliven the energy and bring a little 'edge' to the conversation. And sometimes we'll want to dampen the energy, to support the mindful engagement that allows us to remain in the realm of exploration.

In this field, we also begin to take more account of the entity of the conversation itself, its overall tone and scope. This helps us to see our contribution as an intervention in service to the whole conversation. As we tune into collective energy and experience, our sense of individual self may loosen – we've come to the gateway of Field IV.

If a conversation does become a Field IV experience, listening becomes a palpable sense of attending, receiving and holding lightly. Collective voice is spoken through individuals. It doesn't matter who speaks; each contribution reflects an expression of the conversation itself and is offered for exploration and contemplation. In this field, the act of intervening loses meaning and relevance. While the collective energy of mindful engagement is sustained, the conversation is holding itself and what needs to happen, happens.

This collective energy is, paradoxically, both tangibly profound and somewhat delicate. The collective conscious holding is finely balanced, which means that it can be unsettled if there's a break in someone's attention. For a period of time, it's as if several minds become one. And then, as one or two people drift and get caught up in a personal narrative, conscious holding is diluted and energy may shift into one of the other fields. What's most important in this field is that we actively intervene in 'self', and become even more mindful of our presence and engagement.

When conscious holding does become diluted and collective presence is lost, we can intervene by inviting those present to pause and regroup, possibly by centring together. This may support us to recapture the energy of Field IV.

### Thresholds

Overall, as we move in and through the fields, we can be thoughtful about whether an intervention will reinforce current patterns and energies or disturb them. In addition, we may begin to notice when the energy of a conversation changes.

These thresholds are important, representing a kind of 'tipping point' between one field and the next. In these moments, there may be a natural pause, a sense of openness and/or confusion. This may feel uncomfortable – and someone might make a joke to relieve tension or fill a perceived gap, or might try to usher a conversation back to familiar territory. If, instead, we navigate these thresholds with courage and composure, a conversation can shift into different territory.

At these thresholds, the way we steward ourselves is important and can make the difference between a conversation evolving into a new phase or returning to a familiar pattern. As ever, the short cut to being skilful in these moments is to use the four-part centring practice (Appendix B). The act of centring takes 'self' out of the equation and naturally introduces a spacious, calm and inclusive energy. This enhances collective capacity to hold whatever is present – and means that, if we add something provocative into the mix, it's more likely to land in a useful way. There's no downside to centring – a sentiment I'm happy to repeat.

In fact, there's an upside – centring not only changes our relationship with self, it also changes our relationship with others. As we centre, we expand our personal space to include others. In addition, we can consciously shape our personal space to reflect our intentions, and this significantly influences the impact of any intervention we make. We'll explore this in what follows. First, let's reflect.

## Over to you …

What new insights or questions have arisen from revisiting the fields of conversation?

How much attention do you typically give to the 'ambience' of a conversation, its collective vibe? Can you recall an occasion when you witnessed or experienced a 'shift' in collective energy that either allowed a conversation to blossom or stifled a sense of potential? How might you more often tune in to such changes in energy?

311

Let's turn our attention to the way an intervention may affect others.

## Intent–impact: everything is entry

We first met the intent–impact framework when we were working with Case Study 2 (Chapter 18). It invites us to pay attention to the reality that we can only know our own intent and the impact of another person's words on us. Unless we inquire, we don't know someone else's intent or how they're affected by what they're hearing. In a group, these gaps in knowing bring great complexity – within a conversation, much of the experience of others is unavailable unless we specifically ask.

To further complicate matters, most of us (certainly me) are likely to 'colour' (or flavour) what others say by assuming that we know both their motivation and what they mean. This muddies the waters. Based on partial information such as an expression or gesture, we make inferences about the way that others are making sense of a conversation. For instance, when someone is silent, it's easy to assume they're in agreement when they're simply processing what they've heard. When we make assumptions about what others do and/or say, and about how/whether they're taking in an experience, we obscure what's actually unfolding. This takes us further away from any shared understanding.

It therefore pays to be circumspect about our left-hand column – the stories we're telling ourselves as we listen to others – and to practise centred inquiry (Appendix D). This supports us to consciously seek to discover the intentions of others, what they're trying to convey and how they're being affected by what's unfolding. If we inquire, we surface more of what's not known and we also 'clean up our own act' by becoming more aware of our personal intentions and experiences. If we don't inquire, we're really in a conversation with ourselves, based on our preferences, assumptions, projections, biases and misunderstandings.

In terms of intent–impact, we had a fairly detailed look at intent as part of convening self (Chapter 28). Our intentions shape what we say and this has an influence on the impact we have. However, the impact of our words is significantly influenced by the shape and quality of the energy we bring to them. In order to align the impact of our words with our intent, we'll work with our body and energetic presence, and build on the experience of our energy extending beyond our physical body into a 'personal space' (Chapters 11 and 21). This space is formally known as our peri-personal space, and we'll now explore how we can consciously shape it so that an intervention reflects our intentions. The way we do this depends on whether we're advocating or inquiring.

In general, when at rest and out of consciousness, our peri-personal space tends to be broadly spherical in nature, extending in all directions, including up and down. However, it may be uneven – or, at least, our awareness of it may be incomplete. You may have explored your personal experience of this space in Chapter 11.

One reason that our resting space may seem to be irregular or lopsided is that, as humans, we place great emphasis on what we see. Often, we attend only to our visual field, a broad shape that fans out in front of us. We tend to pay less heed to the rest of our 360° experience – unless we actively develop the capacity to do so.

One method for paying attention to our whole peri-personal space is to adopt the Leadership Embodiment practices outlined in these pages and use them regularly. We can also practise activating our peripheral vision by shifting our attention away from specific objects and 'taking in' the whole room. This 'softens' our gaze and creates space for other forms of sensory awareness. Together, paying deliberate attention to space and softening our gaze lessens our focus on the visual field. We expand our perspective, both visually and in our mind. When our peri-personal space is circular, this supports the 'receiving' practices of listening, suspending judgement and respecting. It also supports inquiry. When our peri-personal space has the triangular shape of advocating energy, the same principle applies.

As we become more aware of our peri-personal space, we can develop our capacity to enlarge it. We can do this by training our imagination or by regular use of a tool or piece of equipment. In Chapter 20, I described the way that a physical tool becomes part of us if we use it regularly: our personal space expands to include it and we 'map' it as part of ourselves. For example, in the case of an artist, their brushes become integral to their being and move as an extension of their body. Further, in elite team sports, players often map the whole pitch and team as their peri-personal space. This attribute – including others in our peri-personal map – is important for our quest to embody dialogue practices.

For example, when we practise centred speaking (Appendix G), we consciously shape our peri-personal space to reflect our intention and whether we're advocating or inquiring. We then extend our sense of space to include others and map them as part of 'me'. When we do this without losing our own centre, we naturally hold others (and their views) in parity. In the next chapter, we'll add one further element to our centring practice – it will support us to balance our own energy with the energy of others.

The capacity to expand our peri-personal space to include others is a great asset when intervening in a conversation. When we include others in our energetic space, what we say doesn't bump up against their sense of self, their beliefs and judgements about what's right or wrong and/or good or bad. This means that they're likely to be more able to consider what we say, perhaps even to be curious about our view – the energies of difference have less traction.

It might stretch your sense of what's tangible, logical and/or practical to embrace the role of opening your peri-personal space to include and accept others. And yet, in my experience, this practice can transform a conversation – for self and others. I encourage you to explore this ground.

## Over to you …

How might you explore your peri-personal space and experiment with the principle of expanding it to include others? You might try this in different circumstances, such as when you're listening and when you're speaking – when you're able do it, what's the impact? How do others respond?

What insights arise from your explorations?

We'll now build on this perspective of the relationship between our peri-personal space and the impact of what we say to explore how we can align our energy and intentions so that an intervention lands well. First, a word of caution: there's a lot of detail in the next section, which describes different aspects of centred and uncentred advocacy and inquiry. As you read, don't try to absorb everything. Instead, consider which of the off-centre interventions most applies to you, and explore what changes if you're able to centre before you intervene in this way. This is an invitation to focus on changing your practice by refining what you do naturally, rather than trying to get everything 'right'. For the other off-centre variations, you might use them to better understand what you observe playing out in your conversations. Our focus is on changing practice – and so we proceed step by step.

The essence of what follows is that, when we're centred and our words and energy are synchronised, the impact of an intervention is more likely to reflect our intent. When we're not centred, we can say the same words but they have a different impact. To explore this, we'll look at four types of spoken contribution, adapted from the speech actions of Kantor's Four-Player Model.[17] They are:

- advocating *towards* a position, a principle, an idea – which Kantor calls a *move*;

- advocating *away from* a proposal, a view, a perception – which Kantor calls an *oppose*;

- inquiring *into* what's been said, seeking information or greater understanding – which Kantor calls a *follow*; and

- inquiring *around* what's been said, seeking broader context and perspective – which Kantor calls a *bystand*.

As we discovered in Chapter 21, advocacy and inquiry each have a characteristic shape and energy and, when these attributes align with our intention, we communicate clearly. When we're out of alignment, others may be confused by what we say. To look at this in greater detail, we'll start with advocating energy.

# Intervening: advocating energy

You may remember that advocacy naturally has a triangular or wedge-shaped energy. This presents a challenge: advocacy can feel ... well ... pointed! We can see the effect of this 'pointed' energy when we (quite literally) talk *at* someone. It's as if we prod them with our finger – and they react accordingly. The pointed energy of our peri-personal space touches or pierces their personal space – whether they're listening, inquiring or advocating.

The diagram below depicts advocating energy from a bird's-eye perspective. In it, Scenario A shows the person on the left as embodying advocating energy, whilst the person on the right is embodying the receptive energy of listening or inquiring. The pointed nature of advocacy contrasts sharply with the circular receiving energy, and this may be unsettling for the person on the right.

In Scenario B, the advocacy of the person on the left is resisted or opposed by similar energy from the person on the right, which may lead to a focus on point and counterpoint. This is the energy of difference, an energetic representation of debate. In both scenarios, being on the receiving end of the pointed nature of certainty and/or insistence can feel personal. This is what creates the sense of prodding.

## Bird's-eye view of energy
### Advocating scenarios

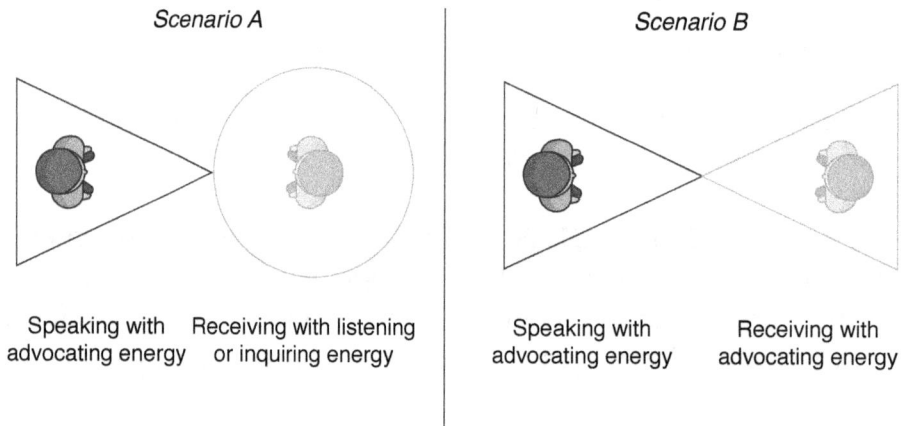

| Scenario A | Scenario B |
|---|---|
| Speaking with advocating energy    Receiving with listening or inquiring energy | Speaking with advocating energy    Receiving with advocating energy |

To advocate skilfully, we centre and expand our peri-personal space to include others. This applies whether we're speaking for or against a point of view, and is the essence of centred advocacy (Chapter 21). First, we tune in to a triangular or wedge-shaped peri-personal space, with strong supporting sides and a clear, incisive point or leading edge. Then we consciously enlarge this space so that the point or leading edge reaches into the distance, and widen the sides and the space behind us proportionately. We continue the expansion until those present are included in our energy, whilst staying connected to our centre. This is depicted in the diagram below.

## Bird's-eye view of energy

Centred advocacy

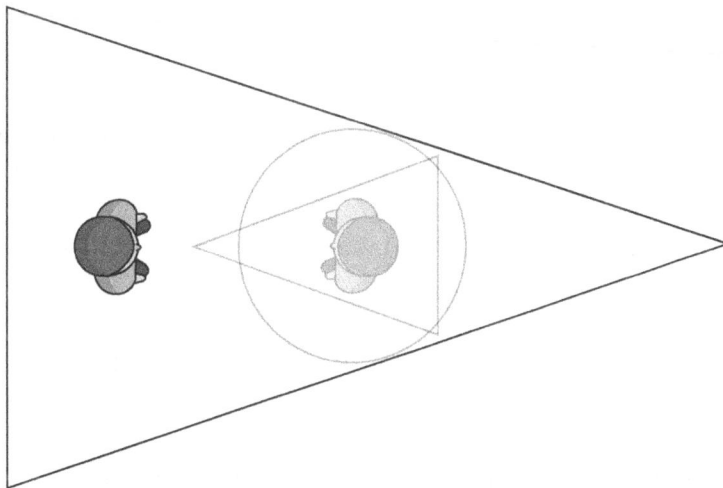

Key:

Centred advocacy, energetic space is expanded evenly to include others and hold them in parity

Included energetically, whether listening, inquiring or advocating

317

In terms of impact, when we embody centred advocacy and include others, we dissolve the energetic boundary between us. This changes the way our words land – they no longer feel personal. The point we're making lies beyond those we've included, and our energy no longer intrudes into their personal space. In the shared energy, whatever we say feels universal and is easier to receive and consider. Our self-interest is lessened: the inclusion of others in our peri-personal space (an aspect of heart) is the energetic equivalent of focusing on the bigger picture (an aspect of core/gut). We can enhance this experience by using the head-heart-core approach to clarify our intentions.

When we embody centred advocacy, we're no longer 'making a point'. Instead, we're offering a view – whether we're advocating 'towards' or 'away from', making a move or an oppose – whilst remaining aware of relationships and the wider system.

In contrast, if we're off-centre when we advocate, our efforts to influence the direction of a conversation can feel either overly insistent or somewhat vague or fuzzy. In each case, we don't hold people and/or views in parity because we lean into either:

- our point of view and/or those we want to win over (conviction); or

- our internal dialogue, overthinking or second-guessing our view (doubt).

In the next two diagrams, these off-centre inclinations are represented by the person on the left. The recipient of the advocacy (on the right) is also shown as embodying advocating energy, but they could be listening and/or ready to inquire.

## Bird's-eye view of energy
Off-centre advocacy with conviction

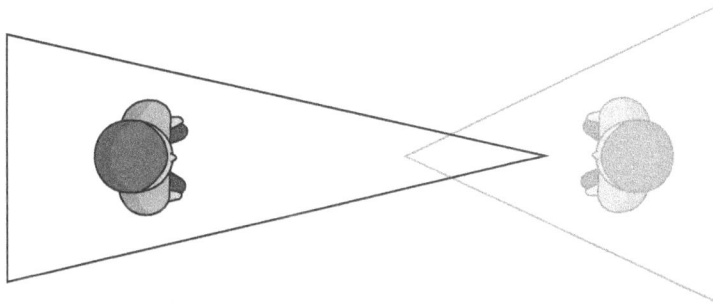

**Key:**

Advocating with conviction, energetic space expands unevenly, overly insistent about own view

Not included energetically or held in parity

Our focus is on the impact of an intervention made with off-centre advocating energy. When we're off-centre and advocating *towards* a position, we may be attached to our view and believe that we're right. If we start to try to convince others, the energy of our triangular peri-personal space intensifies. The shape narrows and becomes more pointed, intruding into their peri-personal space (see the diagram above). The impact of what we say may now feel like a jab or stab, and may even be felt physically. In addition, when we feel certain that we're right, we imply that alternative views are wrong. The energy associated with such conviction is likely to give rise to a fight/flight reaction in others which, depending on their personal tendencies, and situational factors such as relative power, may prompt them to push back or take avoiding action.

## Bird's-eye view of energy
Off-centre advocacy with doubt

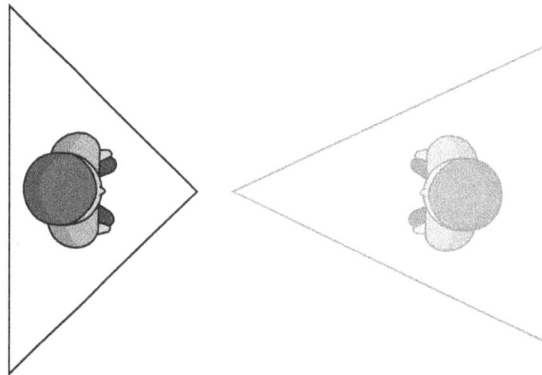

**Key:**

Advocating with doubt, energetic
space contracts in response

Not included energetically
and parity is lost

If, instead of feeling certain of our view, we begin to overthink things and/or to second-guess ourselves, our energy turns inwards and this too affects our peri-personal space (see the diagram above). The point or leading edge of our advocating energy 'pulls in' and is less incisive. When we doubt ourselves, our words may be vague and/or tentative. In addition, we've withdrawn our energy, and this also lessens the impact of what we say. Others may experience this as disconnection or lack of interest, which may prompt a fight/flight reaction in them. In addition, off-centre advocacy can seem closed to alternative views.

Overall, when we're off-centre, and regardless of how confidently it's expressed, advocacy *towards* a view can divert attention from shared purpose by narrowing the focus of a conversation.

Similar changes to our peri-personal space occur when we're off-centre and advocating *away from* a view, countering someone else's advocacy. When we're caught up in the rightness of our perspective, our attempts to query something or to suggest an alternative are likely to feel obstructive or critical. On the other hand, if we're unsure of ourselves, the way we contribute may feel flippant, resigned or defensive. When we intervene with off-centre energy, advocacy *away from* a view can feel like an expression of resistance, directly or indirectly, and put others on alert.

In summary, when we advocate, we may intend to propose a direction or to offer an appropriate challenge, but if our energy isn't aligned, the impact can feel:

- insistent and/or aggressive (heightened energy, advocacy towards);

- critical and/or obstructive (heightened energy, advocacy away from);

- tentative and/or fuzzy (dampened energy, advocacy towards); or

- defensive and/or resigned (dampened energy, advocacy away from).

You can find a summary of the impact of centred and off-centre advocating energy in tabular form at Appendix K.

When we intervene, the shape and quality of the energy we bring to our advocacy matters – especially when different perspectives are being expressed. When advocacy meets advocacy, and we start to champion one view or refute another, we're in the territory of debate. Without care, the energy of point and counterpoint escalates into conflict or collapses into constrained politeness. If we're to channel the energy of our differences towards something generative, we must build capacity to harness our personal energy skilfully whilst 'in the fray'. The LE centring practice (Appendix B) offers a reliable way to do this.

Whether we're advocating *towards* or *away from* a point of view, the impact of an intervention can be enhanced by inviting others to inquire into it. We can do this by actively creating opportunities for those present to ask for more information about the thoughts and feelings that are shaping our perspective. Their questions may uncover data, beliefs, assumptions and experiences that, outside our awareness, are influencing what we think and feel. As we discover and reveal more of this hinterland, we create more room for common ground. Without inquiry, differences remain in the structure of debate, which tends to narrow the scope of a conversation and to widen divides. This leads us naturally to an exploration of inquiring energy. First, let's pause and digest.

## Over to you …

When you're explaining what you think, what you know or believe to be true, do you tend to be ardent and certain, or reflective and circumspect? You might choose other words, but try to appreciate whether you tend to be over-confident in your view or to be so aware of potential pitfalls that you become tentative. On balance, do you tend towards persuading others or holding back?

Next time you're aware of the energy of persuasion or of holding back, try doing a centring practice before you speak. What changes?

Let's now consider the energy we bring to intervening to discover what we don't yet know.

# Intervening: inquiring energy

You may remember that the natural shape of inquiring energy is circular, indicating a willingness to listen and receive (Chapter 21). When we inquire, we hold space for others to speak, and the challenge of this circular, receptive energy is that it can feel somewhat amorphous, blurring the distinction between speaking and listening.

When we inquire, we can be met with receiving energy or with advocating energy, as represented in bird's-eye form in the diagram below. In it, Scenario A shows the person on the left as embodying inquiring energy, which is met with receptive energy from the person on the right – both people are open and curious, yet there may be no real sense of shared interest. Two people can be engaged in separate lines of inquiry, and this has a different quality of energy to that of seeking shared understanding.

In Scenario B, the inquiry of the person on the left is met with advocating energy from the person on the right. An inquiry may naturally invite advocacy – however, if the person who's inquiring hasn't included the person who's advocating in their energetic space, their words can feel like an attempt to persuade or correct.

## Bird's-eye view of energy
### Inquiring scenarios

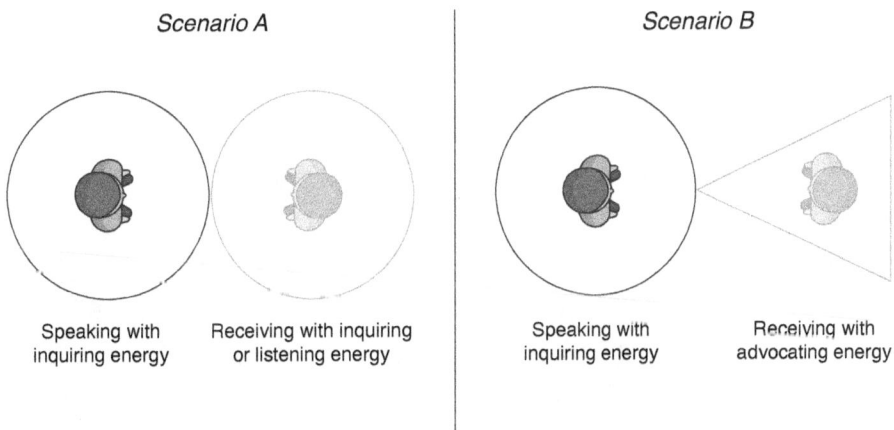

| Scenario A | Scenario B |
|---|---|

| Speaking with inquiring energy | Receiving with inquiring or listening energy | Speaking with inquiring energy | Receiving with advocating energy |
|---|---|---|---|

To inquire skilfully, we centre and expand our circular peri-personal space evenly in all directions, including others whilst maintaining our personal alignment. In doing so, we dissolve the energetic boundary between our words and those who receive them. The diagram below depicts a bird's-eye view of the energy of centred inquiry and represents the culmination of the wall–window activity outlined in Chapter 10.

## Bird's-eye view of energy

### Centred inquiry

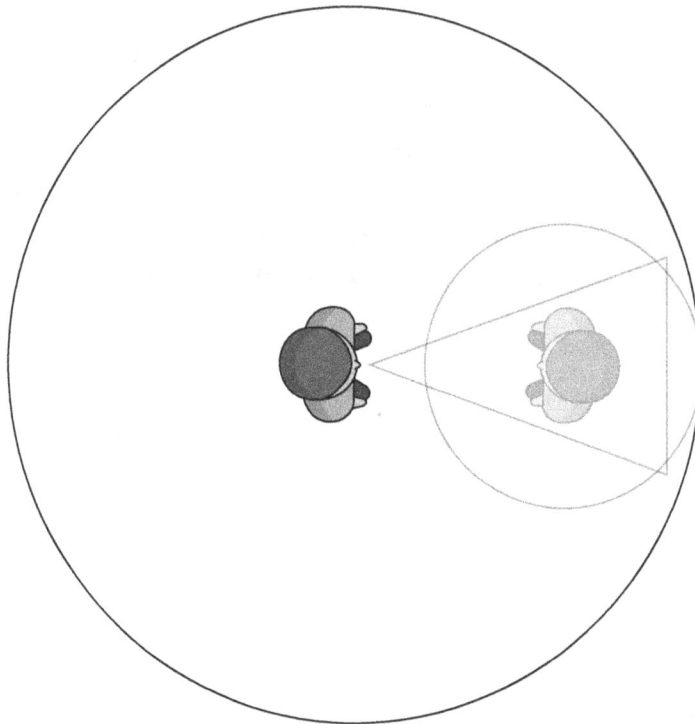

**Key:**

Centred inquiry, energetic space is expanded evenly to include others

Included energetically, whether listening, inquiring or advocating

If you recall, in the wall–window practice, we set aside our position for a moment and we're willing to look at what someone else sees. We express interest, seek information and/or ask them to elaborate on their thinking: we practise centred inquiry. We do this whether we're inquiring *into* what's being said or *around* it. When we inquire *into* something, it's as if we spiral downwards into more detail and/or meaning: we draw out the rich layers of someone's view. When we inquire *around* something, it's as if we spiral upwards to consider wider perspectives, inviting others to join us.

When we embody centred inquiry, we connect to the conversation as a whole, rather than focusing on individual people or views. We're inquiring to enhance shared understanding, and self-interest diminishes. We can enrich an inquiry by using the head-heart-core approach to align our intention and to attend equally to immediate concerns, relationships and the bigger picture. This supports us to express interest in an individual view whilst remaining aware of collective experience. Whether we're inquiring into or around a view – offering a follow or a bystand – we're open and inclusive, inviting others to speak.

In contrast, if we're off-centre when we inquire, our efforts can feel like we're overly interested in a single perspective or person, or that we're satisfying our personal curiosity about something. In each case, we don't hold people and/or their views in parity because we lean into either:

- a particular view and/or person (external focus); or

- our internal dialogue and our own concerns (internal focus).

In the next two diagrams, these off-centre inclinations are represented by the person on the left. The recipient of the inquiry (on the right) may be advocating, inquiring or listening.

**Bird's-eye view of energy**

Off-centre inquiry with external focus

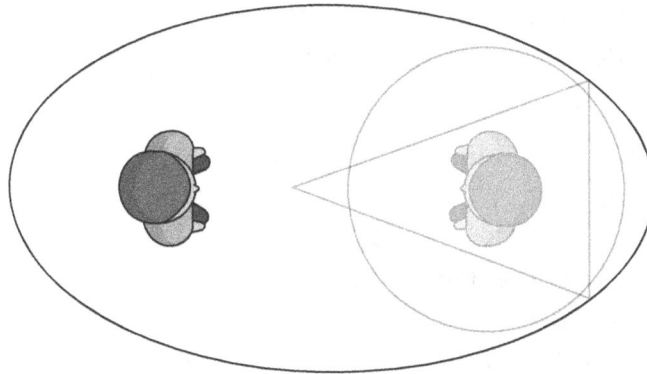

**Key:**

 Inquiring with external focus, energetic space expands unevenly, overly interested in one aspect

 Included energetically, yet not held in parity

Our focus is on the impact of an intervention made with off-centre inquiring energy. Broadly, when we're off-centre and inquiring *into* a subject, our attention may be drawn into the details of a particular view and we lose sight of the wider context. If we're absorbed by one element of a conversation, the shape of our peri-personal space changes to reflect this: it lengthens and becomes elliptical (see the diagram above). As we lean into one aspect of a conversation, we lose our alignment: we're no longer holding views and people in parity. When we inquire with this energy, we focus on the details of a single view, which can feel partisan and/or stifling to others.

In a variation of this aspect of being off-centre, we sometimes ask a question that's advocacy masquerading as inquiry. This kind of question has a pointed, directional energy – and there are many examples of it on television and radio. These 'questions' are often posed in the form of a statement followed by the phrase '… don't you agree?'. Or they begin 'can we agree that …?' Such questions are closed and they attempt to lead an exchange in a particular direction: their energy is advocatory in nature.

## Bird's-eye view of energy
### Off-centre inquiry with internal focus

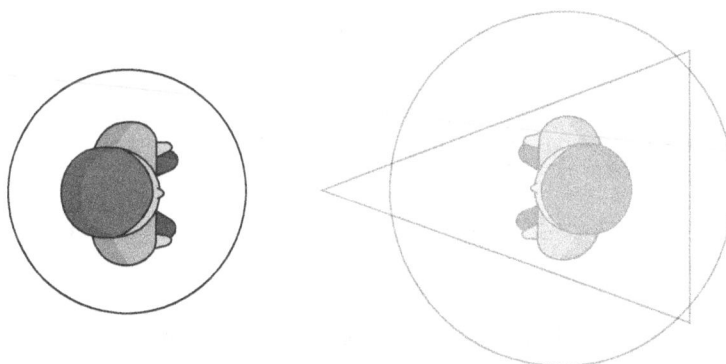

**Key:**

Inquiring with internal focus,
energetic space contracts in response

Not included energetically
and parity is lost

To return to inquiring energy, if we get caught up in an internal train of thought, we turn inwards. This too changes the shape of our peri-personal space. It contracts into self, excluding others (see the diagram above). With this energy and focus, a spoken inquiry may not seem relevant to others, and/or they may feel that we're not really engaged. The impact of our words is diminished.

Overall, when we're off-centre, an inquiry *into* a topic can divert attention from shared purpose by seeking unnecessary detail about a single view, whether our own or someone else's.

When we're off-centre and inquiring *around* a topic, similar changes in our peripersonal space occur. If we're externally focused on a particular issue, angle or person, an inquiry tends to reflect this: the perspective we seek is likely to be limited and/or one-dimensional. When we're referenced internally, and circling personal preoccupations, others may experience our inquiry as tangential and/or our energy as disengaged. When we're off-centre, an inquiry *around* a topic can divert attention from shared purpose by being too narrow or too abstract.

In summary, when inquiring, we may intend to seek more information or to invite a broader perspective, but if our energy isn't aligned, the impact can feel:

- stifling and/or partisan (heightened energy, inquiry into); or

- arbitrary and/or one-dimensional (heightened energy, inquiry around); or

- irrelevant and/or disengaged (dampened energy, inquiry into); or

- tangential and/or unrelated (dampened energy, inquiry around).

You can find a summary of the impact of centred and off-centre inquiring energy in tabular form at Appendix L.

When we intervene, the shape and quality of the energy we bring to our inquiry matters – especially when we're inviting others to express the how they see the world in a different way. If our inquiry is self-interested, superficial or deferential, a conversation will tend to dance around differences rather than bringing them into the light so that they can be explored. In the absence of real engagement with difference, a conversation can be a series of separate monologues.

To draw out the differences that are naturally present when human beings meet to talk, we foster an energy of respectful and heartfelt curiosity towards the views of others, whilst not losing contact with our own voice. The LE centring practice (Appendix B) supports us to access this receptive and open energy and to communicate a spirit of inclusion.

Whether we're inquiring *into* or *around* different perspectives, we can enhance the impact of an intervention by introducing advocacy into the mix. When we do this, we invite others to voice what they're thinking and feeling, whilst being ready to offer our own view. If we withhold our voice, the interest we express in the views of others will lack reciprocity, which they may experience as an unequal exchange. Advocacy provides focus and traction – without it, a conversation can become nebulous, quite literally pointless, and engagement diminishes.

Over to you ...

Recall a handful of occasions when you've invited someone to say more or to explain their thinking – what was your motivation? Were you seeking common ground? Satisfying personal curiosity? Scrutinising the value of what's been said? Asking for clarification that might be useful to all present?

For each example, reflect on the quality of the energy you brought to your inquiry – how did it affect the response offered?

What insights arise from these reflections?

As mentioned earlier in the chapter, we've covered a lot of detail in this exploration of the impact of centred and uncentred ways of intervening in a conversation. With a focus on changing practice, please work with whatever feels most relevant to the way you typically intervene in an exchange. In addition, try using the general principle of the relationship between the energy of an intervention and its impact to gain insight into what can cause a conversation to stutter or derail or support it to flow.

## Intervening skilfully

As we discovered when we revisited the fields of conversation earlier in this chapter, an awareness of the nature and energy of a conversation can give us some context for how we intervene. We can make a conscious choice about whether an intervention will reinforce or disturb the patterns and energies currently playing out. We can advocate to propose a direction or raise a challenge. We can inquire to invite more information or a broader perspective. To intervene skilfully we try to be aware of the impact we might have on the wider conversation.

Further, as we gain more insight into what constitutes a skilful intervention, we discover a relationship between advocacy and inquiry. When we intervene, whether to advocate or inquire, our intent is likely to be open to interpretation by others which means that the energy we bring to what we say matters. If our words land in a way that prompts reactivity in others – whether pushback or compliance – we reduce the possibility that differences will be brought into the open. If we intervene skilfully and bring a 'just right' energy to our words, they'll land well and invite engagement from others.

For example, between advocating energy that's too pointed or too tentative, there's a quality of energy that supports a proposed direction without insisting on it. And, between inquiring energy that's overly referenced on others or self, there's a quality of energy that invites elaboration or new possibilities. 'Just right' energy comes naturally when we centre – we create the conditions for a response, rather than a reaction. When we make a skilful intervention, its impact reflects our intention, as summarised in Appendices K and L.

When we advocate skilfully, we draw on the four dialogue practices of listening, respecting, suspending judgement and authentic voicing. We embody these practices in a way that includes self and others. We listen to both other and self; we respect both other and self; and we suspend judgement of both other and self. This creates a foundation for holding all views in parity (including our own). The LE centring practice (Appendix B) offers a short cut for doing this.

When we adopt an orientation of parity amongst and between voices, we can speak what's true for us and extend that privilege to others. Even when we speak of something that we hold dear or feel passionate about, we do so in a way that allows space for others: we expect difference. In addition, we know that a personal truth is not *the* truth: we offer our view in a way that invites others to probe it, to explore it. When we advocate skilfully, we express our perspective and opinion *and* create space for other perspectives and opinions.

And so, skilful advocacy contains the seeds of inquiry.

If we turn to inquiry, to be skilful in seeking to discover what others see and hold to be true, we again draw on the four dialogue practices. We listen to both other and self and suspend judgement of both other and self, allowing what we think and feel to inform our inquiry. When we inquire, there's a risk that we attend too closely to either our own view or the views of others – this risk dissolves when we respect both other and self.

Skilful inquiry listens deeply (both internally and externally), checks assumptions, coherence and meaning (both internally and externally), and seeks clarification (both internally and externally). And, because we're human, an inquiry will be in service to something – perhaps we're drawing out information, seeing how something fits, or looking for a different angle. Our inquiry has some intention, some direction, even if this is an aspiration to be open and curious.

And so, skilful inquiry contains the seeds of advocacy.

## Over to you …

Think of a time when someone has said their piece and you've felt able to question it, ask for more information and/or suggest alternatives. What made this possible?

Now think of a time when someone invited you to say more and drew you into an exploration of the differences in your respective views. What made this possible?

How might these reflections influence the way you advocate and inquire?

331

Ultimately, a skilful intervention balances advocacy (what I think/believe/feel) with inquiry (curiosity about what you think/believe/feel), whilst attending to the nature of the whole conversation. We're aware, as often as possible, that the meaning we attribute to what we're hearing and saying is personal and may not be shared by others. We're thoughtful about the words we use to frame what we say, so that we reflect this inherent ambiguity and create space for other perspectives. In addition, we aim to embody the four dialogue practices – and we naturally do this when we centre.

When we don't centre, we have to work harder to bring the dialogue practices to our thinking, speaking and listening, and to calibrate the intensity of the energy we bring to an intervention. We're at the mercy of our habitual tendencies, fuelled by the autonomic nervous system. This means that we're susceptible to enacting any tendency to win, argue, tussle, overcome and/or be right, or any tendency to go with the flow, accommodate, adapt, hesitate and/or seek harmony. When we speak from this everyday state, the impact we have on others is less likely to reflect our intention. For me, this reality offers a compelling reason to embrace the embodied practices in these pages – I hope you concur.

This completes our detailed look at the three tenets and how they can support us to embody dialogue practices. As we've covered this ground, you may have noticed resonances between the tenets – in fact, when we fully inhabit the essence of each one, we find there's no difference between them. Let's look into this.

# Chapter 32  Three become one

**Three tenets**

Three become one

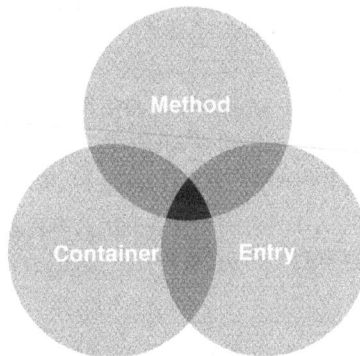

Initially, it's useful to work with the three tenets one at a time. This offers insight into the way each one can support us to embody dialogue practices. However, as our practice evolves, we may see that making distinctions between them is artificial: they're interdependent and represent different facets of a single practice. In this chapter, we'll explore this ground. In addition, we'll bring greater stability to our centring practice by adding one further element to it.

To explore the interdependencies between the tenets, let's start with 'entry is everything' (Tenet 3), which we've considered as both an individual and a collective practice. The individual practice has strong links to our embodied presence – how we carry ourselves and participate. This is the essence of 'we are the method' (Tenet 1) and the principle that there's no separate method for being in dialogue. Instead, a conversation is shaped by the motivation, energy and contribution of those present, and their willingness to explore the differences that arise. The

333

collective practice of 'entry is everything' asks us to pay attention to this reality and to consciously create the initial conditions for our important conversations. Then, as things unfold, we do our best to embody what we've agreed – we 'consciously hold' the container (Tenet 2).

If, instead, we start with 'we are the method' (Tenet 1), it's pretty clear that the way we carry ourselves influences the look and feel of the shared space, the container that's forming as we engage with each other. When we pay attention to this, and actively foster the environment for our conversation, we're in the territory of consciously establishing and holding our container (Tenet 2). In addition, the impact of any intervention we make is affected by our embodied presence and the energy we bring to what we say. The way we contribute matters – everything is entry and entry is everything (Tenet 3).

Finally, we can start with 'consciously holding a container' (Tenet 2) and deliberately fostering the conditions for dialogue. The quality of our shared space reflects the way we speak and listen to each other – we are indeed the method (Tenet 1). The container is also strengthened (or not) by the care, attention and embodied presence that we bring to each contribution or intervention (Tenet 3).

For my part, I use the three tenets to prepare for all my important work-related conversations – whether one-to-one encounters, hosting a workshop or participating in a meeting. I also use them for significant personal exchanges. When something matters, I think about the kind of space that might hold us and what we'll be talking about, and I lightly attend to cultivating it. I think about my intentions and the quality of energy I'll bring to the conversation. And, crucially, I think about what I want to set in motion by the way I begin. Then I do a centring practice.

Ultimately, I see the three tenets as different facets of one thing: being fully present to self, others and what's unfolding. When we work with the tenets separately, we develop greater awareness of the factors that influence the way a conversation plays out, and this supports us to change our practice. However, eventually, they merge into a single embodied practice. When we change our energetic state by using the four-part centring practice (Appendix B), all techniques, methods, skills and/or tactics fall away. We simply become present. The rest unfolds.

A centred state is a flow state, a resourceful and inclusive state that naturally encompasses the essence of the tenets. If we practise, we gradually build our capacity to maintain/sustain this state in moments of intensity, for longer periods of time and/or amongst bigger groups of people. Whatever our level of practice, most of us will regularly get distracted and/or 'space out' – the aim is to catch this quickly, and recover a centred state. As we learn to do this, the working principles of the three tenets can anchor us in what we're trying to bring about.

## Over to you …

Take some time to find your own understanding of the relationships between the three tenets. How might you describe the overlaps between 'we are the method', 'consciously holding a container' and 'entry is everything'?

As you reflect on the overlaps, what connects them? If there's one unifying theme, how might you articulate it?

In summary, our capacity for being in dialogue is enhanced by using the four-part centring practice. To realise the potentials of this practice as fully as possible, we can add one further element to it: enhancing the stability of our peri-personal space as we expand it to include others.

## Strengthening our centring practice

To recap, as part of the four-part centring practice (Appendix B), we intentionally shape and extend our peri-personal space. When our attention lapses, this space returns to its natural resting state (whatever is most typical for us) – and we return to our habitual focus (often the visual field, right in front of us). We can strengthen our expanded, centred energy by consciously drawing on sources of inspiration and support, imagining them in the space behind us. This helps us to sustain our peripheral awareness, a sense of the 360° field. It's a kind of 'ballast' that helps keep our attention active – and it may support us to hold centre for a moment or two longer. Personally, I like to think of this aspect of the practice as 'crowd-funding' energy.

To draw on sources of inspiration and support, we identify people that we hold in high regard and call on their positive qualities to bolster our energy. With her American origins, Wendy Palmer, the founder of Leadership Embodiment, referred to this aspect of the practice as the 'posse'. In the Wild West, a posse was a group of good and true citizens who were temporarily called up by the sheriff to assist in preserving the peace. If the word 'posse' doesn't sit comfortably with you, you can substitute any word that reflects a sense of calling up positive energy and encouragement. My clients have used words such as clan, tribe and crew.

Let's look at how we can use this principle to strengthen our peri-personal space, whether it's in circular/spherical or triangular/wedge-shaped form.

We'll begin with the circular/spherical shape that supports centred listening or centred inquiry – the activities where we're open to receiving what others say. As we centre, we extend this energetic space in all directions so that it includes those we're with, dissolving the energetic boundaries between us. Since our attention tends to be drawn to, or to lean towards, people in our visual field, we imagine 'backup' behind us to balance this tendency. For example, we imagine a host of people who inspire and/or support us crowding into the space behind us to cheer us on. At some stage, it's likely that our expanded peri-personal space will shrink or collapse – or that we'll space out. This is OK. We simply regroup and centre again and, as we open to include others, we recall our posse of inspiration and support.

How do we resource our posse? If possible, we identify people who inspire us and/or those who love and support us. The practice of recognising the positive qualities of others counterbalances any tendency to be critical and to focus on shortcomings. It's often easier to name those we disapprove of, oppose or reject than to express our appreciation for those we admire and respect. In the LE approach, we actively train our minds to develop less-used attributes so that we can be more flexible in what we say and do. So, in a cultural setting that tends to more readily find fault with people than to celebrate their merits, we develop the habit of seeing the good in others. We intentionally look for those who embody qualities that we value and/or those who make a positive contribution in the world.

The people we select for our posse can be public figures, or from our family, workplace or community. They can be living or not. They can even be fictional. We simply choose those with qualities that we admire, and those who lift our spirits when we think about them. When we call them into our personal space, it's as if we borrow their attributes and energy for a moment. Over the years, clients have called up people like Nelson Mandela, Ruth Bader Ginsberg, the Dalai Lama and Mo Mowlam, as well as athletes, grandparents, musicians, teachers and mentors. In the realms of fiction, characters from *Star Trek* and *The Lord of the Rings* have made an appearance, as have the Knights of the Round Table. Feel free to be creative!

For some – and, initially, this applied to me – it can be too big a challenge to identify inspiring people. If so, we can call on other sources of inspiration, such as elements of the natural world – mountains, seascapes, rivers, birds, animals, trees and so on. Or we can draw on pieces of music, artworks and other human creations. Personally, I began with landscapes and moved on to music. Through exploration, I found that the vibrational nature of music energised me more than visual references. It may be different for you – the key is to play with the approach and find out what lifts your spirits and boosts your energy.

After a time, and because I'd become an LE teacher, I applied myself to populating my posse with inspiring people. As a stepping stone, I imagined lineages, such as all the people who'd contributed to developing T'ai Chi and teaching it to others, culminating in my teacher teaching me. I could imagine this flow of commitment, wisdom and training and be inspired by it. Now, I'm at ease with acknowledging the qualities of individuals – and can feel their support and encouragement when I'm trying to do something worthwhile.

As with everything in this book, I'm offering a template and inviting you to find your own way to apply it. The template for calling up inspiration and support is to identify what uplifts and resources us, so that, whatever the nature of the incoming energy, we're more able to be present to it.

One practical way we can begin to gather a personal posse is to consider the qualities that might support our three archetypal centres of energy and presence: the head, heart and core/gut. Let's explore this.

337

## Over to you ...

Take some time to reflect on people you think highly of – what is it that you appreciate, admire and/or respect about the way they conduct themselves? What might this inspire in you?

More generally, what qualities do you value in others? Who most embodies each quality and might act as an archetype for it? To gather a posse, reflect on the following questions:

Head/thinking – whose quality of presence might inspire and support clear perception and thinking?

Heart/values – whose quality of presence might inspire and support an open and compassionate heart?

Core/gut – whose quality of presence might inspire and support a sense of confidence deep in your being?

Having identified three candidates for your posse, do a four-part centring practice (Appendix B) and call up their energetic presence – what changes?

In addition to using a posse to balance our listening and inquiring energy, we can call on it when we're shaping our energy to advocate and express what we think, feel or believe. It's the same principle, with a slightly different emphasis. As we prepare to offer our point of view, we do a centring practice and tune in to a triangular or wedge-shaped energy, imagining strong supporting sides and a clear, incisive point or leading edge. We expand this energetic shape by imagining that the point or leading edge extends into the distance, with the sides widening proportionately until we include those present (Chapter 21). We then imagine the back of the triangle as open, and fill it with our chosen sources of support and inspiration. We can also add those who'll benefit from what we're proposing so that, in essence, we're speaking on their behalf.

The next step is to tune in to this crowd-funded energy and imagine that it flows though us and our words. This flavours what we say with a sense of something bigger, something universal. At some stage, it's likely that our attention will contract to focus on a particular person or view, particularly if they're challenging or opposing what we say. This is OK. We simply regroup and centre again, clarifying our advocating energy towards what matters most and expanding it to include alternative views (Appendices G and H).

To build on the suggestion that we can include those who'll benefit from our advocacy in our posse, here's an example from a coaching client who worked in the National Health Service. Based in a particular locality, the client was preparing to recommend a change in practice in an environment where there were concerns about cost. To support her to make her point, we were exploring the centred advocacy practice and I asked who'd benefit if her proposal was put into action. She began with all her patients, who were being treated for a particular condition. Then she included their families. Then came all those who might need treatment in the future, which took in the whole population of the locality. Finally, we considered that the change in practice might be shared with other localities, and the potential beneficiaries became the population of Scotland. Crowd-funding indeed!

Having done this groundwork, the client practised centring and shaping her energy into a triangular shape, then expanding her peri-personal space to include all potential nay-sayers. She called up the population of Scotland to cheer her on and, inspired and energised by the reach of what she believed to be possible, she spoke with great confidence and power. Her view was no longer based on what she believed to be right, but what she believed would benefit the greatest number of people. With this change, her voice became compelling.

This element of the LE centring practice completes it by enhancing the stability of our peri-personal space, which supports centred inclusion. The full practice is set out below. In preparation for it, take time to reflect on who (or what) you might draw on as a source of inspiration and support, and note the quality of energy that they offer you. This practice is also shown at Appendix M.

# ⭐ Embodied Practice 8

## *Centring with inspiration and support*[†]

### 1. Posture and breath

> Become uplifted and aligned in your posture, with your spine easing to its natural length and curve. As you do so, exhale slowly and imagine the breath spiralling down through your body and into the ground.

> Inhale softly, imagining that the gentle inflow of air lifts each vertebra from the one below it, bringing a sense of lightness into the spine.

> Exhale slowly, imagining the breath flowing down, softening the front of the body, and forming a root in the earth below.

### 2. Balancing and opening personal space

> Become aware of the space you occupy – pay attention behind you as well as in front of you, to the left and right, below your feet and above your head. What would it be like if this space was a little more equal and even, a little more balanced?

> And what would it be like to consciously enlarge this personal container in all directions so that it includes those around you, whilst holding you gently at the centre?

> Now, in the space behind you, imagine the people* who inspire you, those who've helped you develop and grow, those who love you, those who support you and will cheer you on, and/or those who will benefit from what you say and do.

> Feel the presence and energy of your posse …

## 3. Softening

> Whilst maintaining an uplifted posture, soften your forehead, your jaw and your shoulders – imagine they're melting, like butter, and succumbing to gravity …

## 4. Cultivating beneficial energy

> Invite a little more ease (or other beneficial quality) into your being – where do you experience it, and what difference does it make?

## 5. Drawing on the energy of your posse

> Now imagine your back becoming a little more open, a little more porous, and allow the energy of your posse to flow into your being. Let this energy hold, support and/or move you …

\* *You can also draw on aspects of nature, art, music or any other inspiration.*

† *Based on the work of Wendy Palmer.*

When we centre, we sit or stand (or walk) a little taller, extend our presence to include others and amplify our leadership spirit – and this enhances all our interactions. Over the course of this book, we've gradually deepened our understanding of this practice. Let's review how we've introduced each new layer of it, building our capacity to embody dialogue practices and to approach difference differently.

## How we've developed the centring practice

To develop the centring practice, we began with a light description of it in Chapter 9. We linked it to the flow state or 'being in the zone', which most of us have experienced at some stage in our life. In centring we're seeking to access this innate capacity, and to use it in moments that matter. We met the four parts of the foundation practice and briefly explored them. Then, in Chapters 10 and 11, we added to our understanding and applied the practice to centred inquiry and centred listening. In all three chapters, there were opportunities to try out the practice and reflect on the impact of it.

In the next few chapters, we touched on the way centring could support us to handle ourselves well in our conversations. We noted its role in groups, in holding diverse views in parity, and in zooming out to bystand our experience. In Chapter 20, we focused on how we might embody the four dialogue practices and discovered that centring naturally embraces all of them. Centring supports us to create space for, and hold, our differences. We were becoming more familiar with the practice and adding to it, step by step.

In Chapter 21, we introduced the element of consciously shaping our energy to reflect whether we're advocating or inquiring. We added the embodied practice of centred speaking, with the opportunity to explore the impact of this with a partner. This practice supports us to say what's true for us in way that acknowledges that others will see the world differently.

In Chapter 28, we added the three energetic competences of centred speaking, centred listening and centred inclusion. We saw that, when we practise them, we automatically embody the four dialogue practices of listening, respecting, suspending judgement and authentic voicing. To expand on this, when we practise centred speaking, we speak clearly and without attachment: we're respectful of self and other and we suspend judgement of self and other. We're listening to, and for, how our words land. This is the essence of authentic voicing.

When we practise centred listening, we listen spaciously, without taking things personally. In doing so, we naturally offer respect and suspend judgement, which encourages others to speak with authentic voice. This is the essence of the deep listening that characterises dialogue.

And when we practise centred inclusion, we include and accept others whilst maintaining our own centre. We hold all voices in parity, and wonder what's *right* about them. We offer our own voice, trusting others to receive what we say. In doing so, we embody listening, respecting and suspending judgement: we communicate acceptance at an energetic level.

In Chapter 31, we refined our understanding of centred speaking and centred inquiry, and looked in detail at the way we can use our peri-personal space to support the way we intervene in a conversation. We explored the relationship between intent and impact, comparing the way our words might land when we're off-centre with how they land when we're centred and including others, holding them in parity. And now, we've added the element of calling up inspiration and support, enhancing our capacity to expand our space whilst maintaining our alignment and centre.

In summary, we've gradually increased the complexity of the centring practice alongside opportunities to experiment with it. Going slowly lets both body and mind acclimatise to the centred experience and build capacity for it. Instead of presenting the whole practice in one go, a mind-based approach, we've allowed for the fact that the body learns through repetition. We've taken our time to add layers of meaning for the mind and layers of experience for the body.

This process reflects the way that we build capacity for any new practice. It also explains my frequent repetition of key elements of the approach. I've been applying the same broad approach throughout the book – first embracing an idea, then exploring how it works. If we decide to adopt the idea and change our practice, we experiment and then reflect and refine our approach. We then try it again, reflect again, and further refine it. To prepare you to continue to build your practice as you go forward, we'll explore this process more fully in Chapter 35.

This concludes our exploration of the ways we can embody dialogue practices. And so, it's time to bring our conversation to a close and to consider what lies beyond it. This is the ground for Part IV.

# Part IV

**Ending with the beginning in mind**

# Chapter 33 Ending with the beginning in mind

I often say that a conversation doesn't end when everyone leaves the room – whether this is a physical or virtual space. When people talk together, things are set in motion – for better or worse. Each of us will pay attention to different aspects of a shared conversational experience, and remnants of it will lodge in our minds for further reflection, exploration or analysis. Essentially, any interaction with others leaves a trace – perhaps something we found interesting, annoying, puzzling or frustrating, or perhaps something we want to celebrate, share, check out or verify. We're left with reactions, questions and other forms of unfinished business. We ruminate or reflect (or not) and our thinking develops or becomes entrenched. Sometimes, we talk things through with others – colleagues, friends or family – which further shapes our view.

One way or another, our mind changes between the end of one conversation and the beginning of another. This is so obvious as to be both obscure and easily overlooked. It was certainly obscure to me in my early working life – back then, I genuinely expected that Project Meeting 2 would build seamlessly on the end of Project Meeting 1. In my naivety, I made assumptions about both the way one conversation had concluded and the way the next would start.

While what I've just outlined relates to all kinds of conversation – even those we find tedious – it's particularly relevant to dialogue. In dialogue we tend to be talking about complex matters and we can expect to be tested by some of what's said. We'll also encounter difference – which we may experience as a challenge, an invitation to change our perspective and/or anything in between.

An experience of being in dialogue might prompt us to do some research or seek a sounding board to help us fully absorb our reactions and/or appreciate the implications of what we've heard. We might reflect on our experiences and wonder what underlies them. We might also be curious about the experience of others – what's informing their view, what might they be seeking, how have they been affected by what took place?

Deliberations like these can raise questions, alter our perspective or further cement a dearly held view. When the next conversation is convened, our personal starting point will be different – and we can expect that the same will be true for others.

When we pay explicit attention to the reality that the end of one conversation doesn't correlate with the beginning of the next, we can see the importance of the practice of check-in (Chapters 3 and 4). In addition, we might wonder how we can end a conversation in a way that prepares for reopening it well. This invites us to make a practice of 'checking out', taking stock of where we're at, individually and collectively. This is one way of ending with the beginning in mind.

Another is to circle back to the beginning of a conversation and reflect on our original purpose(s). In doing so, we can calibrate what's changing, in terms of both our intentions (the 'what') and our container (the 'how'). We may already end our conversations with a summary of the ground covered and a list of actions (the 'what'). However, to check out skilfully, we reflect on the 'how' of our experience as well.

Full disclosure: I'm very poor at creating time and space for endings in workshops and conversations. Even though I know it's good practice and understand the benefits of harvesting key experiences and reflecting on what's taken place, I don't allow sufficient time for it. When I'm hosting, I plan for a good closing, and then get engaged in the conversation and time disappears. This is especially true for workshops, as there's always something more to say or share, whether by me or others. My saving grace is that I pay close attention to checking in, which goes some way towards compensating for a hurried and incomplete ending in a previous workshop. Which is all very well … until I'm bringing a series of conversations to a close and there's no further beginning. While this isn't ideal, no conversation really ends – when we've set something in motion, it's carried forward in some form or another within all who participate.

Thankfully, in our book-based conversation, I can ensure that we check out. In this chapter, we'll consider one way of doing this and apply it to our conversation. Along the way, we'll discover some of the things we've set in motion, for ourselves and each other. Then, in the remaining chapters, we'll engage with the thorny matter of making time to change our practice.

Done well, the practice of checking out mirrors that of checking in. We can explore this by reversing the phases of the Gibb approach to building trust (Chapters 3 and 4). This offers a framework for revisiting the way a conversation began and preparing the ground to begin again in some way, in due course. To check out in this way, we reflect on:

- the quality of our container and the way we've consciously held it (how we've engaged with each other);

- where we stand with our intentions, individually and collectively, and the questions we now have (what we've done together); and

- who we are now – individually and collectively.

As we inquire into these aspects of our experience, we take note of matters that might otherwise be carried into the space between conversations. If we don't make them conscious, such things are more likely to be lost or forgotten and so, by checking out, we increase the likelihood that there'll be some degree of shared foundation for the beginning of the next conversation. In particular, it's helpful to articulate any areas of frustration and dissatisfaction and to explore how these might be navigated in future. It's also helpful to acknowledge what's going well – and to invite each other to build on this.

Implicit in the invitation to check out is an underlying question: what's changing in and through our conversation? To develop this theme, we might ask: what's changing in our thinking, in the way we're showing up, in the way we're holding our container? We might also ask: what are we hoping to fulfil in and through our conversation? And/or: how is the shape and quality of our conversation changing? And/or: how are we changing, personally? These questions are simply examples of what we might consider, and we don't need to cover all this ground each time we check out. However, it's a useful guiding principle to reflect on the 'what' and the 'how' of a conversation and on the personal experience of those present. Within this general approach, we can check out in a way that suits us.

## Over to you …

Take a few moments to reflect on the way your conversations typically end, in terms of content, pace, style, expectations and the quality of the relationship(s)? What flows from ending a conversation in this way? What might be overlooked?

Can you identify a recent conversation that might have benefited from using some of the ideas set out in the previous paragraphs? What prompted your choice of conversation?
What might you do differently when similar circumstances next arise?

## Checking out: our book-based conversation

And so, for our book-based conversation, how do we end well, with future beginnings in mind? For you, a future beginning might include revisiting parts of the book and/or experimenting with some of the material in it. I hope your future *will* include changing your practice in your conversations. For me, future beginnings might include describing the book, sharing some of the content in workshops and/or writing another book – and will certainly include continuing to change my practice in my conversations.

Let's reflect on our journey together – the quality of our container, what we've learned and might put into practice, and who we are now.

### *How have we engaged?*

We'll begin with how we've stayed present to our conversation and established and held our container. Our experiences may vary significantly because we're doing this reflection in different time frames, and with different starting points and intentions. However, I believe we'll find parallels in the processes of writing and reading because the words on these pages represent a shared exploration of dialogue and its practices. For example, whilst writing, I've had periods of frustration and elation. I've encountered both profound self-doubt and over-inflated confidence. From time to time, I've confused myself and both over-complicated and over-simplified things. I've been both excited and bored. And I'm assuming that you'll have had similar moments. As a reader, you may have loved some bits and questioned others; enjoyed my style of writing and been frustrated by repeated messages; had periods of absorbed engagement and superficial scanning; and/or had moments of clarity and complete bewilderment.

This assortment of experiences arises partly because of who we are as individuals, partly from our capacity to sustain presence and attention, and partly through our relationship in this book-based conversation.

For my part, when I get frustrated with my slow progress and it's hard to stay engaged, I remember that writing is, in itself, a practice. It requires work, and rework ... and then more rework. This can be dull – and yet, when I commit to the process, I can always find positive changes in the evolution of whatever I'm writing. And so, I persevere.

Over to you ...

What do you notice about your capacity to be present to, and engage in, the material in these pages? When were you absorbed and invested, and when less so? From these experiences, what can you learn about what inspires you to engage and what causes you to lose interest?

How might you apply this process of reflection more generally?

### *Have we fulfilled our intentions?*

Having reflected on the part we've each played in holding our container, let's consider how well we've fulfilled our intentions, personally and together. For you, this may involve revisiting some of your responses to the 'Over to you …' inquiries in Chapter 4 – or it may simply be a process of reflection about what's been of value in these pages. You might recall why you bought the book and what you hoped to gain from it – to what extent has this been met? From your end, what has our book-based conversation offered you?

For my part, I set out to write and publish a book that would offer food for thought about how to embody the practices of dialogue and to approach difference differently. I hoped to encourage readers to pay attention to the 'how' of conversations alongside the 'what'. I aspired to equip you to change your practice in your important conversations. In particular, I intended to share what I've learned about the role of the body in conversations, and to offer some embodied resources to support you to act skilfully when differences arise. I believe I've covered this ground and hope that the way I've done it has been of value to you.

In terms of a shared purpose, in Chapter 4, I boldly assumed that we both wanted to explore practices for approaching difference differently. Have we met this aim together? For my part, I feel we have.

I also had some aims as a writer. I wanted to write in way that enticed you into conversation with me, with yourself and with the world around you. I hope I've accomplished this and that all these conversations have enriched your understanding of how people talk and listen together. I wanted to write in a way that encouraged you to try out different ways of engaging with others and learn from these experiences. I too have been trying out new things – of which, more in the next section.

My bigger aspiration was (and is) to sow some seeds that might germinate a wider change in the way we handle difference in our conversations. As I wrote in the Preface, I have a sense that the skills for handling diverse ideas are falling into disuse. Without capacity to explore our differences and use them as a catalyst for new thinking, our world shrinks and the quality of our decisions deteriorates. We run the risk of recycling familiar habits of thinking without taking account of changes in circumstances and context. When we do this, adverse unintended consequences become the norm and we spend more and more time clearing up the aftermath of suboptimal decisions.

The alternative to being caught in this restrictive cycle is that we condition ourselves to expect difference, and learn how to work more skilfully with it. What if we were to invest time and energy *up front* to understand the factors that influence the shape and quality of a conversation and to develop (or redevelop) our personal capacity for handling difference? What if we were to practise doing the preparation that supports a group of people to be in dialogue and to channel the energies of difference creatively?

This train of thinking adds another dimension to ending with the beginning in mind: that we bring an end to current (habitual) practices and begin to foster new practices. To begin afresh, we put an end to ineffective ways of engaging with each other. What will it take? We'll explore this in Chapter 35.

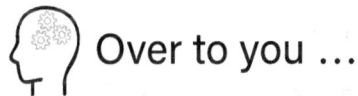

## Over to you ...

Take a few moments to revisit why you bought this book – what did you hope to discover? What has surprised you? What has challenged you? What has delighted you? What will you take on and develop further? What will support you to persevere in this?

### What is changing within us?

The final element of checking out when using the 'reversed' version of the Gibb approach is to wonder: who are we now and who am I now? Have we been changed by the conversation, and if so, how? Let's consider this possibility in a general way and then reflect on our book-based conversation.

While I think we're changed by most conversations – whether negatively or positively – I *know* we're changed by being in dialogue. When we participate in a conversation that balances advocating energy and inquiring energy, our bodies and minds respond and we're almost compelled to reflect on what we heard and said. At least, this is my experience – when I'm moved by a conversation (whether favourably or not), I usually mull over the causes and explore the potential implications. I may change my mind about an issue, expand my horizons to include new possibilities and begin to see myself differently.

When a provocative or incisive question has been raised, my curiosity is activated and I can't help but wonder about it. This reflects a more general matter: a pertinent inquiry tickles the imagination of those present, catalysing fresh thinking and insights. Neuroscience backs this up – a question prompts a process called 'instinctive elaboration', a mental reflex in which the brain picks up on the cues of what, how, why, when, where and who, and sets aside other concerns while it diverts resources to seek resolution. A note: I like to acknowledge my sources, but I've been unable to find the origins of 'instinctive elaboration' – it seems to be an accepted and well-used term. Please explore its provenance if this matters to you.

The reflex of instinctive elaboration means that, if we intervene in a conversation using words like 'I'm wondering what, how, why …' we activate the minds of those present, stimulating their interest and/or curiosity. This is a biological process, an embodied process – it's automatic. There's a pause whilst the brain goes about retrieving connections, and this is what underpins my assertion that the quality of a question is revealed by the length of the silence that follows it (Chapter 19). In such a silence, new possibilities may arise and our sense of self may change.

And so, I hope to tickle your imagination and prompt a silence by asking: how are you changing as a result of what you've found in these pages?

## Over to you …

To what extent has our book-based conversation – and any conversations prompted by it – influenced the way you think about yourself? Who are you, as we approach the end of our conversation? What has changed within you?

How have these changes in your sense of yourself affected your conversations and/or other aspects of your life?

For my part, I've clarified and developed my thinking about dialogue, difference, embodied practices and the impoverished nature of much societal conversation. As with dialogue itself, there's no method for writing a book like this or for bringing it to publication. Largely, I've chosen to write in a way that doesn't sit easily with more conventional forms of book. This isn't a reference book, an academic thesis, or a conventional 'self-help' or leadership development offering, although I hope it has elements of each of these genres.

Throughout the process, I've been (and continue to be) challenged by traversing my chosen terrain in a way that's resonant with Tenet 1 (there's no method). I have a compass and a sense of my bearings, but no map. In seeking to write the book and to bring it to publication in a way that's resonant with dialogue, I've come to engage with myself in a profoundly new way. I've been in dialogue with you, with myself, with friends and associates and with the publishing world. And I've been changed by the process.

As the book comes to completion, I'm coming to realise that, while my primary focus has been this book-based conversation, the scope of all the related generative conversations has been both broad and deep. I'm wondering if this is a natural consequence of being in dialogue? Dialogue stretches, confronts, inspires and generally exercises us, and the changes it catalyses within us permeate other exchanges. The impact of dialogue reaches beyond the immediate and into our wider domain.

Finally, I've been moved and humbled by the willingness of friends and colleagues to give up time to read and comment on drafts of my writing. For many reasons, this book has been challenging to write – and I'm not sure I'd have managed to complete it without the insights and encouragement of others.

## Looking forward

As we approach the end of our book-based conversation, let's begin to think about what happens next and how you might develop your practice as you move beyond these pages. In the remaining chapters, we'll explore how we can identify which conversations might most benefit from the effort involved in changing practice. We'll take a clear look at the hard graft that's involved when we set out to embody a new practice. And, along the way, we'll look into one of the main impediments to making these changes: the mind-set of I (or we) 'don't have time for this'.

We touched on this mind-set in earlier chapters, in the context of spending more time on matters such as:

- paying attention to, and revisiting, the quality of our container;

- extending invitations to join a conversation; and

- generally 'getting ready' for a conversation.

Each of these activities asks us to slow down so that we can embrace new leadership practices – and yet we seem to find this difficult to do. Since it also takes time and effort to adopt and inhabit the embodied four-part centring practice (Appendix B), this too may be something we feel we don't have time for. So, let's explore the impact of a 'don't have time' mind-set and its consequences. By the time we say our farewells in Chapter 36, I hope you'll be thinking: we don't have time *not* to do 'this stuff'.

# Chapter 34  Beginning: making time to prepare

Before considering ways of getting ready for an important conversation, it bears repeating that we don't need to prepare thoroughly for *every* conversation. Many exchanges involve routine updates, agreeing and coordinating actions and/or requests for information. Many more simply nurture our network of relationships. Yet others require some thought and skill, whilst still being within the ordinary run of things. However, a few of our leadership conversations have the potential to significantly influence thinking, actions, relationships or outcomes: it's these that will benefit from greater investment in preparation. How might we identify them?

## Conversations: three contexts and three modes

One approach is a framework that describes three archetypal contexts for conversations and their related conversational modes. The framework draws on the work of many people, and was developed many years ago with a colleague. The diagram overleaf shows the three contexts for conversations, and the related modes are shown in a second diagram later in the chapter. The same axes are used for both diagrams: each is a continuum, briefly described below.

- horizontal axis – contexts for conversation, spanning situations from:
  - clear, linear relationships between cause and effect; to
  - non-linear, dynamic and interdependent relationships between elements of the system and between action and outcome.
- vertical axis – range of outlook within a conversation from:
  - low diversity of view (and people); to
  - high diversity of view (and people).

## Three archetypal contexts for conversation

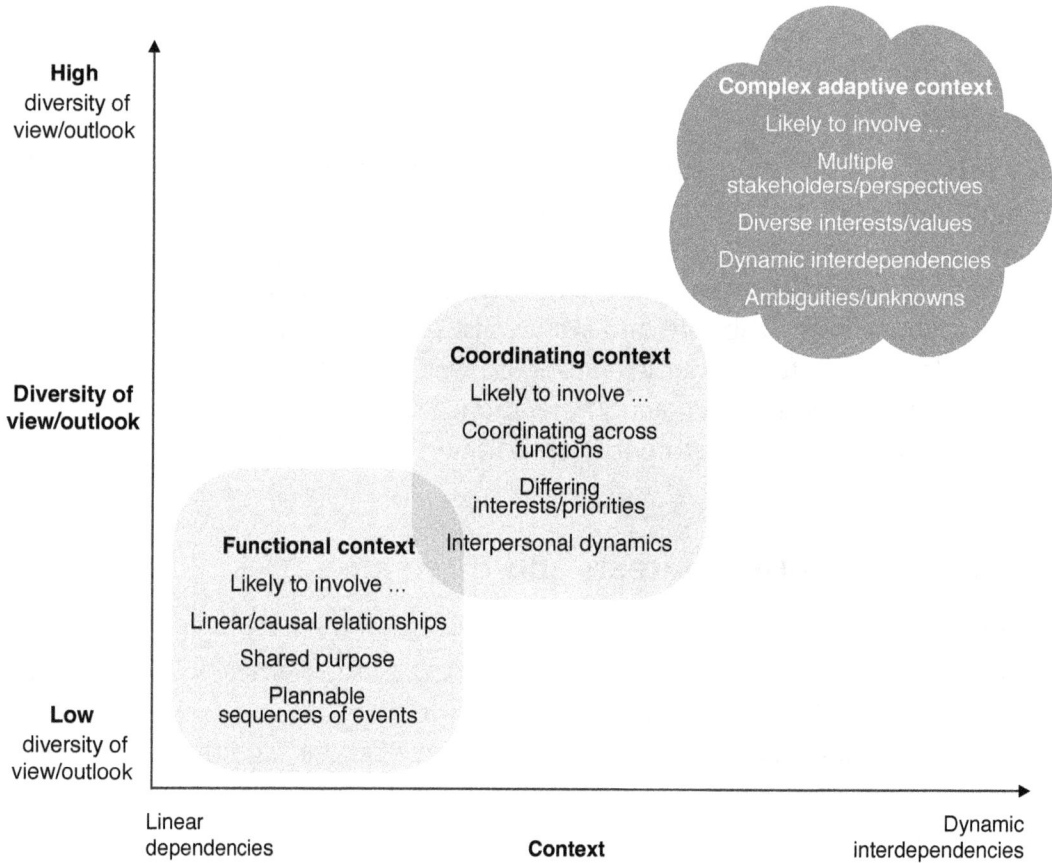

**High**
diversity of
view/outlook

**Diversity of
view/outlook**

**Low**
diversity of
view/outlook

**Complex adaptive context**
Likely to involve ...
Multiple
stakeholders/perspectives
Diverse interests/values
Dynamic interdependencies
Ambiguities/unknowns

**Coordinating context**
Likely to involve ...
Coordinating across
functions
Differing
interests/priorities
Interpersonal dynamics

**Functional context**
Likely to involve ...
Linear/causal relationships
Shared purpose
Plannable
sequences of events

Linear
dependencies

**Context**

Dynamic
interdependencies

Key:

'Tame' issues

'Wicked' issues

Inspired by the work of Ralph Stacey and Caryn Vanstone, Margaret Wheatley, Ed Schein and others

Both axes represent a spectrum of possibilities and so there are an infinite number of nuanced combinations within the space they delineate. In terms of contexts for conversations, the diagram opposite selects three as archetypes. These range from situations in which dependencies are linear in nature and a conversation involves relatively familiar people and ground, to those in which there's complexity of context, perspective and people, and it's important to gain shared understanding of a wider system. Of the three archetypes, two overlap. The third is a step-change in orientation and approach. The selected archetypes are:

- functional context – settings that are familiar and involve everyday concerns and colleagues in a discipline or team with a high degree of shared knowledge;

- coordinating context – settings where people are working across such groupings, calling for some cooperation and coordination to deliver collective ambitions; and

- complex adaptive context – settings that include many stakeholders with differing perspectives, interests, values and paradigms who, together, are navigating uncertainty, ambiguity and non-linear relationships between action and response.

Each context calls for a mode of a conversation in which the time, energy and effort involved is appropriate to the desired purpose or outcome, and these modes are set out in the diagram overleaf. The diagram is followed by a brief description of the attributes of each mode of conversation. These, when combined with the contexts for conversation, can support us to identify the kinds of circumstances that will benefit from significant preparation.

# Three archetypal modes of conversation

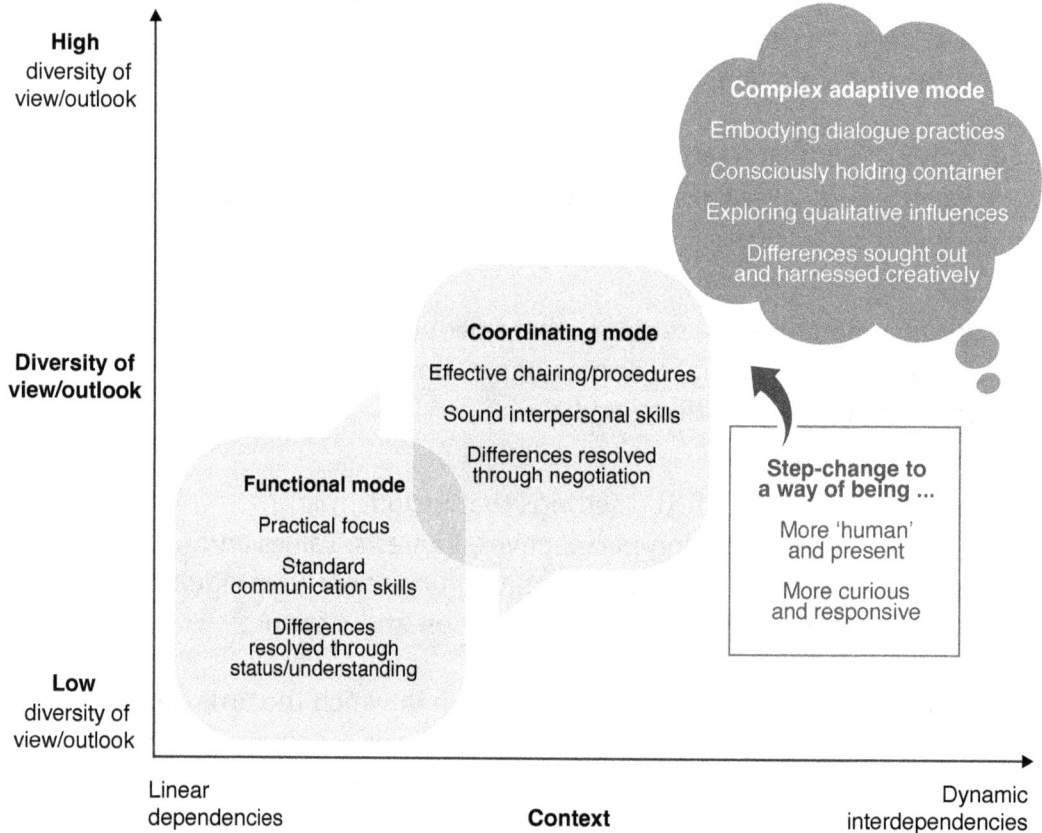

*Functional mode*

Conversations tend to be about practicalities like exchanging information, agreeing actions, and raising and solving local problems. Difference is most likely to surface as alternative courses of action, which will be argued out, with the relative status of individuals influencing the outcome. These conversations call for standard communication skills.

*Coordinating mode*

Conversations tend to be about the cross-functional aspects of working on a shared purpose or project. These too are about exchanging information, allocating actions, and raising and solving problems. With a range of stakeholders, this often involves negotiating agreement, agreeing responsibilities, monitoring progress and other forms of cooperation. There are likely to be both overlaps and differences amongst people, interests, tasks and outcomes. Difference surfaces in a variety of forms, and is likely to be navigated through trade-offs and finding middle ground. Coordinating conversations tend to address matters that are more complicated than those in functional mode, and may involve a wider range of personal and professional relationships. This calls for greater interpersonal skills and the use of methods of containment such as an agenda, a chairperson and record keeping.

*Complex adaptive mode*

Conversations tend to be about gaining some shared understanding of the nature of an issue and how it has arisen. Alongside gathering information, these conversations are likely to involve an exploration of qualitative influences, uncertainties and ambiguities. Difference will be apparent in what's being said and may also arise in less obvious forms, such as a variety of principles, values, perceptions and risk-appetite. These nuanced differences may need to be deliberately surfaced so that they can be taken into account. They're unlikely to be resolved – instead, they'll be accommodated as stakeholders agree to 'live with' an outcome. This kind of conversation calls for dialogue and a shift of attention and energy.

In the diagram on page 360, we're invited to regard dialogue as a change in modality, rather than a progression from even the most sophisticated of more conventional conversations. Essentially, we shift from handling matters skilfully to being present. This asks us to bring more of ourselves to the conversation, and to be more human and more available to others. It involves being open, receptive, generous and curious towards what others think and say, and being less attached to our own position. We seek to include others and hold them and their views in parity, and to focus on gaining shared understanding of an issue rather than reaching a decision.

A further dimension of the diagram showing the archetypal modes of conversation is that it marks a separation between 'tame' and 'wicked' issues. Predicaments that fall into the tame category usually have a single formulation with substantial agreement on material points: there's a known issue to resolve. There may be a range of solutions to be explored and assessed before planning and implementing a chosen path, but the issue is tractable and amenable to being resolved. Whilst it may be very complicated, a tame issue tends to involve systems of linear relationships, and these can usually be navigated within the usual range of leadership communication skills.

In contrast, a complex adaptive or wicked issue is one in which the relationships between different factors and facets are non-linear and dynamic. If one aspect of such a predicament changes, the whole issue changes. A wicked issue is intractable and is deeply rooted: it can't be addressed by linear means. Not only is there no solution, there's no single coherent formulation of the issue: the way each stakeholder sees it depends on their perspective. The framing of a wicked issue is open to question, which invites us to gain greater shared understanding of the conditions giving rise to it. This calls for a change in practice and a shift into the modality of dialogue.

In summary, in terms of context, a wicked issue is in a different category to a tame issue. Similarly, as a mode of conversation, dialogue is in a different category to even the most skilful conventional conversation.

{ } Over to you ...

What do these ideas evoke in you? Can you find an example of each of the contexts described? How do conversations in each context typically play out?

What questions are raised by your reflections?

## To prepare or not?

With clarity on these different modes of conversation, we can see that those in a functional context may need little or no preparation. Conversations in a coordinating context will benefit from the kind of preparation we probably do already, like considering our purpose, potential sticking points and some possible tactics.

The conversations that will benefit from the additional preparation described in these pages are likely to have some combination of the following factors:

- subject matter that's complex, with multiple stakeholders and many uncertainties, interdependencies and ambiguities;

- complex relationships amongst stakeholders;

- a broad range of perspectives, interests and concerns, giving rise to very real differences in outlook and/or desired outcome; and

- high stakes in the form of the potential impact being material in both size and scope for the system(s) involved.

When any one of these components is present, we're in the territory of the unfamiliar, which tends to put our human system on alert. In addition, there are likely to be differences within each component and this too tends to activate our survival instincts. And, even if we're calm, composed and at ease with difference, when we think ahead, it's clear that addressing this kind of subject matter in a coherent way calls for a conversation that takes time and meaningful engagement.

In summary, it's the combination of complexity and difference that calls for dialogue and for the investment in preparation that makes it possible. When this realisation dawns, clients often tell me that they don't have time for 'all this embodying dialogue stuff'. This feels like an instinctive reaction to something that appears daunting. In response, I observe that they seem to have plenty of time to deal with the fallout when their reliance on an existing conversational form results in confusion, inaction, conflict, disruption, resistance and/or misplaced effort. Although they smile wryly, our exchange doesn't seem to spur them into taking action.

Over the years, I've wondered about this inertia and what might underlie it. My best guess is that two factors get in the way. The first is that many approaches to learning and development emphasise models, frameworks and ideas. These are easily grasped – we're smart people – and sometimes a new perspective is sufficient to change the way we operate. However, such 'quick wins' play into a cultural mind-set accustomed to the availability of ready meals, which allow us to avoid the faff of looking out a recipe, buying ingredients and preparing food from scratch. If we're offered a 'packaged' nugget of learning, we might prefer it to the effort of building competence and capacity over time.

The second factor is that we rely on conversation for so much of our leadership and personal activity. Without much thought, we have so many successful conversations – or good-enough conversations – that we might overlook the fact that some of them aren't really fit for purpose. We overestimate both our knowledge and our skill on the basis that we use them pretty well on most days. We think they'll be sufficient in every circumstance and so we simply crack on. We're then surprised when things go pear-shaped.

With all this in play, I don't underestimate what I'm asking when I invite you to prepare for your important conversations. It means clarifying who you'll invite into a conversation and why, and then attending to how you'll contact them. It means being thoughtful about where and when you'll meet and taking time to establish a container. This all takes time and energy. However, when we don't pay attention to these things, there's a risk that a crucial conversation will flare up, implode or have undesirable consequences. This is true even when we 'know this stuff' … and sometimes, perhaps, *especially* when we know this stuff and assume that others know it too. What follows is an example of the way things can go amiss: it relates to a conversation between three people (including me), each with considerable experience of supporting others to develop their capacity for dialogue.

As three practitioners in the field, we met to explore how we might work together to design and jointly host a programme of workshops to widen access to dialogue practices across a large organisation. The conversation began quite well, although we didn't attend explicitly to our container. However, things got a little testy when one practitioner suggested that the next step was to set up a workshop. I demurred, saying I didn't think we'd sufficiently explored how we'd be working together. In essence, I thought we were moving too quickly.

My two potential colleagues felt I was being too cautious and wanted to move to action. As a reflective practitioner, I felt 'hustled' by the pace being proposed, and was also influenced by a previous experience of joint hosting (Chapter 22). When my dissenting voice went unheard on the matter of pace, I didn't feel able to express my unease about our hosting container. The conversation moved on to practical considerations for the workshop. I felt torn between contributing and keeping faith with my practice. In the end, believing that I had to commit or step away, I chose the latter.

The work proceeded without me and, as far as I know, met the desired aim of widening access to dialogue practices across the organisation. However, at my end, there were unintended consequences. A long-term working alliance with one of the practitioners was fractured, and took time to repair. The practitioner that I knew less well seemed to take my withdrawal personally and actively excluded me from other dialogue-related work. Overall, I felt sad that we'd been unable to walk our talk.

When I reflect on this example, I wonder if the discipline of slowing down is actually the hardest aspect of embodying dialogue practices. The wider container for all leadership development, conversations and activities is often characterised by moving 'at pace'. To do otherwise is countercultural and difficult to bring to life. Instead, in the aftermath of conversations that aren't fit for purpose, we spend time and energy fighting fires.

In the context of this book, it may be helpful to think of doing things 'at pace' as a collective habit of thought and behaviour. If we notice an 'at pace' habit around us, we can centre, and choose whether or not to be influenced by it. As individuals, we may also have an inner 'at pace' tendency, and we can work with this in the same way – notice, centre and choose. We can apply this strategy to any characteristic or approach that's become habitual: it will be useful in some circumstances and problematic in others, and centring can help us to discern which applies.

If we're able to loosen the grip of the 'at pace' tendency, we can consider how we might develop a practice of going slowly. Personally, I take inspiration from a Taoist saying:

> There is so much to do. There is so little time. We must go slowly.

## Over to you …

Think of a conversation in which moving quickly to action led to a significant problem, setback or crisis. How did you and those around you deal with this adversity? How much time, energy and money was involved in the process?

If you'd taken time to properly 'put your heads together' before taking action, what might you have been able to foresee?

When similar circumstances occur, what might inspire you to go slowly?

## Hastily reversed decisions

To further illustrate the consequences of being caught in a culture of quick decisions, we can revisit an example from Chapter 13. To recap: an artist's work was removed from a gallery shop because they were reported to have expressed views counter to today's moral code. When robustly challenged, the leadership of the gallery hastily reversed this decision.

Whilst we have very little information about the actual circumstances, we can use this predicament as a general case to explore how such situations arise. As an archetypal pattern, something has been said that, in current times, can be taken as insensitive or offensive, prompting a leadership team to feel it has to act. Let's speculate about what might have been going on, in service to recognising that it could easily happen to us.

As a focus for inquiry and reflection, we might ask: how do experienced leaders find themselves in the position of having to overturn decisions? We might first reflect on the reality that our societal landscape is changing – as is always the case. It seems, though, that the rate of change is accelerating, making it harder to keep track of current mores. This is the general container in which events and conversations take place – how might it shed light on the predicament of the gallery leadership?

One possible narrative is that, until recently, the predominant frame for leadership was cognitive, with an emphasis on cause-and-effect reasoning and comparing the (perceived) costs and benefits of a course of action. For those of us who are getting on a bit, it's likely that our progression into leadership was rooted in this kind of 'business case' thinking, which assumes a largely predictable, linear (and therefore plannable) future. This was certainly the case for me. However, this type of thinking was always an oversimplification of how the world worked. As we made sophisticated estimates and forecasts, and then used them as a basis for creating and delivering a plan, any uncertainties and assumptions were quickly forgotten. The plan then took on a life of its own. To me, even back then, this approach always seemed to be 'a wing and a prayer'. In addition, factors such as values, experience, emotions and (perhaps) vested interests and personal ambition flavoured leadership decisions and actions to some degree, whether consciously or not. Often, these influences were discounted, concealed or explained with post-hoc logic.

367

In the usual way of things, this 'operating system' has remained in place, largely unexamined, and it's been carried into a changing environment. The assumption of a predictable, linear future is even less fit for purpose in a world that's becoming increasingly connected, nuanced, values-based and complex. The way we describe and evaluate choices hasn't really evolved to include textured, qualitative and systemic assessments and decisions. For many in leadership roles, this creates a (largely unrecognised) gap of knowledge and experience when it comes to dealing with values-based societal narratives.

In this context, a leadership group might react in line with their perception of public expectations when the reputation of their organisation seems to be threatened. Perhaps this is what happened in the gallery. Without fully understanding the complexities of the situation, and without collectively thinking through the potential implications, it probably seemed straightforward to remove the artist's work from sale. At face value, leadership were aligning with current proprieties.

However, they may not have considered the potential impact of their decision and what it might communicate to others. They were, in effect, setting in motion a public conversation. Unintended consequences followed in the form of a challenge, what we might call a backlash. At that point, there was an opportunity for the leadership group to acknowledge that they might have misjudged the situation, to apologise and then to pause to reflect. It was time to go slowly. Instead, the pattern seemed to repeat: see a reputational threat and react quickly, without considering what this might communicate to others.

How many times have we seen this pattern, usually dubbed a U-turn, play out in recent times? When we realise that an action was ill-conceived, what might constitute a more considered response? For the leadership of the art gallery, excluding the artist contradicted the organisation's espoused commitment to equality, diversity and inclusion. By simply reversing their decision, they succumbed to an either/or dichotomy – to ban or not ban the artist. At either stage, they might have found a way to better honour the organisation's principles and to make their point, whilst continuing to include the artist's perspective and work. With thoughtfulness and skill, it's possible to acknowledge different views in a way that makes it clear that we don't agree with, or endorse, them. It requires courage, clarity and creativity, all of which are more likely to arise when people think together in a way that includes the voices of head, heart and core/gut (Chapter 12).

## Over to you …

To what extent does this exploration of a hastily made decision and its later reversal resonate with you? Have you been in this position yourself, or been on the receiving end of a similar sequence of events? Drawing on what you're learning in these pages, how might you describe (or bystand) the underlying pattern of what took place?

In the future, how might this influence how you approach a complex issue with societal implications?

In this chapter, we've looked at some of the circumstances that invite us to go more slowly in our conversations. Sometimes moving quickly will be the best option – and sometimes it may be the only option. However, moving 'at pace' can be habitual and can have unintended adverse consequences. If we can be discerning about how and when this habit occurs, we can pause to assess whether it might be beneficial to go slowly and create the conditions for dialogue. In addition, we can support ourselves to go slowly by making time to embrace and embody new practices. Let's explore the practicalities of this.

## Chapter 35 Beginning: making time to embody new practices

The subtitle of this book implies that the practices in these pages will transform your leadership conversations. In reality, embodying them can transform *all* our conversations, whether we're in dialogue or simply in a tricky exchange with a colleague. I have some supporting evidence for these claims, which I hope will inspire you to invest time and energy in building your capacity to embody the practices of dialogue.

## Leadership conversations transformed

Some years ago, I hosted several Dialogue Practice Development programmes for cohorts of senior leaders in the National Health Service in Scotland. The first two groups took place concurrently, as a pilot. Afterwards, the sponsor did a full evaluation, asking participants about their experiences of changing practice. In addition, she surveyed their colleagues, inviting them to describe any changes they'd observed in the way participants engaged with others. The evaluation report became the basis for an article published in the *Health Service Journal* in 2012.[24]

Here are some examples of the changes described by participants:

'I had often wondered why I couldn't get what I wanted out of certain conversations. Through my case-work I realised that my "entry" into conversations could come across as aggressive, impatient and patronising, thus lessening my impact.' Nurse Leader

'When faced with difficult and confrontational situations, I always knew *intellectually* that I should understand the other person's perspective. But I see now that this didn't always inform what I did.' Associate Medical Director

'The programme brought out bits of me that had fallen into "disuse" because of circumstances/culture.' General Manager

The theme of these experiences is an increase in awareness – noticing a pattern and the potential impact of it. This is a change in our relationship with 'self' (we are the method) and is a first step towards changing practice. When we realise something isn't working, we'll often find ways to address it. Later in the chapter, we'll look at a framework for building on this initial awareness to begin to embody a new practice.

First, here's a summary of themes distilled from the changes that colleagues observed in the participants:

- meetings and conversations were more productive – participants contributed more positively, working relationships were improved and less time was spent 'smoothing ruffled feathers';

- positive leadership choices – participants were more discerning about what they paid attention to, letting go of matters they usually fought 'to the end'. This created capacity for everyone to engage more constructively;

- more inclusive working – participants were seen to work with/ through allies rather than independently, and to bring isolated people into the fold; and

- improved reputation – participants gained greater respect as they listened more and managed themselves skilfully in meetings.

These changes arose from six day-long workshops over six months and from the willingness of participants to try out new approaches. For my part, the programme ran for several years, stretching and delighting me in equal measure.

In terms of stretch, when I was packing up after the third session of one of the pilot programmes, a participant returned to the group room. She felt that the relationship between the two of us was uncomfortable and she'd decided to leave the programme. My heart leapt into my mouth and my tendency to 'fight' kicked in. In my left-hand column (thankfully not said), a flash of judgement appeared as I automatically tried to protect my reputation and blame her for any discord.

And then I remembered the four-part centring practice (Appendix B) and, in particular, the 'letting land' practice (Appendix F). Exhaling, and becoming more uplifted in my posture, I consciously imagined my peri-personal space to be circular. I then extended it to include this courageous participant, who'd come back to tell me she was struggling. I let her words land in the space around me and, when she paused, I asked: is there anything I can do differently that might make it possible for you to stay?

In the conversation that followed, we each acknowledged the moments of friction that sometimes arose between us. I gently mentioned that the aim of the programme was to equip us to remain present to such moments and to work through them – and I asked if we could each use our experience as a live case study.

Reader, she remained … and got a great deal from the experience. In fact, we both did.

In terms of delight, I was deeply moved by a participant who shared the story of a conversation with her child. Her young daughter came home from school one day and said, 'Mummy, I hate you'. You can imagine the participant's reaction – hurt, confused, angry. Then she remembered to exhale, uplift and open her peri-personal space, and she recalled the Ladder of Inference, which we'd explored in the previous workshop. She said, with curiosity: 'Can you tell me a little bit about what you mean?'

It turned out that her daughter didn't know what 'hate' meant – she was simply repeating a phrase she'd heard in the playground. When her mum gently explained the meaning, she said 'Mummy, I don't hate you … I love you.'

I cherish this story because, although my dialogue work relates solely to organisational settings, we can use the practices in any conversation. Dialogue skills are human skills and, when we pay attention to them, we may rehabilitate forgotten parts of ourselves, as described by the General Manager in the evaluation of the programme.

{brain icon} Over to you ...

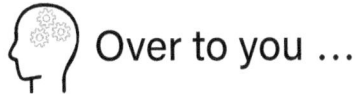

While you've been reading this book, have you had an experience that, afterwards, made you think 'I could have used ... [centring, a dialogue practice, or ...]' What prompted this reflection? How might you recognise a similar situation in future?

And, if you'd been able to use the resource that you identified, what difference might it have made? How can you prepare for the next opportunity to use it?

{lightbulb icon}

## Three expansions of practice

To change our practice, we first notice something that we think might work for us. Then, we try it out. If we decide to adopt it, we refine the new practice and, eventually, come to embody it. I think of this process as three expansions of practice, radiating outwards from an initial inspiring idea. As we actively change our practice, we literally grow into it, amplifying our presence, energy and peri-personal space. This may then influence others to change their practice too.

These three expansions of practice are inspired by a framework of learning containers, developed by Peter Garrett[3] and outlined in my earlier book, *Pause for Breath*.[1] In the diagram overleaf, I've used concentric circles to represent the expansions from an initial, central circle. The boundary of each circle progressively lightens to reflect an increase in our energetic reach as we inhabit a new practice more fully. I've adapted the language of the Garrett's framework to focus on the messy realities of transforming an idea into an embodied experience.

The seed that motivates us to make a change in practice is often sown by an experience. We become intrigued by something someone else is doing, or we read a book or watch a video that makes us think, or we're on a development programme and an approach catches our attention. We're inspired by an idea or

## Embodying a new practice
### Three expansions

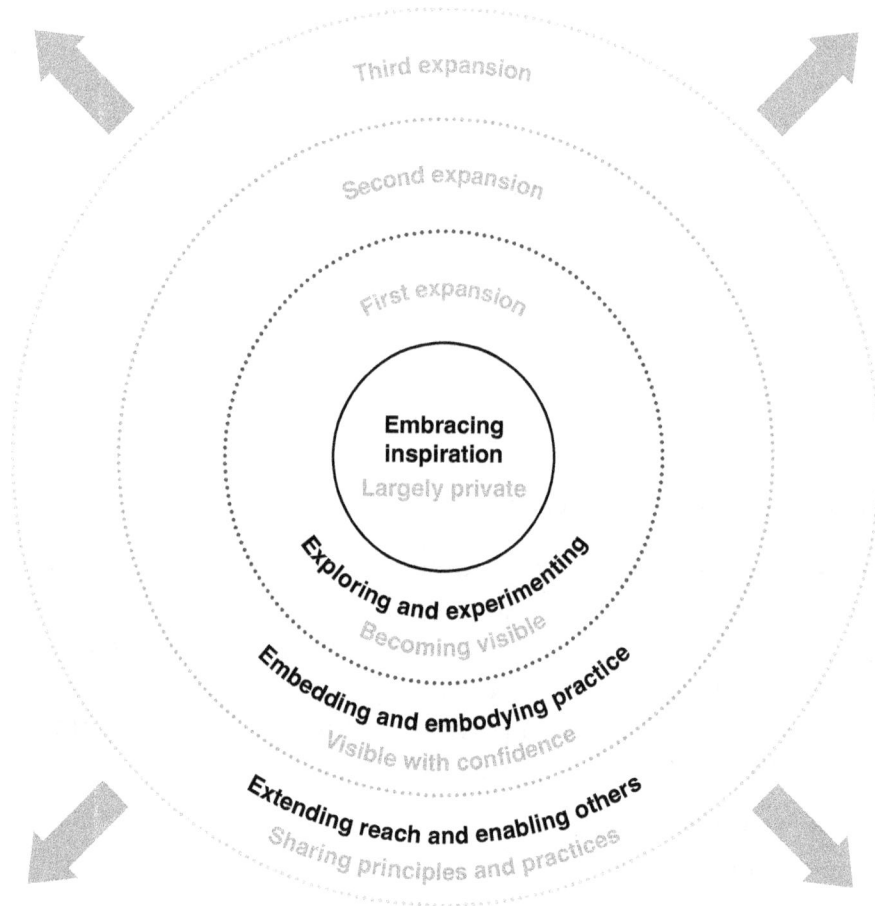

Third expansion

Second expansion

First expansion

**Embracing inspiration**

Largely private

*Exploring and experimenting*

Becoming visible

*Embedding and embodying practice*

Visible with confidence

*Extending reach and enabling others*

Sharing principles and practices

Inspired by the work of Peter Garrett

concept and can see the potential of it. We may decide immediately that we want to include it in our repertoire – or we may reflect and/or do some research, gathering information and weighing up the effort and possible benefits. This pre-practice phase is largely internal and, unless we talk to others about it, it won't be visible externally.

### *First expansion of practice*

The first expansion begins when we decide to try out the approach, or part of it. In doing so, we're likely to become more visible to others, and there's some risk involved in this. When we don't know how something will work out, we can feel a little exposed. In effect, we're piloting something – and we can choose whether or not we let this be known. Personally, I lean towards being transparent. This has several benefits – we can ask others to help us to understand the impact of what we're doing; we reduce the pressure on ourselves to 'get it right'; we raise awareness of something new and/or different; and we communicate that we're still learning and developing.

The purpose of the first expansion is to get a sense of how an approach works for us and for others. Some changes in practice might come easily and feel like a natural next step. Others may sit less comfortably with our current habits, personal style and ways of working. We may need to play with aspects of an approach (such as language) to create a more workable fit with our character and/or our leadership practice. The frame of experimenting – which I once heard described as 'poking it with a stick and seeing what happens' – is really helpful: we can adopt the stance of a scientist researching the effect of making a change. The key question to ask ourselves is: what's the impact of this new approach, and how will I evidence it? The frame of experimenting can help us to develop some confidence in using a new practice.

To get the most out of this expansion (and those that follow), we engage in reflective practice and refine what we're doing. This often means circling back to the beginning, to the original impetus for change. As we embrace an idea and select what we'll work on, it's important to note our starting point and our direction of travel. This provides a baseline against which to assess change. Whether we're a relative beginner or a seasoned practitioner, each repetition of a practice can yield data, and this allows us to refine what we're doing.

The process is similar to the 'small tests of change' approach, also known as plan-do-study-act or PDSA cycles (Dr W. Edwards Deming[25]). Essentially, we prepare to try out a new approach, choosing a low-risk situation. We take a step, study the effects, reflect, make small adjustments and repeat the cycle.

How might you step into this expansion with some of the material we've been exploring?

## Over to you …

Within our book-based conversation, what's caught your attention as something you might adopt? Perhaps it's the centring practice? Perhaps it's an approach like 'check-in'? Perhaps it's something like listening more skilfully or finding a better balance between advocacy and inquiry?

Choose just one thing, note its potential merits and develop a testing strategy. Where might you try this out? How will you prepare? How will you assess the impact? What will you do next?

### *Second expansion of practice*

In the second expansion, we aim to inhabit the new approach and make it integral to our leadership practice. We're in the realm of repetition, which can be dull and hard to maintain. We also become more visible, which brings the risk of a fall – if we're not consistent in our efforts to change, we may be judged by others. However, there's no short cut. We have to put in enough repetitions to embed our chosen practice in our mind, body and spirit so that we can improvise when we meet the unexpected. We want to be confident that the new approach will be readily accessible when circumstances call for it.

As we put in the repetitions, we'll have variable experiences. To learn from them, we continue the process of small tests of change (PDSA cycles). We reflect on what happened, refine our practice, then repeat. In addition, we change how we measure what's 'right', assessing progress by the impact we have instead of by 'doing it right'. For example, in Chapters 19 and 33, I described the measure of the quality of a question as the length of the silence that follows it. The skilfulness of an inquiry is determined by the 'pause' that indicates people are thinking, not the finesse of what we say.

In this expansion, progress is likely to be slow and is sometimes hard to see. When I was struggling with this aspect of my T'ai Chi practice, a senior student offered me the metaphor that, each time we practise, we lay down a layer of rice paper. Viewed edge-on, each layer is almost invisible, but once you have a stack, you can see the difference. We can use this image to help us keep faith with any change we're making, even when the immediate results are small and/or unclear.

In this second expansion of practice, we can enhance our repetition of any dialogue practice by centring and shaping our peri-personal space to support it. This brings us into alignment and places our attention on the quality of our energy and presence, increasing the likelihood that our efforts will be skilful. Combining embodied practices and dialogue practices reinforces the neural pathways of both our mind-set and our body-set (Chapter 19), which accelerates the process of inhabiting a new practice.

## Over to you …

As you begin to consider – and even embrace – the idea that embodying a new practice requires repeated effort, how might you make time to begin the process?

If you decide to proceed, how will you make repetition interesting?

### Third expansion of practice

The bedrock of the third expansion is continued repetition. As we truly embody a new practice, we naturally become a standard-bearer for it. We extend our reach as others notice what we're doing, which may inspire them to explore the same ground. The effect can be almost viral, radiating beyond our immediate circle. We begin to affect a wider field.

We don't need to do anything additional in this expansion – we simply become increasingly consistent in the way we embody our practice. We continue to reflect and refine, learning from encounters that go well and those that don't. We keep a practice alive by doing it, and our ongoing attention keeps it fresh.

As we refine our practice, we circle back to experimenting and even revisit the original idea. We make modifications, test them, reflect and refine again. Essentially, we embody a new practice through action-learning. We have to work out how we (in all our human reality) can put an idea (in all its conceptual idealism) into practice (in a messy world that involves the human realities of others). This takes time, application … and good humour.

This brings me to one of the most important things I've learned on my journey into this territory: to take myself less seriously. In our initial exploration of the four-part centring practice (Chapter 9 onwards), we discovered a pattern in the way we react to stress, pressure or anxiety – we tend to fight, flee or become immobile. When we come to appreciate that this unresourceful state is simply part of our humanness, we can acknowledge and accept it each time it recurs. Wendy Palmer encouraged her Leadership Embodiment students to recognise the inevitability of this reaction by saying 'Ah! There I am again', accessorised with a wry smile. As I learned to accept the reality that my embodied reactive pattern would show up again and again, I also learned to accept the repeating thought patterns that derail my good intentions. Ah! There I am again. And again. And again.

Over time, I've come to see my predictable patterns as (mostly) endearingly ridiculous. Since these habits of body and mind are deeply ingrained, they'll probably be with me for life – and so I can choose either to befriend them or to fight them. Mostly, I choose the former, accepting my foibles with kindness and compassion. This doesn't excuse them – I resolve to do better, whilst knowing that this will take time and practice. In the meantime, I smile, do a centring practice and see what changes. And, as I accept myself and my experience more warmly and graciously, I'm more often able to extend compassion, generosity and acceptance to others.

In this third expansion of practice, we may be inspired to support others to realise similar benefits. Some of my dialogue clients have done this by hosting a kind of 'book club' for a small group of colleagues centred on *Pause for Breath*. The group

378

worked through the book together, and the client found it helpful to revisit the principles and practices outlined in it. You'll find brief guidance for how you might do this at Appendix N.

Which brings us back to repetition (again) and my promise to deliberately repeat things, again and again (Chapter 4). My reason is (and was) that we pay different attention to the same thing, depending on when, where and how we read it (or hear it). We also perceive things differently as our knowledge and understanding grow and as we try things out. This means that something we skipped over in an early chapter might make new sense and/or have greater significance when we see it again.

From my heart, I encourage you to embrace the discipline of repetition and seek the potential in it.

## Applying the expansions

We can apply the process of changing practice to a whole new approach or to individual aspects within it. For example, I adopted Leadership Embodiment wholesale. I was primed to be receptive to it because I was already trying to develop some embodied activities of my own. As a result, the 'embracing ideas' phase was very short. I threw myself into an intensive period of training (the first expansion) and, because of my martial arts experience, quickly grasped the essentials of the approach. However, embedding the practices (the second expansion) took time, many workshops with Wendy Palmer, and many repetitions of the individual activities. This work is ongoing.

In contrast, in the field of dialogue, my development path focused on selecting individual aspects of the approach. Early on, I realised that much of what I said was advocacy. In fact, it was nearly always advocacy 'away from' what others were saying – opposing, questioning, challenging. Whilst my intention was usually to improve the coherence of decisions, my energy was very 'pointed'. Most of my challenges left casualties in their wake. Others often experienced my input as critical, obstructive and/or competitive (Appendix K).

To work on this, I took time to prepare for important conversations and to clarify my intentions using the head-heart-core approach (Chapter 12). I built my capacity to steward my energy by using the centred advocacy practice, expanding my peri-personal space to include others so that my 'point' landed beyond them. Gradually my challenges became both more skilful and more impactful – energetically, they reflected my intention, which was nearly always to be helpful. In addition, I added more 'towards' advocacy into my repertoire: I more often said what I was 'for', as well as what I was 'against'.

Finally, I applied myself to adding some inquiry into my interactions. Initially, I didn't worry too much about the quality of my inquiry – I simply asked others for their perspective, rather than assuming I knew best. I tried out different questions and reflected on the responses – nearly all of which enriched my thinking. This motivated me to use even more inquiry in my conversations.

The twin track of refining what I did naturally, and adding something that I did much less often, led to more interesting and effective exchanges. I practised in my all conversations, not just those that might be 'dialogue', which reflects the principle that we can embody dialogue practices in any situation – remember the mother whose daughter said 'I hate you'?

As I inhabited my new practices, I had more influence. In addition, my mind-set changed to lean more towards accentuating positives rather than identifying potential problems. These days, most people are surprised to hear that I have a combative nature. I've affected the field around me.

## Over to you …

What do you already do a lot of in your conversations? How might you refine this natural tendency so that you have more influence and impact?

What might you add into your conversational practice in order to enrich your exchanges?

How might you use the centring practices outlined in this book to support the changes you introduce?

We began this chapter by looking at the benefits that can flow as we start to embody dialogue practices. As we become more aware of *our* part in the way a conversation plays out, we tend to reconnect with our values. We may then try to reflect them in what we say and how we say it. We're also more likely to include others and work collaboratively on things that matter. Generally, we see positive changes in ourselves and in those around us.

As we continue to make changes to our practice, it can be useful to have a sense of a destination, an idea of what might characterise a dialogue practitioner. The foundation is, I think, an ongoing commitment to engaging in the 'inner work' that helps us to see ourselves clearly. As we gain compassionate insight into the bundle of wisdoms and warts that makes a 'me', we're more able to hold others and their views in parity. As we recognise and accept difference within ourselves, our capacity to hold the differences of others grows. We begin to consciously hold our personal container.

In our conversations, as we come into this new relationship with ourselves, we begin to pay attention to the 'how' alongside the 'what'. We see that we have a part to play in establishing and holding a collective container. We actively engage in this and, to support our continued learning, we regularly reflect on our experience by wondering (Chapter 7):

- what's happening for individuals, between individuals and collectively?

- what's my part in this?; and

- what might I change in the way I contribute?

We can reflect on any kind of conversation in this way: whether we're hosting or participating, these questions offer a rich field of learning. They support us to prepare for our conversations, and to refine the way we approach them and intervene in them. We begin to recognise ourselves in others and to embrace, fully and transparently, our shared humanness, and this is then reflected in the quality of our interventions.

As we embody dialogue practices, we naturally start to 'live' them, at home, at work, at play. It may be that this kind of coherence is the mark of a specialist practitioner, one who desires to influence others and the field. A more generalist practitioner may simply wish to accrue enough knowledge, experience and practice to improve their conversations in their community or workplace. Personally, I don't think it matters: to change the world, one conversation at a time, we need both specialists and generalists. I believe that, when any one of us is intent on having better conversations, we contribute to a better world. Each effort to change practice, however small, is a step on this journey. Perhaps this belief is what characterises a dialogue practitioner.

And so, we've come to the final chapter. In it, we'll use the three expansions of practice to reflect briefly on our journey. Then, we'll say our farewells.

# Chapter 36  Bringing our conversation to a close

I'd like to end by circling back to the beginning of our book-based conversation and using the three expansions of practice to get a sense of the road we've travelled together.

## The road travelled

We began with William Isaacs' description of dialogue as a way of 'harnessing the energy of our differences' to create something new. From this we inferred that, if difference is present, dialogue is the most appropriate form of conversation to realise the potential within it. To engage in dialogue, we pay attention to the 'how' of a conversation alongside the 'what', and this invites us to make changes to our practice.

In Part I, we used the Gibb approach to check in with each other and begin to journey towards dialogue. As part of this process, I proposed three tenets that invite us to pay attention to the 'how' of our conversations. Together, they offer guidance on the way we hold conversations and handle ourselves within them.

In Part II, we prepared the ground for deeper consideration of the tenets. We explored some ideas, frameworks and perspectives that can help us to describe the shape and quality of our conversations. We drew a distinction between advocacy and inquiry, and used a case study as a mental rehearsal for using this framework in practice.

In Chapters 9 and 10, we began to look into the role of the body in our conversations, particularly those in which we're dealing with difference or something unfamiliar. We considered the possibility that the way a conversation unfolds is significantly affected by the energy we bring to it, the way we carry ourselves. We discovered that we can influence our presence and energy by using the Leadership Embodiment four-part centring practice (Appendix B). If we adopt this practice and become skilful in accessing centre, we can transform our leadership conversations.

To test this claim, or to adopt any new approach, we have to move beyond the realm of ideas and into the first expansion of embodying a practice: we start to try things out. We might conduct some initial experiments covertly. However, if we make a deliberate change in our practice, it's likely that others will notice. As we become more visible, it can feel uncomfortable, especially as the results of trying something new can be variable. We can use the LE centring practice to weather any ups and downs as we experiment again and again: it will support us to reflect on the impact of each change in practice and consider how we might refine it.

In Chapters 11 to 13, we considered a broader context for the dance between neat ideas and the messy realities of putting them into practice. We looked at some of the factors that influence our conversations, emphasising the importance of the way we carry ourselves as we talk and listen. From this ground, we began to distil some steps for moving towards dialogue, culminating in five such steps. This prepared us to engage more explicitly with practices from the field of dialogue.

In Chapter 14, we began to explore Scharmer's Four Fields of Conversation. This framework offers a language for describing the interplay between individual voices and the currents and tides of collective energy. We began to pay attention to the whole conversation alongside our personal concerns.

This set the scene for Part III, in which we considered how the three tenets outlined in Part I can support us to build capacity to embody dialogue practices, individually and together. As we worked with each tenet, we began to move from the realm of exploring and experimenting (the first expansion of practice) into the realm of embedding and embodying a chosen approach (the second expansion).

Through the lens of the tenets, we came to appreciate the way that our relationship with ourselves affects the way we engage with others. We came to understand that, when a conversation matters, we don't do it justice if we just 'turn up and see what happens'. We also discovered that the way we begin has a disproportionate effect on how things unfold. We found that the quality of presence that we bring to our conversations underpins each of the tenets, reinforcing the importance of the embodied practices contained in these pages.

Finally, in Part IV, we looked at factors that can help us determine which of our conversations might benefit from the preparation that supports us to be in dialogue. We found that such conversations tend to involve important issues, multiple stakeholders and many uncertainties, interdependencies and ambiguities – they're worth additional time, care and attention. Then, approaching the end of the book, we considered ways of continuing to build capacity to embody dialogue practices beyond it. We learned that, when we fully inhabit a practice, we naturally extend our reach and affect others, which may inspire them to change their practice too.

At this point, it really is 'Over to you …'

If you continue to engage in this work, it doesn't matter whether you embrace the whole field of dialogue or simply learn to embody individual dialogue practices in order to enhance your everyday conversations. Each time we have a conversation that's fruitful for all concerned and improves our working alliances, we contribute to making the world a slightly better place.

We've discovered that the road towards approaching difference differently is long and winding. And, as we've travelled some of it together, we've seen that it's full of potholes. However, I believe it's a road worth travelling … and, once we begin to change our practice in our leadership conversations, we find that it's a lifetime endeavour. However accomplished we become, we'll always be put further to the test by changes of context; new people with their preferences and idiosyncrasies; and our own preoccupations and foibles. We keep reflecting. We keep refining. We keep practising.

## Ending with hope

We'll bring our book-based conversation to a close with an example that shows that we can navigate quite challenging differences in a way that strengthens relationships.

The context was an executive coaching programme that was under new leadership. The incoming Programme Lead had changed the way that coaching assignments were evaluated. In my view, the revised approach was both less reflective than the old one and inappropriate in terms of client confidentiality. I raised an objection, not really expecting a response. However, another seasoned coach had also questioned the process and we were both invited into a conversation with the Programme Lead and her colleague.

We began the conversation by checking in, each of us describing what we felt was important – we were all experienced, knowledgeable and prepared to say what we thought. What followed was gritty, intense and sometimes very uncomfortable. However, each of us was respectful towards the others and we all listened carefully. From the different perspectives of coaching relationships and leading a coaching programme, we were each true to what we believed to be essential.

We explored the issues, without trying to reach solutions. After about two hours, the Programme Lead suddenly stood up. She summarised the key points raised and proposed a way forward that substantially met the needs of both professional stances. Within a few minutes, we'd made a few tweaks and were ready to conclude. Afterwards, the Programme Lead and her colleague enacted what we'd agreed, quickly and proficiently. The new evaluation process was robust and stood the test of time.

Whilst tough, this conversation delivered an effective and sustainable outcome and strengthened all the relationships involved – in a single afternoon. As well as improving the evaluation of the programme, we'd enhanced our capacity to handle tricky differences. For my part, I knew that I could raise any future issue with confidence that I'd be 'met' and taken seriously.

From this example, we can see that coming through difficult terrain together builds trust and confidence in one another – it strengthens the container. This insight invites us to change our relationship to difference, and see it as positive and generative. And so, I encourage you to find your own example of a conversation that tested all present, yet resolved with a sense of satisfaction on all sides. This kind of constructive exchange can provide a valuable reference for what can be accomplished as you continue to explore how you might approach difference differently.

In truth, I believe it's important to note each and every favourable experience in our leadership conversations and to appreciate what made them possible. If we're able to accumulate a treasure trove of good experiences, they might inspire us to persevere ... for the road ahead will continue to be long, winding and full of potholes.

For the last time ...

## ... over to you ...

Whatever your stage, how will you continue to build your practice? How will you coach yourself to persevere when the going gets tough? Who might support and/or accompany you? How will you celebrate your successes?

And ... how will you remember to have fun along the way?

In reaching the end of our shared journey, I hope that you feel equipped to take the next steps alone. If you've already started to make changes in your conversational practice, I hope that those around you are reaping the rewards.

My heart's desire is that you come to believe that we don't have time *not* to do 'this stuff', and that you're inspired to take action and to build your capacity to embody dialogue practices. If you do, you'll transform your conversations and play your part in channelling the energies of difference to create something new.

Finally, I wish you many fruitful beginnings and much happy practising. Thank you for your companionship – it inspired me to persevere and to bring this book to fruition.

# Sources and resources

1   *Pause for Breath: Bringing the practices of mindfulness and dialogue to leadership conversations,* Amanda Ridings. 3rd edition, Originate Books, 2024.
2   *Dialogue and the Art of Thinking Together,* William Isaacs. Doubleday, 1999.
3   Dialogues Associates: www.dialogue-associates.com.
4   Amanda Ridings, LinkedIn: https://www.linkedin.com/in/amanda-ridings-6083283a/recent-activity/articles/.
5   Leadership Embodiment: https://leadershipembodiment.com/.
6   *Trust – A New Vision of Human Relationships for Business, Education, Family and Personal Living,* Jack Gibb. Newcastle Publishing Co., Inc., 1991.
7   *The Fifth Discipline: The Art & Practice of the Learning Organization,* Peter Senge. Currency/Doubleday, 1990.
8   *The Fifth Discipline Fieldbook: Strategies and Tools for Building a Learning Organization,* Peter Senge, Art Kleiner, Richard Ross et al. Nicholas Brealey Publishing, 1994.
9   *On Dialogue,* David Bohm. Routledge, 1996.
10  *Leadership Embodiment: How the Way We Sit and Stand Can Change the Way We Think and Speak,* Wendy Palmer and Janet Crawford. The Embodiment Foundation with CreateSpace, 2013.
11  The King's Fund: https://www.kingsfund.org.uk/leadership-development.
12  *Six Thinking Hats,* Edward de Bono. Penguin, 1987.
13  'Unity does not trump a healthy democracy', Kevin Pringle. *The Sunday Times,* 25 April 2021.
14  *Weekly Leadership Contemplations,* Amanda Ridings. 2nd edition, Originate Books, 2024.
15  *Movement in Black,* Pat Parker. Firebrand Books, 1999.
16  *Theory U: Leading from the Future as It Emerges,* C. Otto Scharmer. Berrett-Koehler Publishers, 2016.
17  *Reading the Room: Group Dynamics for Coaches and Leaders,* David Kantor. John Wiley & Sons, Inc., 2012.
18  The Gestalt Centre: https://gestaltcentre.org.uk/what-is-gestalt/.
19  *Virtual Leadership: Learning to Lead Differently,* Ghislaine Caulat and Mike Pedlar. Libri Publishing, 2012.

20  'Virtual Leadership: rethinking virtual teams', Ghislaine Caulat. *Danish Leadership Review*, September–October 2012.

21  *The Universe in a Single Atom*, His Holiness the Dalai Lama. Abacus, 2007.

22  *Unlikely Teachers*, Judy Ringer. One Point Press, 2006.

23  Private email exchange with Timothy B. Kelly, January 2024.

24  'Leadership Conversations', Sharon Millar and Amanda Ridings. *Health Service Journal*, 20 September 2012.

25  Deming Institute: https://deming.org/explore/pdsa/.

# Appendices

# Appendix A

## Pause for Breath mindfulness practice

*This practice is for a group preparing to check in to a conversation, and assumes that those present are sitting on dining chairs, or similar.*

Sit a little towards the front of your chair, so that you're supporting your own back, rather than leaning against the chairback. Place both feet flat on the floor and rest your hands on your thighs, palms down. Imagine there's a silken thread at the crown of your head, drawing you gently upwards into a comfortable upright posture. Now, exhale slowly, imagining the breath spiralling down through your body and into the ground.

As you inhale, imagine the soft touch of a finger moving from the base of your spine to your crown, and sense the breath filling your body. Then exhale slowly, imagining the breath spiralling down through your body, softening the tissues and forming a root in the ground. And, as you inhale, imagine the breath flowing up your spine, gently lifting each vertebra from the one below, so that the body feels light and spacious.

Now, rest your attention on your breath, and simply observe it for a few moments, exhaling, inhaling … rest in the movement of the breath. *[Pause …]*

Now, gently observe your state of mind without getting caught up in the mind's activity. Notice if your mind is busy, scattered, calm, noisy, quiet, preoccupied, settled, distracted, active, sleepy … or choose another word that describes it. You don't need to do anything, simply observe and accept this state of mind. *[Pause …]*

Now, bring your attention to your heart and notice your state of heart as we gather to talk and listen together. Notice if your heart is heavy, light, weary, open, full, tender, closed, raw, radiant … or choose another word that describes it. Gently notice your orientation to being here; perhaps you're whole-hearted, half-hearted or your heart really isn't in it. You don't need to do anything, simply observe and accept your state of heart. *[Pause …]*

And, deep down, in the very core of you, what matters? What called you to be here? How might this calling support you to be present to whatever unfolds? *[Pause …]*

Now bring your attention gently to the sensation of contact between your feet and the floor … and to the contact between your thighs and the chair … and to the contact between your hands and your thighs … and back to the breath, observing it for a few moments. *[Pause …]*

Become aware of the space around you and the people present. Expand your sense of space to include them and prepare to check in, to share how you are and what really matters to you. *[Pause … and then begin to check in to the conversation]*

# Appendix B

# Embodied Practice 1: Foundation four-part centring practice[†]

1. Posture and breath

Become uplifted and aligned in your posture, with your spine easing to its natural length and curve. As you do this, exhale slowly and imagine the breath spiralling down through your body and into the ground.

Inhale softly, imagining that the gentle inflow of air lifts each vertebra from the one below it, bringing a sense of lightness into the spine.

Exhale slowly, imagining the breath flowing down, softening the front of the body and forming a root in the earth below.

2. Balancing and opening personal space

Now become aware of the space you occupy – pay attention behind you as well as in front of you, to the left and right, below your feet and above your head. Notice if this space has a colour or texture associated with it, or even a sound …

… what would it be like if this personal energetic space was a little more equal and even, a little more balanced?

… what would it be like to consciously enlarge this personal container in all directions so that it includes those around you, whilst holding you gently at the centre?

3. Softening

Whilst maintaining an uplifted posture, soften your forehead, your jaw and your shoulders – imagine they're melting, like butter, and succumbing to gravity …

4. Cultivating beneficial energy*

Invite a little more ease* into your being – where do you experience it and what difference does it make?

* I've used 'ease' as a generic quality of energy – you can tailor the practice by choosing a different quality.

† Based on the work of Wendy Palmer.

# Appendix C

# Embodied Practice 2: Centring in action†

1. Recall a recent event that was irritating, stressful or frustrating enough to cause tension and/or discomfort in your body – keep this proportionate and use an event such as getting a parking ticket or someone forgetting an appointment. Don't use a major life event.

2. Notice and acknowledge any specific areas of tension or discomfort, perhaps gritted teeth, fluttering in your belly, tightness in your chest or a sense of heat in some part of your body.

3. Do the four-part centring practice (Embodied Practice 1), taking twenty seconds or so for each step.

4. Once your system is settled and you have a sense of spaciousness, revisit the event – what's different in your body and mind? How do you experience the event now?

† Based on the work of Wendy Palmer.

# Appendix D

# Embodied Practice 3: Centred inquiry with a practice partner[†]

To explore the 'wall–window' activity, work with a partner. Stand facing one another in a place where you can see obviously different things such as a blank wall and a window, or walls of two different colours. You should be about two arm-lengths apart. Decide which of you will choose to approach difference differently.

1. The first step is to create an energetic experience of difference – an argument, if you like. To do this, each person picks a feature of what they can see and briefly describes it as a fact, with the energy of being right. For example: 'it's a red wall' – 'no! it's a window and a tree'.

2. Repeat this exchange – insisting on your chosen details – until you feel some discord and intensity, perhaps some exasperation, frustration, tension or judgement.

3. To approach difference differently, do a four-part centring practice (Appendix B): uplifting, exhaling, opening your sense of space to include your partner, calling up a beneficial quality of energy. This is respectful opposition. Notice what changes.

4. Having centred, step slightly to the side (suspending your position for a moment) and walk past your partner. Once you're past them, turn to look at what they can see.

5. Do another centring practice: uplifting, exhaling, opening your sense of space to include your partner, calling up a beneficial quality of energy. Stand in this experience for a moment – you're willing to see the world the way your partner sees it. Notice what changes.

6. Finally, return to your starting place and reiterate your original words. You still disagree and … notice how the energy of difference has changed.

7. Debrief with your partner – what happened for them as you tried out this activity? What do you conclude from this?

8. Now change roles and repeat …

[†] *Based on the work of Wendy Palmer.*

## Appendix E

## Embodied Practice 4: Centred listening, 'letting land'[†]

1. Do a four-part centring practice (Appendix B)

> Become uplifted and aligned in your posture and exhale slowly, imagining the breath spiralling down through your body and into the ground, forming a root.
>
> Become aware of the space you occupy – pay attention behind you as well as in front of you, to the left and right, below your feet and above your head. What would it be like if this space was a little more equal and even, a little more balanced, holding you gently at the centre?
>
> Whilst maintaining an uplifted posture, soften your forehead, jaw and shoulders – imagine they're melting, like butter, and succumbing to gravity.
>
> Invite a little more ease (or your chosen quality) into your being – where do you experience it, and what difference does it make?

2. Expanding and including

> From this more centred place, allow your sense of space to be circular/spherical and expand it to include whoever is present. Balance the expansion back and front, left and right, above your head and below your feet.
>
> As someone speaks, allow their words to float or fall into the space between you. Simply hear the words, don't take them into yourself. Let them rest in the shared space, whilst wondering what, if anything, you might respond to …

3. Responding

> If you decide to respond, do the four-part centring practice and connect with what matters – repeat this step until you feel ready to speak.
>
> Expand your personal space to include those present, and then say your words into the shared space, rather than delivering them to (or at) someone.

[†] *Based on the work of Wendy Palmer.*

# Appendix F

# Embodied Practice 5: Letting land with a practice partner[†]

To explore the impact of centred listening and letting land, work with a partner. Brief the partner to say something that you find difficult to hear (go for a 2/10 difficulty, not a personal criticism or a major life event). You can now compare and contrast the experience of receiving these words in an uncentred state and in a centred state.

1. In the first step, your partner delivers the words that you find difficult to hear before you've made any effort to centre or collect yourself. Notice the impact the words have on you and your reaction to them. Perhaps there's a physical sensation such as tightening or shrinking; perhaps there's a feeling such as annoyance or concern; perhaps there's an impulse to speak, to put someone right, to explain, to apologise, to hit back. Or perhaps all of these things. Simply notice and accept whatever occurs – does it represent a pattern?

2. Next, ask your partner to wait a moment or two, saying you'll nod when you're ready for them to speak. Do the four-part centring practice (Appendix B), and then expand your personal space to include your practice partner, remembering to expand it evenly in all dimensions. Nod when you're ready and, as your partner speaks, imagine the words falling or floating softly to the table/ground between you. Notice the impact of the words when you listen in this way.

3. When your partner has delivered the words, connect with what really matters – do you need to respond? If so, what is it important to say? Centre again and speak.

4. Debrief with your partner – what did each of you experience in steps 1 and 2? If you responded in step 3, how did your partner experience your words? What insights arise?

5. Now change roles and repeat …

[†] Based on the work of Wendy Palmer.

# Appendix G

# Embodied Practice 6: Centred speaking[†]

1. Do a four-part centring practice (Appendix B)

   Become uplifted and aligned in your posture and exhale slowly, imagining the breath spiralling down through your body and into the ground, forming a root.

   Become aware of the space you occupy – pay attention back and front, left and right, below your feet and above your head. Allow the space to hold you.

   Whilst maintaining an uplifted posture, soften your forehead, jaw and shoulders – imagine they're melting, like butter, and succumbing to gravity …

   Invite a little more ease (or your chosen quality) into your being …

2. If advocating …

   Consciously tune in to the energy of purpose and intention and a sense of triangular or wedge-shaped space that has strong sides and a clear point or leading edge …

   … and then extend this energetic space so that the point or leading edge reaches into the distance, beyond all those present, allowing the sides and back of the triangle/wedge widen proportionately to include them …

3. If inquiring …

   Consciously tune in to the energy of invitation and curiosity and a sense of circular or spherical space …

   … and then extend this energetic space evenly in all directions, back and front, left and right, above your head and below your feet, allowing it to include all those present …

4. Speaking

   Maintaining your alignment within your extended energetic space, connect to what matters, and say your words into the shared space, rather than delivering them to (or at) a person …

   *Advocacy:* offer your point of view, position or opinion, with clarity and without attachment; or

   *Inquiry:* seek to discover what you don't yet know or understand, with curiosity and without attachment.

5. Preparing to listen

   After you've spoken, do the centred listening practice (Appendix E), bringing to mind a circular space in preparation for receiving what others say and letting their words land in the shared space.

[†] *Based on the work of Wendy Palmer.*

# Appendix H

# Embodied Practice 7: Giving unwelcome news to a practice partner[†]

Ask your practice partner to describe something that would represent unwelcome news for them (invite them to choose a 2/10 difficulty, such as a disappointing response to a presentation or request for resources, not a personal criticism or a major life event). Ask them to observe how your words feel when you offer them from an uncentred state and from a centred state.

> 1. First, notice that the news you're about to give is unwelcome to your partner – how does this affect you? Perhaps you're aware of some physical tightening or shrinking or a sense of wariness, discomfort or dread …

> 2. Then, give the unwelcome news to your partner without making any effort to centre or to collect yourself.

> 3. Pause … and do the four-part centring practice (Appendix B), aligning and uplifting, exhaling and consciously shaping your personal space and energy for advocacy: triangular or wedge-shaped.

> 4. Expand this triangular/wedge-shaped personal space so that the point or leading edge extends beyond your partner, widening the sides and back proportionately. Your partner is now included in the 'big triangle' of your personal space, and within your advocating energy.

> 5. Focusing on the point or leading edge of your big triangle and the shared energetic space the triangle defines, say the same unwelcome words again.

> 6. Debrief with your partner – compare how the unwelcome news landed in steps 2 and 5. What insights arise?

> 7. Now change roles and repeat …

[†] *Based on the work of Wendy Palmer.*

# Appendix I

# Practice 20 from Pause for Breath

### *Raising awareness of your internal dialogue*

When you are next in a dilemma about something, find some quiet space and commit to exploring what you really think, feel and sense. Write down the nub of your dilemma. Note the key points of your thinking about it, from any or all perspectives, with any consequences. Now sit in a comfortable and upright posture and bring your attention to your breath for a moment or two. Just notice the inhale and the exhale, one after another. See if you can let your breath 'breathe you' for a while.

Now bring your attention to your dilemma and see what aspect of it arises first. Give this aspect a name or short description and then ask: where in my body does this arise? Notice any sensations arising in your body.

When you feel you have found the source, make a note or two, then return your attention to inhale and exhale for a few moments. Adjust your posture to be upright again and let your breath 'breathe you'.

Now place your attention on your dilemma again and notice what aspect of it arises next. Give this aspect a name or short description and then ask: where in my body does this arise? Notice any sensations occurring.

Repeat this cycle of attending to your breath and your dilemma until nothing more arises. Then ask: what is needed in response to this situation? Wait for a settled sense of acceptance. If your mind jumps in with an answer, thank it and say, 'not right now'. Bring your attention back to your breath and ask again, 'what is needed in response to this situation?'

What are you learning about the way you approach complex situations where there is no single 'right' answer?

# Appendix J

# Practice 29 from Pause for Breath

### *Authentic voice*

Think of a situation where you have something important to say. Perhaps you want to ask for something, or give feedback, or challenge someone.

Sit or stand in a comfortable upright posture. Bring your attention fully to your breath, imagining it flowing up and down. Inhale, lengthening and straightening your spine. Exhale and imagine your breath flowing down into the ground, forming a root, as your shoulders and core relax. Take two or three breaths this way.

Now bring your attention to your mind. Inhale a sense of space and good intent into the centre of your mind and relax as you exhale. Ask yourself, 'what does my head want to say in this situation?' Find a sentence that expresses this and say it out loud.

Now bring your attention to your heart and solar plexus. Inhale a sense of space and good intent into the centre of your heart and/or solar plexus and relax as you exhale. Ask yourself, 'what does my heart/solar plexus want to say in this situation?' Find a sentence that expresses this and say it out loud.

Now bring your attention to your belly, deep down. Inhale a sense of space and good intent into the centre of your lower abdomen and relax as you exhale. Ask yourself, 'what does my gut want to say in this situation?' Find a sentence that expresses this and say it out loud.

Now let your attention flow through your mind, your heart/solar plexus and your belly. Inhale a sense of space and good intent into these places and relax as you exhale. Ask yourself, 'if my mind, heart and gut are aligned, what do I want to say in this situation? What is my truth?' Find a sentence that expresses this and say it out loud.

Take a few moments to rest and reflect on the effects of this practice.

## Appendix K

## Intent–impact summary: advocating energy

| SPOKEN CONTRIBUTION | Bird's-eye view of advocating energy | Advocacy towards/ for a direction of travel (move, propose) | Advocacy away from/against a direction of travel (challenge, oppose) |
|---|---|---|---|
| INTENT | | Direction, clarity, commitment<br>Supported by the practice of centring and authentic voicing | Coherence, precision, fit<br>Supported by the practice of centring and respecting |
| IMPACT WHEN CENTRED<br>Energy is aligned, open | | Offering direction, commitment and clarity – inviting engagement<br>Impact reflects intent; views and people held in parity | Questioning fit, coherence, precision – inviting appraisal<br><br>Impact reflects intent; views and people held in parity |
| IMPACT WHEN OFF-CENTRE<br>Energy is heightened, exaggerating shape | | Pointedness is intensified, and advocacy can feel directive, insistent, aggressive<br>Impact doesn't reflect intent; parity is lost | Pointedness is intensified, and advocacy can feel critical, obstructive, competitive<br>Impact doesn't reflect intent; parity is lost |
| IMPACT WHEN OFF-CENTRE<br>Energy is dampened, subduing shape | | Pointedness is lessened, and advocacy can feel tentative, fuzzy, disconnected<br>Impact doesn't reflect intent; parity is lost | Pointedness is lessened, and advocacy can feel defensive, resigned, resistant<br>Impact doesn't reflect intent; parity is lost |

# Appendix L

# Intent–impact summary: inquiring energy

| SPOKEN CONTRIBUTION | Bird's-eye view of inquiring energy | Inquiry into a view ... spiral in (follow, support) | Inquiry around a view ... spiral out (bystand, perspective) |
|---|---|---|---|
| INTENT | | Discovery, inclusion, building<br><br>Supported by the practice of centring and listening | Awareness, perspective, spaciousness<br>Supported by the practice of centring and suspending judgement |
| IMPACT WHEN CENTRED<br>Energy is aligned, open | | Encouraging discovery, inclusion, building – inviting curiosity<br>Impact reflects intent, views and people held in parity | Invoking perspective, spaciousness, awareness – inviting reflection<br>Impact reflects intent, views and people held in parity |
| IMPACT WHEN OFF-CENTRE<br>Energy is heightened, exaggerating shape | | Exploration is referenced on one person or view, and inquiry can feel deferential, stifling, partisan<br>Impact doesn't reflect intent; parity is lost | Exploration is referenced on one person or view, and inquiry can feel narrow, arbitrary, one-dimensional<br>Impact doesn't reflect intent; parity is lost |
| IMPACT WHEN OFF-CENTRE<br>Energy is dampened, subduing shape | | Exploration is referenced internally, and inquiry can feel irrelevant, disengaged, self-absorbed<br>Impact doesn't reflect intent; parity is lost | Exploration is referenced internally, and inquiry can feel tangential, unrelated, abstract<br><br>Impact doesn't reflect intent; parity is lost |

## Appendix M

## Embodied Practice 8: Centring with inspiration and support[†]

1. Posture and breath

> Become uplifted and aligned in your posture, with your spine easing to its natural length and curve. As you do so, exhale slowly and imagine the breath spiralling down through your body and into the ground.

> Inhale softly, imagining that the gentle inflow of air lifts each vertebra from the one below it, bringing a sense of lightness into the spine.

> Exhale slowly, imagining the breath flowing down, softening the front of the body, and forming a root in the earth below.

2. Balancing and opening personal space

> Become aware of the space you occupy – pay attention behind you as well as in front of you, to the left and right, below your feet and above your head. What would it be like if this space was a little more equal and even, a little more balanced?

> And what would it be like to consciously enlarge this personal container in all directions so that it includes those around you, whilst holding you gently at the centre?

> Now, in the space behind you, imagine the people* who inspire you, those who've helped you develop and grow, those who love you, those who support you and will cheer you on, and/or those who will benefit from what you say and do.

> Feel the presence and energy of your posse …

3. Softening

> Whilst maintaining an uplifted posture, soften your forehead, your jaw and your shoulders – imagine they're melting, like butter, and succumbing to gravity …

4. Cultivating beneficial energy

> Invite a little more ease (or other beneficial quality) into your being – where do you experience it, and what difference does it make?

5. Drawing on the energy of your posse

> Now imagine your back becoming a little more open, a little more porous, and allow the energy of your posse to flow into your being. Let this energy hold, support and/or move you …

*You can also draw on aspects of nature, art, music or any other inspiration.*

[†] *Based on the work of Wendy Palmer.*

# Appendix N

# Guidelines for a *Pause for Breath* 'book club'

A proposal

> What follows is a hybrid of a book club and an action learning set and is intended to offer a relatively safe framework for members of a small, self-directed group to explore ways of changing their practice in their conversations.

> The approach is centred on the six 'parts' of *Pause for Breath*. Each part has six or seven chapters, each with supporting fieldwork (or practice) to support inquiry and learning.

How it might work ...

> A group of four to six people agrees to meet every month for seven months. The aim is to read *Pause for Breath* and explore the ideas in it and to share any learning from the practices and fieldwork.

Session one: getting started

> Meet and agree the tone for your sessions and how you're going to conduct yourselves. You can adopt the four dialogue practices (respecting, listening, suspending judgement, authentic voicing) and/or any other qualities that seem relevant. If possible, avoid rules.

> Aim to balance advocacy with inquiry (see Chapter 4 of *Pause for Breath*) and ensure that everyone gets a chance to speak. Then commit to reading 'Part One' and allocate one practice or piece of field-work to each person. It doesn't matter if two people do the same thing, but try and cover all aspects if you can.

Sessions two to seven

> Check in briefly – how are you today? To settle into a session, you might try reading Practice 6 from *Pause for Breath* to support people to arrive and become present. Remind each other of the tone you agreed in the first session and lightly monitor how well your conversation matches your aspirations.

> Explore what you've read and share any learning from the practices/fieldwork. You might agree some standard inquiry questions for the 'book-club' aspect, such as:

> - what challenged me from this section? Why?
> - what attracted me? Why?
> - what might I try out and what would support me to do that?

As with any book club, let each person have their say and see what emerges. At the end, agree to read the next 'part' and share out the fieldwork.

Remember: people run book clubs all over the country – have confidence that this will be OK. Have fun!

Finished? Either continue by exploring books in the resources section of each 'part' of *Pause for Breath* or ... you could each form another group and repeat the process – you'll learn even more the second time around.

# Acknowledgements and gratitude

For the gift that gave me the freedom to begin writing this book: my thanks to Pamela Molyneaux.

For reading a very early draft: my thanks to Sam Anderson, Ruth Dorman, Tim Kelly, Elaine Mottram. Your insights radically reshaped the book.

For reading later drafts: my thanks to Sam Anderson, Aileen Brown, Susan Burney, Peter Casebow, Ray Charlton, Marianne Dee, Rhona Graham, Tim Kelly, Catriona Morrison, Allana Sheil, Barbara Wallis. You encouraged me to believe.

For the many insightful conversations that helped shape my writing: my thanks to all the readers above and to Dorothy, Lorna, Kay, Monica, Renata, Steve and Tania.

For those from whom I learned on the job: my thanks to my coaching and supervision clients, and to those who participated in my Leadership Embodiment workshops, Dialogue Practice Development programmes and Pause for Breath retreats.

For her wisdom and support, and for developing the amazing Leadership Embodiment practices: my thanks to the late Wendy Palmer.

For her support, encouragement and continued commitment to Leadership Embodiment practices: my thanks to Tiphani Palmer.

For her design and layout expertise, and her flexibility, encouragement and support: my thanks to Heather Macpherson.

For her copyediting expertise, insightful questions, thoroughness and patient support: my thanks to Helen Bleck.

For transforming my diagrams: my thanks to Sai Cook.

And … for two people who didn't work on this book, but without whom there would have been no books: my thanks to Murielle Maupoint and Bek Pickard.

# About the author

Amanda Ridings is based in the Cairngorms National Park in Scotland. She is in the process of discovering a different rhythm of life after many years working as an independent executive coach, coach supervisor, dialogue guide and Leadership Embodiment teacher. She intends to walk more, write more and spend more time enjoying the company of friends. She continues to practise T'ai Chi Chuan and to study Buddhist teachings.

Amanda has published two previous books, *Pause for Breath* and *Weekly Leadership Contemplations*. *Pause for Breath* received a Silver Nautilus Award in the category of Conscious Business and Leadership. Nautilus Awards aim to recognise exceptional literary contributions to fields such as spiritual growth, responsible leadership and positive social change.

You'll find Amanda's blog – and occasional updates about her writing projects – on her website: www.originate.org.uk.

# Also by Amanda Ridings

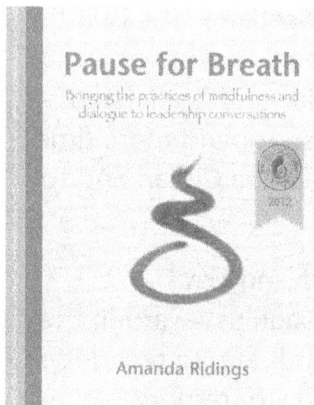

## Pause for Breath

Most leadership is conducted through the medium of conversation – whether meetings, presentations or one-to-ones. And yet, short of time, we often rely on a few 'go-to' strategies for the way we approach them. Mostly, this serves us well. And sometimes there's a gap between our intentions and what actually transpires.

This book is for all those who are intrigued by such gaps and want to achieve better outcomes in their leadership conversations. Each chapter describes ideas from the field of dialogue and invites you to reflect on how they play out in practice.

Within these pages you'll discover:

- How mind, body and spirit influence your impact in your conversations;

- How your internal dialogue affects your interactions with others; and

- How to be more composed and versatile in your most challenging exchanges.

Taken together, these themes will shed light on the shape and quality of your leadership conversations and inspire you to make changes in your practice. They will support you to involve others in dialogue – germinating systemic change, one conversation at a time.

# Also by Amanda Ridings

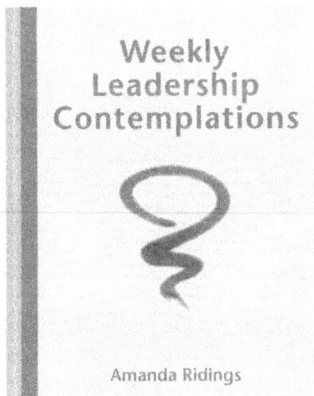

## Weekly Leadership Contemplations

This is a book for our times. It is for leaders, coaches and other practitioners who are searching for inspiration as they reflect on their leadership experiences and practice.

Each of the fifty two short pieces in this collection is shaped by the author's personal experiences and by thought-provoking themes raised by her executive coaching clients or by events in the world. The contemplation questions accompanying each piece invite you to explore how these relate to your own life and work.

You will be gently challenged to hold yourself to account when you discover a 'gap' between your leadership aspirations and your ability to live up to them. You will also be encouraged to make contact with your finest leadership spirit, to inhabit it and to anchor your choices in it.

This book is meant to be read slowly – each piece is a written 'thought for the week'.